HERESY AND MYSTICISM IN SIXTEENTH-CENTURY SPAIN

The Alumbrados

Alastair Hamilton

University of Toronto Press
Toronto   Buffalo

For Carlo Bo

First published in North America in 1992 by
University of Toronto Press Incorporated
Toronto and Buffalo

ISBN 0-8020-2943-4

First published in the UK by James Clarke & Co., 1992
with whose permission this edition is published
Copyright © Alastair Hamilton, 1992

Canadian Cataloguing in Publication Data
Hamilton Alastair, 1941-
Heresy and mysticism in sixteenth-century Spain
Includes bibliographical reference and index.
ISBN 0-8020-2943-4

1. Alumbrados. 2. Inquisition - Spain. 3. Spain - Church
History. 4. Mysticism - Spain. 5. Heretics, Christian - Spain
I. Title

BX1735.H35 1992   272'.2'0946   C92-095210-0

Printed in the UK by
The Cromwell Press, Melksham

Contents

Acknowledgements iv
Introduction 1
I.   Reform and Enthusiasm 7
II.   The Piety of the *Alumbrados* of Toledo 25
III. Tradition and Discussion 43
IV.   The First Arrests 51
V.   The *Alumbrados* between Two Heresies 65
VI.   Humanism Attacked 77
VII. The Fear of Novelty 91
VIII. The *Alumbrados* of Llerena and Seville 115
Conclusion 129
Abbreviations 133
Notes 134
Index 148

List of Maps

1. Spain (showing the territories of the Crowns of Castile and
   Aragon) and Portugal 6
2. Guadalajara and the surrounding area 24
3. Andalusia and southern Extremadura 90

Acknowledgements

Since I started working on the *alumbrados* almost twenty years ago I have benefited from much assistance and advice. In Spain my special thanks are due to the late Professor Pedro Sainz Rodríguez and to the Fundación Universitaria Española for providing me with a research grant and many other kindnesses. I am also most grateful to Professor Eugenio Asensio, the late Professor Marcel Bataillon, Professor Jaime Contreras and Professor Ignácio Tellechea Idígoras. Professor Miquel Batllori, Professor J.H. Elliott and Dr Dermot Fenlon read earlier versions of my typescript and made valuable comments. I thank Fr Edmond Lamalle for his help in the Jesuit archives in Rome, Dr Carlos Gilly, Professor Augustin Redondo and Mr Michael Walsh and the Heythrop College Library. Dr A. Gordon Kinder has generously supplied me with bibliographical information. I owe much to my colleagues Dr Burcht Pranger at the University of Amsterdam and Professor María Rosa Saurín de la Iglesia at the University of Urbino, while the maps were kindly drawn by Dr Peter Davidson at the University of Leiden. I am indebted, finally, to Dr Geoffrey Nuttall for pressing me to complete this book and for reading it before publication.

Introduction

In the early sixteenth century few European countries provided so ideal a setting for religious enthusiasm as Spain. Effectively united since 1479 by Ferdinand of Aragon and Isabella of Castile, with imperial possessions scattered over Europe and the prospect of still greater ones in the New World, Spain could aspire to leadership among the Christian nations of the west. It could claim to have accomplished one of the objects of all the Christian powers since the Middle Ages: a successful crusade against Islam. After the conquest in 1492 of the kingdom of Granada, the last Muslim stronghold in western Europe, Spanish churchmen and politicians dreamed of pursuing the Muslims into North Africa, and even of pressing as far as Jerusalem to recover the Holy Places, put an end to Islam, and unite the world under a single Christian rule. The vision of Spain as a world power was accompanied by plans for a widespread and thorough reformation of the Spanish Church. After gaining impetus in the course of the fifteenth century these plans seemed on the verge of a formidable outcome: the conversion to Christianity of the Spanish Jews, the reform of the religious orders, the diffusion of works of piety throughout the nation, and the renewal of Biblical scholarship.

Against this background there arose what has gone down to history as a single native heretical movement - the movement of the *alumbrados*, of men and women 'illuminated' by the Holy Spirit. Its origins lay in the circles of Franciscan friars who produced some of the first great works on mysticism to be published in Spain. It started in the area of Guadalajara in about 1512 under the leadership of a Franciscan tertiary, Isabel de la Cruz, who was joined slightly later by Pedro Ruiz de Alcaraz, an accountant in the service of the local nobility. It was detected by the Spanish Inquisition in 1519, and its members were known as the '*alumbrados* of Toledo' after the tribunal which investigated and condemned them.

Isabel de la Cruz and her followers taught the practice of *dejamiento* or 'abandonment'. They were accused of claiming that those who surrendered themselves to the love of God had no need of the ceremonies or sacraments of the Church, that they should desist from all activity, being cleansed of sin in their union with the Deity. In fact the *alumbrados* of Toledo based their beliefs on a remarkably thorough study of the Scriptures and they attracted people with a true desire to improve the state of the Church. Their views on justification were in many respects similar to Luther's solfidianism - the teaching that the first step in the process of salvation was faith alone which preceded, and was independent of, any good works. This, their emphasis on the working of the Spirit in the individual, their pessimism about human nature, their interest in St Paul, and their quest for greater simplicity in religion suggest that they were part of the tendency known as evangelism, a Catholic desire for reform prompted above all by the study of the New Testament, found in many parts of Europe at the time of the Reformation.

After the arrest of the first *alumbrados* in 1524 and the edict of faith defining and condemning their doctrine, *alumbradismo* took on a number of meanings and uses for the authorities. Isabel de la Cruz and many of her followers descended from *conversos* or Jews converted to Christianity. The charge of *alumbradismo* was thus often applied to other members of this social group, which was both successful and vulnerable, the object of jealousy and prejudice. It could be held against the readers of Luther (and of Erasmus), and was an ideal means of attacking men of *converso* origin who had studied or taught at the university of Alcalá, who were attached to the imperial court, and who were resented by the more conservative elements in the Spanish Church. The accusation could even be extended to some of the most distinguished Catholic reformers - St Ignatius Loyola, St John of Avila, Bartolomé Carranza - who endeavoured to revive Catholicism with ideas suspicious on account of their novelty. The *alumbrados'* use of the language of mysticism, moreover, their proximity to the Franciscan mystics, and their advocacy of complete passivity, the 'quiet' of the senses which the Church had long regarded with distrust, meant that the accusation of *alumbradismo* could serve to discredit other mystics, even the greatest mystical writers of the Spanish Golden Age such as Luis de Granada and St Teresa of Avila.

Over fifty years after the *alumbrados* of Toledo had been investigated other groups were detected in the south of Spain, in Extremadura and Andalusia. The '*alumbrados* of Llerena' (in the late sixteenth century) and the '*alumbrados* of Seville (in the early seventeenth century) had certain superficial similarities with the *alumbrados* of

Toledo: they assembled at prayer meetings unauthorised by the Church and they believed in their own impeccability. They too rejected any form of activity which could hinder their union with God and basked in the security of grace. Made up of priests and female penitents, the later groups of *alumbrados* combined lasciviousness with spectacular exhibitions of their mystical experience. In contrast to the movement led by Isabel de la Cruz, they encouraged ecstasies and trances. The edicts issued in Llerena in 1574 and in Seville in 1623 contributed to the dissociation of the *alumbrados* from Lutheranism and identified them, rather, with pseudo-mysticism and imposture. Besides being used well into the eighteenth century for fraudulent visionaries, lecherous confessors, and mystics whose inspiration was of dubious origin, the term *alumbrado* lingered on as a generalised bugbear in the works of writers on mysticism. From the late seventeenth century onwards the charge was gradually replaced by the accusation of Quietism or Molinosism, but the leader of the new movement, Miguel de Molinos, defended his own mystical teaching by deploring the heresy of the *alumbrados*.

Alumbradismo had many facets. We have the beliefs of the heretics themselves who assembled in identifiable groups. Yet the groups differed from one another. Even if those investigated in Baeza led by the disciples of John of Avila can be said to have held an intermediate position, the *alumbrados* of Llerena and Seville are a far cry from those of Toledo. At the same time *alumbradismo* led a more or less independent existence as an accusation, usually combined with other accusations, against individuals who had no direct connection with any of the existing *alumbrado* groups. The different aspects of the heresy and of the term are examined in this book.

My study opens with a brief survey of the spiritual climate in which the *alumbrados* of Toledo developed their beliefs. They did so at a time when various plans to reform the Church were afoot. Some, such as the foundation of the Spanish Inquisition, were decidedly coercive, but others, such as the spread of devotional literature in the vernacular, the establishment of new seats of learning, and the encouragement given to mysticism as a universally accessible way to God, were of a gentler character. The most prominent figure behind these enterprises, Cardinal Francisco Jiménez de Cisneros, was also attracted by the messianic prophecies so widespread not only in Spain but throughout Europe, and he admired the more spectacular expressions of mysticism. These were phenomena against which the *alumbrados* reacted, but they nevertheless had their own origins in the same movement of religious revival which he promoted at a time when the barriers between orthodoxy and heterodoxy were far more fluid than they were to become under the impact of the Reformation and the Council of Trent in the 1540s.

I then deal with the piety of the *alumbrados* of Toledo. What were they accused of thinking, what were their true beliefs, and what were their sources? Although we have writings of some of their later followers, such as Juan de Valdés, no work by the first *alumbrados* would seem to have survived - no catechism or spiritual alphabet similar to those produced by the advocates of other 'arts of reaching God'. We must rely on their trials in order to define their beliefs, on the letters they wrote in their defence and about which they were often advised by their counsels, and on the statements made by witnesses, many of whom were overtly hostile. Yet the Spanish Inquisition was a punctilious institution whose object was indeed to uncover the truth. Compared to the secular magistrates the inquisitors went about their duty with an astonishing thoroughness. In the end the trials, in which the statements of witnesses both antagonistic and well-disposed to-wards the accused are recorded in the greatest detail, are a reasonably reliable indication of the beliefs under investigation.

The next question I discuss is how these trials were conducted: first the events that prompted the *alumbrados*' arrest, their treatment in prison, and their sentences; then the attitude of the inquisitors. The inquisitors' aim may well have been to get at the truth, but the interrogations were often organised in order to discover whether the defendants were guilty of Judaizing, a heresy familiar to the Holy Office, or whether they in fact held views closer to the new heresy which the inquisitors were bracing themselves to combat but of which they still had little experience, Lutheranism.

The threat of Lutheranism explains not only the initial decision to prosecute the *alumbrados*, but also the manner in which *alumbrado* tenets were ascribed to a far wider circle of men and women in the 1530s. I therefore show how *alumbradismo* was used as an accusation against courtiers and scholars who declared their admiration for Erasmus and against Catholic reformers. Even if the charge in itself was seldom justified, it does demonstrate the widespread opposition to attempts to introduce novelty into the Spanish Church.

The last section of this book concerns the later *alumbrado* groups, those of Llerena and Seville. The information about them is almost entirely hostile. The transcriptions of the full judicial proceedings which we still have for the first half of the sixteenth century, so cumbersome but so precious as a source of knowledge, were being replaced by brief summaries of the trials, *relaciones de causas*, which tell us little about the defence of the accused. We are also left with the extensive reports by the *alumbrados'* Dominican enemies, but these are one-sided accounts, and so our view of the later *alumbrados* remains one-sided. Nevertheless these descriptions explain the future of the term as it survived into the eighteenth century and make it possible to compare the movements with similar ones elsewhere in Europe.

The bibliography on the *alumbrados* is vast. The *alumbrados* of Toledo in particular have been the subject of numerous studies stretching back to the nineteenth century when they were regarded as the precursors of later movements of religious non-conformity.[1] In the last fifteen years research has been facilitated by the publication of some of the most relevant documents, the trials.[2] Much material has also recently been published on the later *alumbrados* of Extremadura and Andalusia.[3] There are, however, few surveys of the heresy as a whole, from the early sixteenth to the seventeenth century, and none in English. I hope to remedy this lack with the present study.

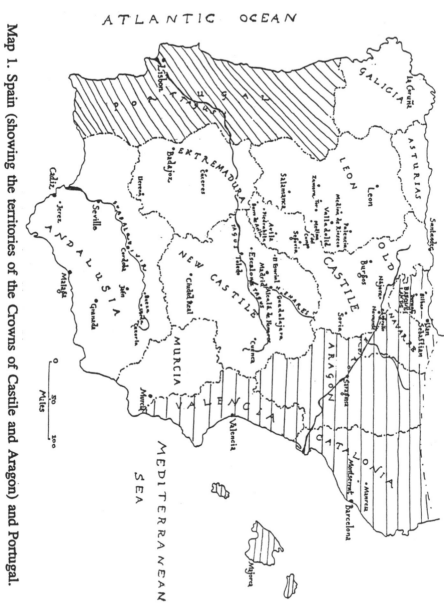

Map 1. Spain (showing the territories of the Crowns of Castile and Aragon) and Portugal.

Chapter I

Reform and Enthusiasm

Whatever similarities the *alumbrados* of Toledo may have had with contemporary religious movements elsewhere in Europe, they developed their ideas and were themselves investigated in an atmosphere peculiar to Spain alone, where enthusiasm went hand in hand with prejudice and where dogmatic flexibility and uncertainty were accompanied by a deep suspicion of diversity.

The Spanish Inquisition

For the greater part of the Middle Ages religious diversity had been tolerated in Spain. Although the invasion of the peninsula by the Arabs in the eighth century was followed by the gradual reconquest of Iberia by the Christians advancing from the north, the Arabs, who had been pressed as far south as Andalusia by the thirteenth century, left a tradition of peaceful coexistence between Jews, Muslims and Christians. This ended in the 1390s. Economic resentment of the Jews in Castile, Aragon and Catalonia, together with religious hatred fostered by preachers such as the Dominican Vincent Ferrer, led to the first substantial pogroms Spain had ever known.

The conversion of the Spanish Jews to Christianity began after the pogroms of 1391 and accelerated at the beginning of the fifteenth century as the anti-Jewish legislation became more rigorous, the converts and their descendants being known as *conversos* or New Christians. In 1477 the Catholic Kings (as Ferdinand and Isabella were later named by the pope) became aware of large communities in and around Seville of Judaizers, *conversos* who had reverted to their former religious practices. When they were codified by the Inquisition these practices could be divided into three categories. The first was the observance of traditional Jewish feasts, such as the Sabbath, Yom Kippur and the Passover. The second was the deliberate violation of the commandments of the Church - refusal to attend mass, the eating of meat on days of abstinence, failure to go to confession or to take communion, and the third was the abuse of sacred objects, whipping crucifixes or insulting images of the Virgin Mary and the saints.

Influential figures in Castile urged the establishment of an inquisition whose purpose would be to chastise recalcitrant *conversos* and forestall the pogroms. The most ardent advocates were 'Old Christians' (Spaniards who claimed to have no Jewish blood), many of whom resented the growing success and prestige of the converts. But there were also New Christians themselves, such as Fray Alonso de Espina, who encouraged the foundation of the Holy Office so as to safeguard Catholic orthodoxy from the insidious influence of more recent converts often baptized out of expediency rather than conviction.[1]

The Spanish Inquisition, which was founded by the Catholic Kings in 1478, was established in Andalusia by the end of 1480. A tribunal was set up in Ciudad Real in New Castile in 1483 and transferred to Toledo a couple of years later. In 1487 the Holy Office was introduced into Aragon. In the areas belonging to King Ferdinand - Aragon, Valencia, the Basque countries, Navarre, Catalonia, Sardinia and Sicily - it was regarded as an instrument of Castilian colonisation and was accepted after strong resistance. Only in Naples was it never imposed.

As an organisation the Spanish Inquisition was a novelty in more than one respect. Castile had known no medieval inquisition, although Aragon had. In contrast to the medieval institution, the Spanish Inquisition was not predominantly in the hands of the mendicant orders, the Franciscans and the Dominicans, but allowed a far greater influence to the secular clergy. Moreover, the inquisitor general, the head of a supreme council, the *Consejo de la Suprema y General Inquisición* (known as the *Suprema*), which always remained in Castile, was appointed by the Spanish Crown. The new organisation was thus essentially a national one, although the right of appeal to the pope continued to exist.

The first targets of the Inquisition were *conversos*, a vast category of individuals who, as we shall see in chapter V, accepted the new faith with varying degrees of sincerity. The most recent converts had been faced with a choice between baptism or expulsion from Spain after the fall of Granada in 1492. Thereafter in the sixteenth century the converts of the first generation were mainly Jewish exiles seeking readmission into Spanish territory after a period spent abroad, usually in Portugal or North Africa. After the expulsion of adult practising Muslims in 1502, they were joined by *moriscos*, converts from Islam. But in the centre of Castile, where the *alumbrados* flourished, the tribunals of the Inquisition were concerned above all with the converted Jews and their descendants.

The policy of edification

The choice between baptism or exile was coercive, and the methods of the Inquisition - the confiscation of property, imprisonment, the occasional use of torture, and, particularly in the early years, frequent sentences to the stake - were even more so. Yet there were various ecclesiastics who believed that the Jews and Muslims should be converted, and the New Christians edified, by example and persuasion. This was the view, in the late fifteenth century, of the archbishop of Toledo, Cardinal Pedro González de Mendoza, and of the archbishop of Granada, the Hieronymite Hernando de Talavera. To achieve their object they encouraged the composition of manuals and catechisms. The printing press was a new and valuable instrument for the transmission of their ideas not only to the *conversos* but to the laity in general.

At the beginning of his *Luzero de la vida christiana*, dedicated to Ferdinand and Isabella and first printed in 1493, Pedro Jiménez de Préjano, bishop of Coria, referred to the forcible conversions of the late fourteenth century approved by Vincent Ferrer.

> In the time of that great preacher St Vincent many elderly Jews and Jewesses were converted to the faith, some of them against their will, by force and fear. Brought up in the Mosaic Law they taught this law and its ceremonies to their children, grandchildren and families, so, although they were baptised, they never abandoned the Jewish rites which they had learned in their infancy. Distressed by the blindness and perdition of humanity and of the faithful, which have been caused above all by the aforesaid ignorance, moved by the most pious and Catholic behest of Your Highnesses and by love and zeal for the Holy Catholic Faith and salvation of so many souls damaged in this way, I . . . decided to try to write in our Castilian tongue so that a brief summary of the things necessary for our salvation might be placed at the disposal of the faithful of all estates, ages and conditions.[2]

Besides commenting on the Gospels the bishop of Coria explained the sacraments and the laws prescribed by the Old and New Testaments. Other writers confined themselves to descriptions of the life of Christ, endeavouring, as Juan de Padilla said in the first canticle of his *Retablo de la vida de Christo*, to describe it simply and devoutly, without the 'high style of orators and vain poets'.[3]

Popularisation of scenes from the Gospels was accompanied by popularisation of the words of the Gospels. In 1485 the Gospels and Epistles, with commentaries by the French Dominican William of Paris, were printed in Saragossa in the Castilian translation of Gonzalo

García de Santa María, a lawyer protected by Ferdinand of Aragon. An even greater contribution was made to the vulgarisation of the New Testament by Ambrosio Montesino of the Franciscan Order. By 1501 he had finished the translation of the *Vita Christi* by the Carthusian Ludolph of Saxony: the four volumes were printed over the next two years in Alcalá de Henares. Sentences from the Gospels were quoted in Castilian and followed by extensive glosses by the author, the Church Fathers, and more recent exegetes. Ten years later, in 1512, Montesino concluded his *Epistolas y evangelios por todo el año con sus doctrinas y sermones*, a work undertaken at the command of the king to improve on Gonzalo García de Santa María's version.

Cardinal Jiménez de Cisneros

Of the princes of the Church who supervised and encouraged this propagation of devotional literature in the vernacular the most active and influential was Cardinal Francisco Jiménez de Cisneros.[4]

After a promising career which ended in his appointment as vicar general to Cardinal Mendoza, Cisneros retired from the world, withdrawing to the Franciscan *recolectorio* of La Salceda close to Guadalajara, a convent intended for meditation, and in 1484, at the age of forty-eight, joined the Friars Minor, entering the newly founded convent of San Juan de los Reyes in Toledo. His asceticism, the austerity of his retreats and his evident sanctity led to his being recommended to Queen Isabella by Mendoza and, in 1492, he became her confessor. Two years later he was nominated provincial of the Franciscans in Castile; in 1495·he succeeded Mendoza as archbishop of Toledo and primate of Spain. In 1506, after the death of Ferdinand's son-in-law and heir Philip of Burgundy, he ruled briefly as regent of Castile, and in the following year he was made cardinal and inquisitor general.

Still more than Hernando de Talavera, Cisneros managed to acquire a mythical reputation. Not only was he the ascetic 'eschewing the society of men', searching 'barefooted for the silence of the forests, dressed in sackcloth and content to sleep on a bed of straw' as he is described by the humanist Pietro Martire d'Anghiera;[5] he was also a warrior, a crusading cardinal who personally accompanied the Spanish forces to North Africa in 1509 to fight against Islam. For many he was the providential figure designated by prophecies over the centuries, a desirable candidate for the papacy who would convert or crush the Muslims and reconquer Jerusalem.

An enlightened patron of learning, Cisneros revolutionised schol-

arship in Spain. In Alcalá de Henares he founded the academy known
as the Complutensian University after the Latin name of the town.
Absolute priority was given to theology. There was no civil law faculty,
a feature prominent in most other Spanish universities, and to the
professorships of Thomism and Scotism Cisneros added one of nominalism, which was altogether unprecedented in Spain. He thus encouraged the study of the teaching of the German nominalist Gabriel Biel
(whose influence on Luther was considerable). In accordance with
humanist principles the statutes of the university of Alcalá introduced
a Greek professorship and also made provisions for chairs in Hebrew
and Arabic, although the latter was never filled. At the new university,
whose first constitutions were issued in 1510, the cardinal assembled
the scholars who were to contribute to his most ambitious project, the
publication of a polyglot Bible with the purpose of establishing a more
perfect text of the Scriptures than the one contained in the standard
Latin translation of St Jerome, the Vulgate. It was the first of a series
of multilingual editions issued throughout Europe for the next two
centuries. The Greek and Latin texts of the New Testament were
completed in 1514, while the Old Testament, with versions and
paraphrases in Latin, Greek, Hebrew and Aramaic, was printed three
years later. By founding the Complutensian University as a training
ground for the study of the Biblical languages and texts Cisneros had
sanctioned scholarly investigation into the Scriptures. The university
soon became a lively centre of theological debate and it was there that
the first *alumbrados* encountered the world of learning.

Another development in which Cisneros played a prominent role
and which was closely connected with the growth of Spanish mysticism was the reform of the religious orders. The movement in many
parts of Europe to reform most of the existing monastic and conventual
houses, to suppress the laxity and the wealth they had acquired since
their foundation, and to bring them back to the original rule of their
founders, started in the late fourteenth century. Spain was no exception, and Benedictines, Dominicans, Franciscans and other orders
endeavoured, in the course of the fifteenth century, to revive the true
spirit of monastic discipline. The process gathered impetus gradually,
and it was under the Catholic Kings, above all during the primacy of
Cardinal Cisneros, that the reformers achieved the greatest number of
their goals.

Although Cisneros promoted the reform of every order in Spain, his
first concern was with his own order, the Friars Minor, and the
Franciscans, more than any others, became the bearers of his spiritu-

ality. One by one the conventual houses, with their property and easier way of life, were replaced by observant houses practising St Francis's rule, and by the time of Cisneros's death in 1517 the conventual houses had disappeared.[6]

Mysticism

An essential aspect of Franciscan reform, especially in the late fifteenth century, was the practice of meditation. There is no way of identifying the meditative methods which existed under one of the first reformers, Pedro de Villacreces, at the beginning of the fifteenth century. However, the exercise of *recogimiento*, the 'gathering' of the senses which became characteristic of the order, seems to have developed in the 1480s partly as a reaction against the excessive anti-intellectualism and devotion to liturgy prevalent during the earliest phases of the reform.[7] The encouragement of this method led to convents being reserved for its practice. They came to be known as *recolectorios*, and it was to one of the most important, La Salceda, that Cisneros withdrew from his secular life and there that he decided to become a Franciscan.

For a definition of *recogimiento* we have to wait until the 1520s. By then the Franciscan methods of meditation had been perfected and we can identify the various sources on which their practitioners drew. Contemporary exercises devised outside Spain were imported, particularly those followed in the Netherlands by members of the Brethren of the Common Life such as Wessel Gansfort and Jan Mombaer.

The man who appears to have introduced Mombaer's ideas into Spain was in fact a Benedictine, Cardinal Cisneros's cousin García Jiménez de Cisneros, prior, and later abbot, of the monastery of Montserrat in Catalonia. He probably encountered Mombaer when he accompanied a diplomatic mission to Charles VIII at Amboise in 1496. On his return to Spain he used the printing press installed at Montserrat in 1499 to produce a far earlier work from the circle of the Devotio Moderna, Gerard Zerbolt's *Tractatus de spiritualibus ascensionibus*, and in November 1500 he published his own book, the *Ejercitatorio de la vida espiritual*.

García de Cisneros's *Ejercitatorio* draws heavily on the most popular texts on mysticism in circulation: on Zerbolt and on Mombaer's *Rosetum exercitiorum spiritualium*, with its mnemotechnical devices to assist the reader at his various stages of spiritual progress; on Hugh of Balma (the editor of the Pseudo-Dionysius); on Richard of St Victor,

Bonaventure, Gerson and the Valencian mystic Francesc Eiximenis. It contains instructions on the three mystical ways, the *via purgativa*, the *via illuminativa* and the *via unitiva;* provides subjects of meditation; and recommends the most suitable place, time, and physical position in which to empty the mind of human cares, to meditate on the humanity of Christ and pass progressively to more abstract themes. In the final stage, the understanding ceases its activity and the highest part of the soul is elevated to God by love.

The work was intended above all for García de Cisneros's fellow Benedictines, albeit for the less learned ones, and the ideal place for meditation remained the monastic cell. In his discussion of those who are most suited to meditation, however, he emphasised the advantages of the unlearned in general, of those who approach God with love rather than with learning. At the end he also alluded to a broader readership. He had written his book in the vernacular, he said, in order to reach *'los simples devotos'*, and not for the benefit of 'proud scholars', *'los letrados soberbios'*.[8] Learning, he insisted, leads to intellectual arrogance, the greatest obstacle to union with God.

That mysticism was the ideal 'theology' for the simple in spirit was already a commonplace by the time García de Cisneros was writing. It was stated in one of the most popular manuals, Gerson's *Mystica Theologia*, and was stressed in other books. Yet although there was no shortage of works on mysticism in the late Middle Ages, few were in the vernacular. The praise of ignorance they contained was reserved for the learned who could read them in Latin. One of the most striking features of the movement for religious reform during the primacy of Cardinal Cisneros was the amount of mystical literature made available in Castilian. Even if it was largely composed by members of the religious orders it was distributed outside the convents and became accessible on a vast scale to the laity.

While the great product of the Devotio Moderna, the *Imitation of Christ*, was being issued repeatedly in the vernacular - in Catalan since 1482, in Castilian since 1490, in Valencian since 1491 - Cardinal Cisneros himself ordered Castilian translations of St John Climacus's *Spiritual Ladder*, of the works of Catherine of Siena and Angela of Foligno, and of the popular version of the Pseudo-Dionysius's *Mystical Theology* by Hugh of Balma translated as *Sol de contemplativos*.

Not only was the mystical way to God generally recommended as being accessible to an unlearned laity, but it was soon presented as both the easiest and the quickest manner of attaining perfection. Though the mystical authors emphasised the necessity for spiritual exercises and preparation, and strove to show that only a small number of persons might experience union with God in the last stage of the mystical process, they nevertheless soon referred to it as an art and as a short-cut, *un atajo*. The first writer to have used these words on a title-page was an anonymous Franciscan, whose *Hun brevissimo atajo e arte de amar a Dios: Con otra arte de contemplar e algunas reglas breves para ordenar la piensa en el amor de Dios* appeared in Barcelona in 1513.[9] A short-cut and an art, the mystical method was easy, brief and sweet, but it had hitherto been known to the few. From 1513 onwards one book after another was to divulge it, to provide 'sufficient rules,' as the Franciscan tertiary Bernabé de Palma wrote, 'for a man to change from carnal to spiritual'.[10]

The majority of Spanish writers on mysticism in the first forty years of the sixteenth century were Franciscans. It was a Franciscan, Antonio de Ciudad Real, vicar of the convent of San Juan de los Reyes in Toledo, who translated Hugh of Balma's version of the Pseudo-Dionysius, published, like *Hun brevissimo atajo*, in 1513, and it was the Franciscans Alonso de Madrid and above all Francisco de Osuna, who described the method of meditation known as *recogimiento*.

Recogimiento

Francisco de Osuna, a native of Andalusia, studied theology at Alcalá and entered the *recolectorio* of La Salceda in the early 1520s. In his *Tercer abecedario espiritual*, the standard manual on the method first published in 1527, he distinguishes between two kinds of *recogimiento*, general and particular. The first type is defined as a virtuous existence led aloof from the 'cares of human affairs'. The second is the specifically meditative exercise practised by the friars at La Salceda. The exercise should be performed, he says, in a dark and silent place, the eyes closed or lowered and focused on one point. This makes it possible to collect or gather the senses. It should be done for at least two hours a day, the first hour before noon and the second later. Although he says that the religious are in a particularly favourable position to practise the method and that few people are chosen to do so, Osuna insists on its universality. It is well suited, he continues, to rich laymen with enough leisure to perform it, and even to merchants frequently engaged in business. All the practitioner really needs is the strength to dominate his appetites, and Osuna is liberal in his advice about how this should be done. The *recogido* must take care of his diet, avoiding spices, garlic, raw onion and anything highly dressed. He must keep away from pungent smells, rinse his mouth to rid it of any strong taste, clean his teeth and drink his wine watered. The test of the right size of a meal, Osuna admonishes, is the ability to pray after it instead of falling asleep.[11]

The practitioner of *recogimiento* should then learn three forms of prayer. The first is vocal, the best being the Lord's Prayer on which Osuna provides a commentary; the second is in our hearts and consists of meditating on the life and passion of Christ; the third and most perfect type of prayer, which corresponds to the last mystical stage, the *via unitiva*, is 'mental or spiritual'. If the first stage perfects the memory and the second the understanding, in the third the will is perfected. The highest part of the soul is raised to God 'on the wings of desire and pious affection propelled by love'. At this point 'an exchange of wills' occurs: 'man only desires what God desires and God does not depart from the will of man'. In this state all intellectual activity must end, but, Osuna reminds his readers, 'not to think of anything is more than it sounds. In no manner can it be explained since God, to whom it is directed, is inexplicable: indeed, I tell you that this thinking nothing is to think of Him entirely.'[12]

With his insistence on edifying company, on fraternal correction, on the necessity of a spiritual adviser, Osuna pays homage to the Church. Like García de Cisneros and in accordance with a venerable tradition in his own order, he rejects the benefits of learning and reminds us that erudition can be an insuperable obstacle to his method. 'Too many books,' he admonishes, 'are nothing but too much dissolution of the mind, excessive labour, lack of rest, weight on the memory, a meat that can never fill your stomach ... Many books make a library of your cell, but not of your memory, for all they leave there are the titles'. 'I do not wish to concern myself with such people,' he writes elsewhere, 'since they are alien to true devotion and place all their learning in talking to God as though they were talking to Lorenzo Valla or someone else who could accuse them of speaking bad Latin.' Mystical theology, on the other hand,

> has nothing to do with familiarity with the knowledge of letters, it does not need a school, as it were, or intellect, but must be sought in the school of the affections through the vehement exercise of virtues. We can thus conclude that there is this difference: even if it is the supreme and most perfect knowledge, mystical theology can be mastered by any one of the faithful, be it a poor little woman or an ignoramus.[13]

In his hostility to learning - a hostility which would seem to be aimed more at the new humanism than the old scholasticism - Osuna resorts to an emphasis on experience, on 'the taste within the soul'. Although he admits that this can sometimes be illusory, he displays the greatest assurance where all signs of divine favour are concerned. He condemns the scepticism towards trances and ecstasies which had been expressed over a century earlier in Vincent Ferrer's devotional manual, the *Tractatus de vita spirituali*. 'While in our days there are many who have been visited with an abundance of grace,' he continues, 'there are also many who are alien to it, and who, seeing in others by certain external signs what they do not see in themselves, think they are mad and deceived or possessed by devils, and the least evil they attribute to them is hypocrisy.'[14]

Optimistic assurance was endemic in the type of mystical manual produced by the Franciscans at this time. The art or method recommended, accessible even to 'a poor little woman or an ignoramus', *'mujercillas e ydiotas'*, those who had not studied theology, was guaranteed to succeed. In his *Arte para servir a Dios* of 1521 Alonso de Madrid informed his reader that, by following his instructions, he would progress much further in one year than he would in ten without them.[15] Those who followed the method enjoyed immense privileges. 'A soul nourished in mystical theology,' wrote the Franciscan Bernardino de Laredo in his *Subida del Monte Sión*, first published in 1535 and revised in 1538, 'will be able to feel and to explain certain problems of the Holy Scriptures more rapidly and with greater profit than any scholastic theologian, however notable, who lacks spiritual wisdom.'[16]

In such an atmosphere the most spectacular manifestations of divine grace were welcomed. Cardinal Cisneros had ordered the republication of Vincent Ferrer's treatise on the spiritual life in Alcalá in 1510 but had removed the chapters in which the Dominican advised caution in judging ecstasies and visions.[17] The rejection of any scepticism frequently engendered an unquestioning faith in the numerous visionaries who arose throughout Spain and whose prophecies confirmed the providential role reserved for the country and its governors.

Prophecy
The inspired were frequently women - nuns or *beatas*, women leading a life purporting to be in the service of the Almighty. Some were tertiaries (members of a 'third order' attached to the Dominicans or the Franciscans but intended for the laity). Others were independent of any order but had taken a vow of chastity and sometimes of poverty. Cardinal Cisneros was particularly inclined to accept the authenticity of their divine gifts. He believed in the ecstasies of María de Toledo,

the founder of the convent of Clarissas of Santa Isabel de los Reyes, and in the miraculous grace of the Benedictine Madre Marta. He believed, too, in the visions of the Dominican tertiary María de Santo Domingo, known as the *beata* of Piedrahita,[18] whose experiences are one of the best illustrations of the spiritual climate at the time.

Sor María de Santo Domingo had attempted, in the first years of the sixteenth century, to reform the Order of Preachers by founding an observantine convent in her birthplace, Aldeanueva near Barco de Avila. The Dominican provincial opposed the plan so Sor María and her followers decided to proceed with support from outside the order - from Ferdinand of Aragon, the Duke of Alba (in whose territories Barco de Avila lay) and Cardinal Cisneros. Her followers observed a type of austerity that had been rigorously prohibited; they wore a habit of their own devising reminiscent of that worn by Savonarola's adherents in Florence. When an attempt was made by the new prior of Avila to visit their convent, the inmates imprisoned him. After a complaint to the papacy by the provincial, a brief arrived in 1509 ordering three apostolic judges to investigate the matter. Sor María's various trials, the efforts to eject the friars from Aldeanueva and to enforce sanctions on the tertiary dragged on for three years until, in 1512, the vicar general of the order in Rome complied with Cisneros's wishes and allowed the remaining friars to stay in the convent. Sor María was formally absolved and acted as prioress until her death.

As with most of the other prophecies so popular in Spain at the time, María de Santo Domingo's utterances were based on a synthesis of medieval traditions. One of them, the Joachist tradition, consisted of ideas attributed to the twelfth-century Cistercian theologian, Joachim of Fiore, though these had been revised and elaborated since his death in 1202.[19] The fundamental conviction was that the Church was about to be reformed and the world converted by 'spiritual men'. Although the members of Joachim's own order had been candidates for the fulfilment of the prophecy, it was adopted with particular fervour by the mendicant orders. There had been revivals of it among the Dominicans since the first movements of reform in the later fourteenth century and these revivals had often led to violence. In Spain, Vincent Ferrer had expressed Joachist ideas in his sermons, while certain beliefs associated with Joachim were probably taken over by Savonarola. Still more than the Dominicans, however, it was the Franciscans who appropriated Joachim's prophecies. Numerous traces can be found in Spain. Joachist Franciscans are reported in Majorca, Valencia, Aragon and Catalonia throughout the fourteenth century.[20] The fifteenth century is less well documented due to the absence of an inquisition in Castile, which meant that the world of the convents there was effectively sealed. Yet there is reason to think that Joachist ideas lost little of their strength: they emerged as soon as the Inquisition began its investigations, and they were held by the Franciscans in the Basque town of Durango to be discussed in chapter III.

Another tradition which frequently accompanied the Joachist ideal of the imminent 'spiritual church' originated in the myth of a crusade which would end with the transference of the papacy to Jerusalem and the reformation of the world under the last emperor. Who the emperor might be was a subject of speculation. For some he was to be a French king, for others a German, and by the early fourteenth century the Franciscan Arnaldo de Vilanova had proclaimed that he would be the king of Aragon, while the mystic Ramon Lull was uncertain as to whether the great crusade would be led by a king of Aragon or France.[21] In early sixteenth-century Castile all the Spanish rulers, Ferdinand of Aragon, Cisneros and Charles V, were suggested.

In the visions of Sor María de Santo Domingo it was Cisneros who recurred. She spoke of a saintly reformer who would become pope with the assistance of the Dominicans and two or three Franciscans. She did not actually specify whether Cisneros was to be the pope or one of the Franciscans who were to help him, but this could be inferred. She claimed that she herself would convert 90,000 Muslims in a day, that she would visit Jerusalem twice and that she had foreseen Cisneros's triumphant arrival in Oran - dreams all in keeping with the cardinal's plans for a new crusade. Proof of the authenticity of Sor María's inspiration was supplied by her miracles. When she had taken communion the elements had supposedly approached her of their own accord. During her trances, she was said to have answered searching theological questions although she was ignorant of dogmatic niceties. A wound had reputedly opened between her ribs on Maundy Thursday. She had been seen struggling with the devil. Christ had presented her with a ring. Countless admirers implored her to wear articles belonging to them in order to benefit from her supernatural qualities and Cisneros himself asked her to wear a Franciscan girdle for his sake.

Such evident sanctity was accompanied by the certitude of both María and her admirers that she was impeccable. God, she maintained, had told her that He would keep her from sin. This belief was to be invaluable when her prosecutors accused her of moral misdemeanours, of embracing her followers and of allowing her confessor to spend the entire night in her cell. Later in the century Sor María's persuasion might have had grave consequences, but as it was she was judged by an apostolic tribunal clearly predisposed in her favour. She was defended fervently by her confessor and a fellow Dominican. She was protected by the king and the inquisitor general, and the Holy Office chose not to intervene. Despite the opposition of several powerful members of her order, including the vicar general, she was fully acquitted, and her judges recommended her as a model of piety.

Cardinal Cisneros welcomed those prophets who foresaw his own triumph. Charles de Bovelles, the French admirer of Lull, stayed with him in 1506 and spoke of the reconquest of the Holy Land due to take place within twelve years and the imminent conversion of the world to Christianity. Three years later, after Cisneros's victory at Oran, Bovelles exhorted him to continue his march through the territory of the infidel, to press as far as Jerusalem and fulfil the prophecy of Jeremiah.

In 1512 Cisneros received reports about a man uttering similar prophecies, Fray Melchor.[22] The son of rich *converso* merchants, Melchor spent his youth at the court of England where he was called to repentance. He returned to Spain with the intention of pursuing his journey into Africa, but remained in the peninsula. After joining one religious order after another he encountered Sor María de Santo Domingo who advised him to become a Franciscan. The vicar general allowed him to travel from convent to convent in his endeavour to fulfil his mission of reform, and in the course of his peregrinations he met a number of *beatas* who amazed him by their sanctity: Cisneros's protégée Madre Marta and, possibly, Francisca Hernández who was to play so important a part among the *alumbrados*. Fray Melchor, like Bovelles, believed in the impending conversion of the Muslims and maintained that the entire Church would be transformed within twelve years: seven had elapsed and in the five that remained the Holy Roman Empire would be destroyed, all the kings of Europe vanishing together with their kingdoms. The whole clergy, with the exception of a few reformers, would be beheaded and the Church would then be re-established in Jerusalem.

Predictions of this kind can be documented throughout Europe at the time, transmitted by every available means - in woodcuts, in broadsheets, but above all by word of mouth.[23] In the world of the *alumbrados* of Toledo they recur again and again. In about 1523, the vicar of the convent of La Salceda stated that Luther was Antichrist but that God would remedy the havoc caused in Christendom by way of a creature with the stigmata who would introduce peace on earth among the Jews, the Muslims and the Christians.[24] Slightly later, when the learned Franciscan Francisco Ortiz justified his devotion to Francisca Hernández before the Inquisition, he emphasised the providential rôle that *beata* was due to play in the reform of the Franciscan order. She had not come to impose a new way of life, he said, but to 'end the blindness' which had led men to concentrate on external things. The revolution she was about to accomplish was purely spiritual: she was to show that the essence of the poverty which God and St Francis had prescribed for the Friars Minor was 'not to refrain from touching money with one's hands . . . true poverty consisted in banishing all covetousness of this world from one's heart'.[25] The plan for reforming the world which another Franciscan, Francisco de Ocaña, divulged to one of the leading *alumbrados*, Pedro Ruiz de Alcaraz, was less spiritual: this time Francisca Hernández was to accompany the friar to Rome and to rewrite the Scriptures while a new pope was installed and the king of France was dispossessed of his kingdom by Charles V.[26]

Orthodoxy and heterodoxy

During the primacy of Cardinal Cisneros the *beatas* and the visionaries were not the objects of local piety alone. The spectacles they provided drew crowds. Their fame spread; they were supported by the court and the nobility and had the approval of a part at least of the ecclesiastical hierarchy. Only some years after Cisneros's death did ecclesiastical tribunals probe the sources of their inspiration and obtain repeated confessions of imposture and diabolical influences.

Mysticism, at the same time, was generally commended as the best means for even the humblest Spaniard to reach God. It was a short cut, described in the vernacular, and open to the unlearned. It was also essentially individual and bred a piety of peculiar intensity.

Intense religiosity tended to be greeted with enthusiasm. Not until the 1520s, with the Lutheran Reformation in Germany, did the fear develop that a particular kind of piety was dangerous, and not until the Council of Trent, which opened in 1545, were dogmatic definitions provided which made a clear distinction between what was Roman Catholic and what Protestant. Certainly previous councils had reached conclusions on many points; there was no doubt in anybody's mind that the convert to Christianity who reverted to Islam or to Judaism was a heretic. The fundamentals of the faith as expressed in the Apostles' Creed had to be respected, but a great deal of space was left for opinions. The various monastic orders were accustomed to fierce debates about matters such as the immaculate conception of the Virgin Mary; other views were discussed at the universities and at the Spanish feudal courts. Justification, a subject which was to come under such suspicion with the Reformation, had long provoked argument. Numerous teachings were admitted and were held by men who were to remain loyal to the Catholic Church in spite of the Lutheran schism.[27]

The uncertainty about what was orthodox allows us to understand how the *alumbrados* of Toledo had been able to proselytise for some seven years, from about 1512 to 1519, before being denounced to the Inquisition, and how they were able to continue their activity for another five years before being condemned.[28] It is also reflected in the attitude of those powerful noblemen who protected them.

Catholic patrons

The ideas of the *alumbrados* of Toledo, it was later claimed, originated in the Franciscan convents in which *recogimiento* was being practised.[29] Soon, however, they were taken outside the convent walls and spread among the laity, and they were accepted with eagerness at the courts of the Spanish nobility with which the *alumbrados* were connected.

The entire area of the early *alumbrado* movement, the town of Guadalajara, the villages and convents in the valleys and hills to the south and south-east, between the Henares and the Tagus, was dominated by the various branches of the Mendoza family, at its head, the Duke of Infantado. The Mendozas were the *alumbrados'* first patrons, employing, protecting and befriending them.

The third Duke of Infantado, Don Diego Hurtado de Mendoza, one of the richest and most powerful of the Spanish grandees, was to be accorded the honour of entertaining the king of France after his capture at the battle of Pavia in 1525. He had formerly been an active warrior, but in his old age he was increasingly afflicted by gout and confined to his apartments. The splendid ducal palace in Guadalajara, built at the end of the fifteenth century by Juan and Enrique Guas, appears to have been a centre of streams of piety. It was later said that the duke had come to agree with Luther's doctrine of salvation.[30] Such a rumour, however, was probably the result of his interest in different religious opinions including those of the *alumbrados*, for the duke was also known for his love of relics and ceremonies. He turned his palace into 'a cathedral or chapel royal',[31] making elaborate provisions for services of extreme grandeur in his private chapel and assembling singers and musical instruments on a scale exceptional among his contemporaries.

The second great nobleman to protect the *alumbrados* was Don Diego López Pacheco, second Marquess of Villena and Duke of

Escalona.[32] The son of Don Juan Fernández Pacheco, the favourite of Henry IV of Castile, Don Diego had taken part in the civil war following the sovereign's death in 1474. He had fought against the new queen of Castile in defence of the dead king's daughter and certain rights to which he laid claim. By 1479 he had to admit defeat. He had lost over half of his numerous possessions, and when he was pardoned the next year he had to be contented with the favour of the Catholic Kings and titles which he held only in name. Nevertheless, he distinguished himself at the siege of Granada twelve years later, obtaining fresh estates in reward for his services. After Isabella's death he opposed Ferdinand's regency of Castile and tried to check the political power of Cisneros, finally committing himself to Ferdinand's grandson who succeeded to the throne as Charles I of Spain in 1516 and was elected Holy Roman Emperor, Charles V, in 1519. Don Diego supported the royal cause in the revolts of the early 1520s[33] and then retired for good to his castle of Escalona.

Villena's castle, some twenty-five miles north-north-west of Toledo on the road to Avila and commanding a bend in the river Alberche, had once contained one of the most magnificent courts in Spain, that of Don Alvaro de Luna. Like the Infantado palace in Guadalajara it was filled by its owner with representatives of different religious ideas. Don Diego shared a devotion to the Franciscans with his second wife, Doña Juana Enríquez, the sister of the Admiral of Castile. He founded churches and convents on his estates, the headquarters of his own spiritual advisers being the observantine convent he built outside Escalona in 1493. Yet it was not only the Franciscans who stimulated the marquess's faith: he was also an admirer of Erasmus. Francisco de Osuna dedicated to him his *Tercer abecedario espiritual*, that standard manual on mysticism, but the marquess also received the dedication of the far less orthodox *Diálogo de doctrina christiana* by Juan de Valdés, who had once attended him as his page.

Although many other members of the nobility are mentioned in the trials of the *alumbrados*, there is a third figure of special prominence: the Marquess of Villena's brother-in-law, Don Fadrique Enríquez, Admiral of Castile.[34] A veteran of the siege of Granada, he was to act as joint regent during Charles V's tours abroad and was to be one of the first governors of Spain to urge the monarch to proceed against the Lutherans. After the defeat of the rebels in 1521 he too withdrew from public life and settled on his estates in Medina de Ríoseco, north-west of Valladolid. He too built Franciscan convents, and to him Francisco de Osuna dedicated another of his books, the *Gracioso Convite*. For all his encouragement of anti-Lutheran measures Don Fadrique too was attracted by all manifestations of true piety. Convinced of the need to reform the Church, he briefly assembled on his estates men who were later to be accused of Lutheranism; he corresponded until his death with Fray Francisco Ortiz living in the convent of Torrelaguna after his condemnation by the Inquisition; and it was to Don Fadrique that the alleged founder of the *alumbrado* movement, Isabel de la Cruz, turned in order to obtain her release from imprisonment in 1529.[35]

Throughout the sixteenth century members of the Spanish nobility encouraged reformers of the Church. A few were implicated in the Lutheran scare of the late 1550s, but by and large they gave their support to orthodox movements. Aristocrats helped John of Avila and assisted the Jesuits. They were attracted by the Carmelite reformers and by other mystics and ascetics who flourished in the second half of the century. Many of their younger children entered convents to practise asceticism themselves, but Francisco de Osuna also wrote extensively on how noblemen, merely by exercising spiritual poverty, had no need ever to suffer from financial deprivation in their quest for salvation. They could keep their riches and still be sure of a heavenly reward.

Even if a high cultural level was by no means characteristic of the Spanish aristocracy in the sixteenth century, those of its members who were sufficiently educated to appreciate the theological ideas being discussed at the time indicate the sympathies current among the ruling classes. Their readiness to protect the *alumbrados* confirms the uncertainty as to what was orthodox and what was heterodox and suggests, as we shall see in the next chapter, a propensity towards evangelism which they shared with many members of the nobility in Italy but which stopped well short of Protestantism and a break with the Church of Rome.

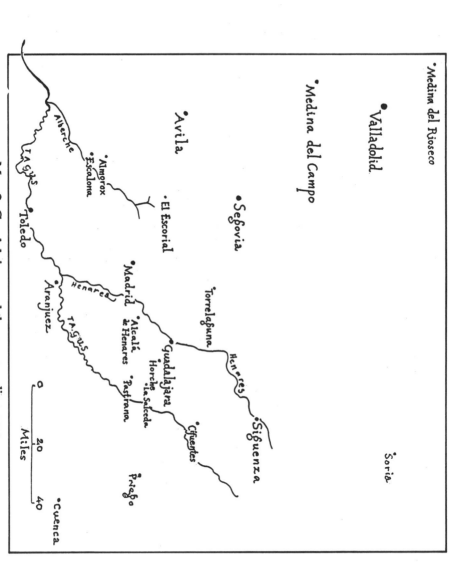

Map 2. Guadalajara and the surrounding area.

Chapter II

The Piety of the *Alumbrados* of Toledo

Born in the last decades of the fifteenth century, the leading *alumbrados* were brought up during the primacy of Cardinal Cisneros. They read the devotional literature the publication of which he had encouraged and they were joined by scholars he had influenced and assisted. Closely connected with the Franciscan *recolectorios* from the outset, they used the language of mysticism which we find in the writings of Francisco de Osuna and Alonso de Madrid. Yet, in a world where ceremonies were lavish and displays of religious fervour frequent, the *alumbrados* formed, in certain respects, a movement of reaction. Their personalities were more typical of the austere nonconformity to be found at a later date in English Puritanism than of the atmosphere of flamboyant ritual frequently associated with sixteenth-century Spanish Catholicism.

The protagonists

Comparatively little is known about Isabel de la Cruz, the *beata* who had become a Franciscan tertiary and had left her family to preach in the Guadalajara region in about 1512.[1] It was she who allegedly first turned ideas which she had assimilated in Franciscan convents into the doctrine of the *alumbrados*, but only excerpts from her trial have survived and our impressions of her are fragmentary. The trials of two of her earliest followers, on the other hand, are extensive and informative: Pedro Ruiz de Alcaraz and María de Cazalla emerge with exceptional clarity.

Self-righteous, tactless and obstinate, ever ready to criticise and eager to admonish, Pedro Ruiz de Alcaraz excelled in making enemies. Yet his refusal to conform, especially in church, to the behaviour of his neighbours (a feature reflected even in the slovenliness of his clothes), the integrity of his views and the strength of his faith, make him an impressive figure and account for his influence and the devotion he inspired in his disciples.

Like Isabel de la Cruz, Alcaraz was of *converso* descent.[2] The grandson of a scribe and the son of a bread merchant, he was brought up in Guadalajara in the household of Don Pedro Hurtado de Mendoza, who bore the title of *adelantado*, or governor, of Cazorla (a small area close to Jaén in Andalusia). The *adelantado*, as he was always known, was a son of the Marquess of Santillana and brother of the first Duke of Infantado. Subsequently, Alcaraz worked for the *adelantado's* son-in-law, Don Diego Carrillo de Mendoza, third Count of Priego, and then for Don Diego's son and heir Don Luis, who employed him as an accountant. After the death of Don Luis in 1522 he departed for Madrid in the service of Don Benito Cisneros, the nephew of the great cardinal.[3] Returning to Guadalajara soon after, however, he received an invitation from the Marquess of Villena to join him in Escalona. The marquess took on his fourteen-year-old son as his page and gave Alcaraz a salary of 35,000 maravedís a year,[4] hoping to profit not so much from his professional services as from his talents as a lay preacher. He seems to have owed his acquaintance to Antonio de Baeza, the *alcalde* or judicial official of Escalona, who was noted for his piety and erudition. Alcaraz remained in the marquess's employment until his arrest by the Inquisition in 1524.[5]

Married, the father of a number of children and the owner of a small property in Guadalajara, Alcaraz was professionally concerned with money matters and led an essentially secular existence. He never attended university or studied theology and he only had a limited knowledge of Latin. Yet he had an immense interest in devotional works. He possessed a library which was large by contemporary standards and included nearly all the religious literature in the vernacular printed under Cardinal Cisneros. He owned the works of 'the Carthusians', almost certainly the lives of Christ by Ludolph of Saxony and Juan de Padilla, and possibly the Castilian translation of Denis the Carthusian's *De Quatuor Novissimis*. His collection included *El estimulo de amor* attributed to Bonaventure, the *Meditaciones* ascribed to Augustine, a *Flos sanctorum*, Hugh of Balma's *Sol de contemplativos*, Bernard's sermons, the book of Angela of Foligno (bound with the Rule of St Clare and Vincent Ferrer's treatise on the spiritual life), a Latin and a Castilian version of the Scriptures, the *Imitation of Christ* (*Contemptus mundi*) and a book to which he referred as St Benedict's *Directorio* but which was almost certainly García de Cisneros's *Ejercitatorio de la vida espiritual*. He was well acquainted, furthermore, with John Climacus's *Spiritual Ladder* and with the letters and prayers of Catherine of Siena.[6]

Alcaraz was known for his asceticism, but this was far surpassed by the austerity of María de Cazalla. The accountant was later to write to the inquisitors that she used to make fun of her brother Juan when he cried because of his chilblains, 'saying that he preached fortitude but did not know how to practise it'. 'For,' Alcaraz went on, 'she attached little importance to the sorrows of this world, even to death, and since I knew our weaknesses I regarded her as presumptuous.'[7] Alcaraz succumbed, during his imprisonment, to that sense of persecution and friendlessness which the Holy Office sometimes succeeded in engendering.[8] María de Cazalla, on the other hand, never did. Until her release she courageously defended herself and others accused, resisting torture and risking ever heavier sentences by corresponding with her friends. The attraction she had for scholars and members of the Mendoza family testifies to a personality of exceptional force.

María de Cazalla, too, was of *converso* descent, but she was of a higher social standing than Isabel de la Cruz or Alcaraz. She came from Palma del Río in Andalusia, where her father had been a merchant and her mother's family had worked in the service of the Count of Palma, Don Luis Fernández de Portocarrero.[9] One of her own brothers, Juan de Cazalla, entered the Franciscan order and became chaplain to Cardinal Cisneros. He was subsequently appointed titular bishop of Verissa in Thrace, visitor of the archbishopric of Toledo and coadjutor of the bishop of Avila. María herself married a rich merchant from Guadalajara, Lope de Rueda. In Guadalajara she became a favourite in the Duke of Infantado's family, and was befriended by the duke's wife, by his illegitimate daughter, Doña Brianda de Mendoza, by his daughter-in-law the Countess of Saldaña, as well as by the Duke of Medinaceli's bastard brother Don Alonso de la Cerda. Through her brother Juan, moreover, her connections extended to elevated academic, ecclesiastical and political circles, and she was well acquainted with some of the most distinguished scholars at the nearby university of Alcalá. These, in turn, provided her with ideas and with reading matter, and by the time of her own arrest (which was not to occur until 1532), she had been able to indulge her considerable intellectual curiosity.

The edict of faith

The ideas which brought about the arrest of the *alumbrados* were listed and condemned in an edict of faith issued by the inquisitor general Alonso Manrique, archbishop of Seville, in 1525.[10] It contained forty-eight propositions, mainly statements or snatches of conversation overheard by hostile witnesses. A number seem to have been recorded by the inquisitors with a notable lack of grammatical precision and they were all presented in a disjointed and isolated form, outside the general context in which they had been uttered. The majority of the propositions were attributed to Alcaraz, and nearly all the rest to Isabel de la Cruz and her other followers: María de Cazalla and her brother Juan; Gaspar de Bedoya, a *converso* priest and Isabel's principal legate in Pastrana; Alonso López de la Palomera, a crippled weaver also from Pastrana; and Rodrigo de Bivar, the cantor of the Duke of Infantado's choir, and, with López de la Palomera, one of the very few Old Christians involved.

The first purpose of the edict of faith was to make known the reprehensible nature of the statements listed - each was accompanied by qualifications ranging from 'heretical' to 'false', 'erroneous', or simply 'mad'. It was read in its final form on Sundays and feast-days in order to put the faithful on their guard against the new doctrine. Drafts of the paper also had other objects, however. The edict dated 23 September 1525 had been preceded by edicts probably going back to the previous year. These contained the same propositions and were designed to elicit further denunciations from anybody who had heard any of the propositions but had not yet reported them to the Holy Office. They also summoned those guilty of having uttered such statements to appear before the inquisitors with a spontaneous confession. Both María de Cazalla and Rodrigo de Bivar responded to the appeal: the former consequently escaped arrest until 1532 and the latter until 1539.[11] Another object of the edict was to prompt the memory of forgetful witnesses during the trials themselves. Indeed, many of the denunciations the inquisitors received from their prisoners, particularly in the 1530s, were the result of a fresh reading of the document of 1525.

The edict was directed against persons 'who called themselves enlightened, abandoned and perfect', '*alumbrados, dexados e perfectos*'. As in the case of so many heresies of the past the names, particularly that of *alumbrado*, were originally terms of mockery and abuse. *Alumbrado* had been used previously to denote excessive piety and to suggest hysteria and hypocrisy or fraudulence.[12] Never, in the history of the different groups making up the heresy, did anyone agree that he or she was an *alumbrado*. The word remained a term of accusation alone.

Because of the manner in which it was composed the edict cannot, at a first glance, be considered a satisfactory definition of a doctrine. At least one of the statements, that the world was to end in twelve years' time (qualified as 'mad'), reflected the views of Charles de Bovelles and Fray Melchor, but was probably attributable to one of the opponents of Isabel de la Cruz and her followers. Other statements, reminiscent of the evangelical movements in northern Europe, were of uncertain authorship and the ideas they expressed had little prominence in what we know of the beliefs of the *alumbrados*.[13] The thirty-fifth proposition runs 'that in no manner is it legitimate to swear' ('*que en ninguna manera se avía de jurar*'), a conviction of the Swiss Anabaptists in the 1520s which spread among the Anabaptists in southern Germany and the Rhineland and was later adopted by the Dutch Mennonites. A further view which was at best of marginal relevance to the teaching of the *alumbrados* was that a work attributed to St Augustine was the fruit of fantasy, '*que los Soliloquios de S. Agustín eran cosas fantaseadas*'. The work in question, *Meditaciones, Soliloquio y manual*, one of the Castilian publications encouraged by Cisneros, was in fact a medieval compilation of texts by Anselm, John of St Victor, Cyprian, Gregory and other authors (including Augustine), and its true authorship may well have been suggested by the learned Juan de Cazalla.

Most of the propositions, however, can be fitted into a more coherent faith. One was that 'prayer must be mental and not vocal'. Many expressed contempt for the cult of the saints, the worship of images, bulls, indulgences, fasting, abstinence and the commandments of the Church. Others concerned *dejamiento*, abandonment, passive reliance on the divine will, a devotional state in which no special form of prayer or place suitable for meditation was required but which brought about a condition of perfection in which 'the love of God in man was God'. No effort should be made to combat temptations - indeed, they should rather be embraced and accepted. All activity was an obstacle to the divine presence in the soul. It was thus wrong to ask anything of the Almighty, to think of the humanity of Christ, or, by exerting the memory, even to remember God.

Dejamiento

The edict of faith presented the most exaggerated and damning possible version of the *alumbrados*' beliefs. So did the bills of indictment submitted during the trials. But we should now examine the condemned teaching in the light of the *alumbrados*' own defences and of what we know of kindred movements of the time.

Dejamiento would appear to have first been devised by Isabel de la Cruz who, Alcaraz was to claim under torture, derived her entire doctrine from the Franciscans.[14] There is no doubt that *dejamiento* had a great appeal in the Franciscan convents of the diocese of Toledo and it is often presented in opposition to the accepted method of meditation described in the previous chapter, *recogimiento*. The danger of such a distinction is that the word *recogimiento* can in fact be applied to any method of meditation and can lose all precise meaning. If, however, it is taken to be the method prescribed by Francisco de Osuna, we can examine the elements common to, and the differences between, these two ways of reaching God.

The main scene of the conflict was the town of Pastrana where Osuna himself and two of his fellow Franciscans, Francisco Ortiz and Cristóbal de Tendilla, were instructing the local laity in the practice of *recogimiento*. It consisted, according to one practitioner, Jerónimo Olivares, in a gathering of the senses which entailed banishing all thoughts and placing the soul in a state of quiet until it reached the stage in which 'it recalled neither itself nor God'.[15] In order to achieve this condition Olivares and his companions knelt for a while and then sat down in a corner with their eyes closed.

Another practitioner, Graviel Sánchez, a curate of Pastrana, was told by Osuna to reserve certain hours for meditation, to endeavour to cease thinking, and to 'abandon his will and heart to God'. If he did this for an hour before and an hour after mass every day he would finally reach the point when he could practise the method continuously, in the choir, in a cell, or while performing any other activity, even in the market-place. Yet another practitioner, Nicolás de Enbid, said he had been instructed to free his heart of anything offensive to God, 'to raise his will to love God'. Once he was 'feasting' in this state of suspension he would need to seek no further but should cast away all thoughts, even virtuous ones. Cristóbal de Tendilla, he added, had told him that it was then a temptation even to think of God.[16]

Doubts about the benefits of *recogimiento* were introduced into the community of Pastrana by Olivares's brother, Francisco Jiménez, who travelled to Cifuentes and was there introduced by Fray Diego de Barreda and Fray Antonio de Pastrana, both Franciscans, to *dejamiento*.[17] Judging from Olivares's account, the principal difference between the two methods lay in the physical circumstances in which they were practised. The *dejados* dispensed with those actions recommended by the *recogidos*. To sit in a corner and close one's eyes was unnecessary. The subject merely had to submit himself to God without forcing himself to pray or even to reject temptations. Temptations, evil thoughts, might come; they might be sent by God to purify the soul. The *dejado* was not to combat them; all he could do was not to consent to them wilfully. This form of prayer - for a form of prayer it was - could be used at all times, in all places and by all people. God, Barreda had reminded Olivares, was everywhere. Wherever the devout happened to be they must be engaged in prayer, with the same reverence as if He were standing before them.[18] Isabel de la Cruz and Alcaraz had also maintained that 'the prayer could be said continuously, wherever or however one liked, even while trading, and that nothing could impede it'. Isabel presented Alcaraz as an example of a layman who was married and constantly engaged in business ' in the market-place', but who let no such detail stand in his way. Another witness recalled Alcaraz as saying that one could pray to God anywhere, just as 'peasants and carpenters prayed as they worked'.[19]

Fray Diego de Barreda had told Francisco Jiménez that '*dejamiento* was a better and a surer way than *recogimiento*.[20] When the Franciscan chapter of Toledo met at Escalona in May 1524 the '*scandalosae inventae viae illuminatorum seu dimittentium*' were condemned. For Fray Diego and the authors of the decree the difference between the two methods was clear, but it was not so for everyone. Both *recogimiento* and *dejamiento* were universal; both were practised by Franciscans; both seemed to lead to the inactivity of the senses, even if writers on *recogimiento* were cautious in their terminology and thus escaped the charge of advocating complete passivity. In the twelfth proposition of the edict against the *alumbrados* which refers specifically to *dejamiento*, the inquisitors seem to have incorporated a part of Nicolás de Enbid's description of *recogimiento*.[21] When the prosecutor presented Francisco Ortiz with the bill of indictment he included this proposition, and Ortiz showed no sign of being aware of the error.[22] Olivares and Francisca Hernández both referred to Alcaraz's method of prayer as *recogimiento*.[23]

The confusion was increased, perhaps disingenuously, by the defendants. On being asked how he defined the two methods, Alcaraz, who had formerly denounced the *recogidos*, said that he understood both words to mean the same thing: a determination not to offend God, to refrain from vices, to avoid vanities and to keep the commandments of God and the Church.[24] When questioned about her preference for *dejamiento* or *recogimiento* when she first visited Pastrana in the early 1520s María de Cazalla also answered that she 'had never held an opinion on what was practised in Pastrana and Guadalajara but simply sought . . . by all means the best way, closest to the doctrine of the saints, to reach God and know His will so as to obey it.'[25] Defences such as these must, of course, be treated with scepticism, but there are also other items of evidence. If the Fray Cristóbal included among the correspondents of Isabel de la Cruz can be identified with Cristóbal de Tendilla, and if the Fray Andrés de Ecija on the same list was the provincial who defrocked the tertiary and was so moved by Olmillos's utterances, it would seem that even those most closely associated with the method of *recogimiento* were prepared to experiment with rival arts.[26]

But can the *alumbrados* be regarded as mystics? In their defence both Isabel de la Cruz and Alcaraz claimed that they could be. Alcaraz possessed the standard manual on mysticism, Hugh of Balma's *Sol de contemplativos*. He quoted it in his defence, albeit not as frequently as the *Imitation of Christ*, and mainly at a later stage in his trial when his letters were being written by his counsel, Fray Reginaldo de Esquina.[27] He also referred to mystical steps.[28] Isabel de la Cruz was even more specific about the mystical and progressive nature of *dejamiento*. She had said there were three types of prayer, vocal, mental and supramental. She informed the inquisitors that she advised the beginners to devote themselves to discipline, fasting, prayer and meditation on the passion of Christ, and that it was only '*los que estavan ynstrutos*', the initiates, who had attained a sufficient degree of virtue, whom she told to pay no heed to these 'base' things but to remain 'for ever suspended in the desire and love of God'. She gave the names of 'beginners' and those 'advanced'. Alcaraz was among the latter.[29]

Scepticism and reaction

Even if they were indeed mystics, the first *alumbrados* were all opposed to the more flamboyant manifestations of religious enthusiasm so popular at the time. Our knowledge of Isabel de la Cruz's attitude rests largely on the testimony of Alonso López de la Palomera, the crippled weaver who had been afflicted by trembling fits when attending the elevation of the eucharist and had been taken to Isabel de la Cruz by the Count of Saldaña's steward. Isabel told him to beware of appropriating 'the gifts of God', for a high price would be exacted on the day of judgement. The recipient of these gifts, she said, should hide them. On no account should they be employed as a display of sanctity.[30] Alcaraz agreed. In support of the assertion that, however great the benefits of human and divine consolations, true virtue was to be capable of dispensing with both, he referred to the *Imitation of Christ*. This is the work he quoted more frequently than any other non-Scriptural source and with such accuracy that he either knew entire sections of it by heart or, more probably, had been permitted to keep a copy in prison. On the subject of spiritual consolations he cited the celebrated passage in the eleventh chapter of the second book: 'Many follow Jesus to the breaking of bread, but few follow Him to the drinking of the chalice of His passion. Many revere His miracles, but few follow the ignominy of the Cross.'[31] In Alcaraz's eyes spiritual consolations were, at their best, spectacular shows of divine grace which the recipient was well advised to keep under control. At their worst they were inspired by the devil.

Such an approach was by no means novel. The majority of writers on mysticism gave the same warning, and they did so with growing urgency in the course of the sixteenth century: John of the Cross and Teresa of Avila are two of many examples. In *alumbrado* circles there was a special interest in the admonitions given by Gerson (who was widely believed, at the time, to be the author of the *Imitation of Christ*). One of Alcaraz's most devoted followers, the learned *alcalde* of Escalona, Antonio de Baeza, translated into Castilian Gerson's tract *De probatione spirituum*. It was written on the occasion of the debate about the canonisation of Bridget of Sweden at Constance in 1415, and dealt with the authenticity of inspiration. Gerson did not deny the value of visions any more than he claimed it was impossible to determine their authenticity. He merely recommended the utmost caution and insisted that only spiritual men, of whom there were few, could judge matters of the spirit.

Yet, however common scepticism about outer manifestations of grace may be in the history of mysticism, it ran against the grain of Cardinal Cisneros's ecclesiastical policy and of the Franciscan mystics who pursued the same tradition after the cardinal's death. Thus Vincent Ferrer's strictures on visions and trances were expurgated from the 1510 edition of his *Tractatus de vita spirituali* and Francisco de Osuna expressed favourable opinions on the subject in his *Tercer abecedario*, even if he punctuated his book with conventional warnings about the possibility of Satanic influence in spiritual excesses. He maintained, probably with Alcaraz and his circle in mind, that to deny the value of spiritual consolations was to express an idea 'forged in the devil's furnace which is accustomed to falsify and impair pious intentions'. Those who, like the *alumbrados*, regarded spiritual consolations as an indirect means of reaching God which tied man down ('*ataduras*'), 'are unworthy of a reply since they equate spiritual consolation with worldly consolation and say they are both self love'. Osuna himself seems to have viewed spiritual consolations in the same light as the humanity of Christ: 'If humanity is a way to reach God, His sweetness spurs us on to run to Him'. It is necessary; the taste of sweetness is a gift of God for which we should be grateful; but it is only a step on the way to union with Him.[32]

The attitude of the first *alumbrados* to the more flamboyant manifestations of mysticism was certainly unpopular in Spain in the early 1520s. It brought Alcaraz into conflict with the Franciscans, and it brought Isabel de la Cruz into conflict with other *beatas* and their followers. It could gain the enmity of rivals such as Francisca Hernández and María de Tejeda, but it could not be considered heretical. Nevertheless it pointed to another side of *dejamiento*, one which bore a resemblance to Lutheranism.

Sin and grace

Isabel de la Cruz and her circle were far from sharing the optimism of Francisco de Osuna. Persuaded of the sinfulness of others, they were equally convinced of their own initial unworthiness. María de Cazalla had a particular liking for the seventh and eighth chapters of the Epistle to the Romans. One of her favourite texts when she commented on the New Testament was Rom 7:19: 'For the good that I would I do not: but the evil which I would not, that I do.' Her deep sense of sinfulness was to make her responsive to the section of Erasmus's *Enchiridion* on the 'inner and outer man'. It also affected her domestic behaviour, leading her to refrain from any sexual relations with her husband. When she resumed them (on the advice of Isabel de la Cruz) she did so with unconcealed distaste. Her feeling of unworthiness was accompanied by an even more intense longing for God. She spoke of an 'anguished desire to see God without a veil and apart from my body'. The statement, with echoes of 2 Cor 3:14-16, was associated by the inquisitors with the heretical claim to see God 'face to face' and was attributed to some of the *alumbrados* later in the century.[33]

It was with the same awareness of human worthlessness and the same aspiration towards communion with God that Alcaraz developed the idea of a double process of man's belief in the love that God has for him, accompanied by his reliance on the love of God. Alcaraz provided a number of Scriptural quotations in support of this process. He referred frequently to the Johannine Epistles, which can be said to have provided the basis of his spirituality. His preference was for 1 Jn 4:16: 'And we have known and believed the love that God hath to us. God is love; and he that dwelleth in love dwelleth in God, and God in him.' Before the inquisitors he quoted Rom 9:16, 'So then it is not of him that willeth, nor of him that runneth, but of God that sheweth mercy', and

2 Cor 10:5: 'Casting down imaginations, and every high thing that exalteth itself against the knowledge of God, and bringing into captivity every thought to the obedience of Christ'.[34]

Love was a gift of God, comprehensible to God alone, which He had bestowed on Alcaraz and which Alcaraz had recognised by its effect. It was dispensed independently of human effort. The will had to be abdicated. Alcaraz maintained that 'all our good works proceeded from God and that man could do nothing for himself but subject himself to God and recognise his own worthlessness, and that even this recognition was a gift of God'. When the inquisitors objected that God had given us knowledge of good and evil together with the freedom to choose between the two, Alcaraz had replied that 'one made far better use of the freedom of will by submitting it to God since no choice could be made without Him.' Reliance on God, abandonment to His will, was to be so complete that there was no point in endeavouring to arouse the human will to resist temptations or to fret about salvation. '*Qui amat animam suam, perdet eam*' (Jn 12:25) was to be taken literally.[35]

Works, Alcaraz believed, were the consequence of the love of God; they never preceded it. If man really loved God he would perform great works, and otherwise he did not love God.

How, the inquisitors wondered, could Alcaraz be so sure that he possessed the love of God? And what was the result of this certainty? In reply to the first question Alcaraz quoted Jn 3:8, '*Spiritus ubi vult spirat*'. He had tasted the love of God and could allow no doubt as to its existence in him, unworthy though he might be. To the second question the replies of both Alcaraz and Isabel de la Cruz have survived. In words reminiscent of 1 Jn 3:9 Isabel de la Cruz admitted to believing that 'as long as she retained this love of God she could not be deceived and that she could not err as long as she remained in this love of God and her neighbour'. Alcaraz too assured the inquisitors that 'love was so deeply rooted in him that it was impossible for him to misinterpret the Scriptures or to err' and added that 'it was impossible for him to lie'.[36]

On the face of it such confidence would seem to justify the charge of antinomianism, and indeed this was to be the principal characteristic of the later *alumbrado* movements: their members were convinced they had achieved such a degree of grace that they could not sin. Isabel de la Cruz's followers, however, always regarded *dejamiento* as the elimination of the desire to sin, and not as a state of impeccability in which sins can be committed but not regarded as such.[37] All that is known of Alcaraz's doctrine in practice confirms the asceticism of his piety. He frequently quoted Col 3:5: 'Mortify . . . your members'. Another passage which he advanced as a source for *dejamiento* was Mt 16:24: 'If any man will come after me, let him deny himself, and take up his cross, and follow me'. When he was asked by the inquisitors how he interpreted these words he said they meant we should deny our own will, refrain from mortal sin, relinquish vanities and refuse to love anything temporal and contrary to the will of Christ in adversity.[38]

Saints, ceremonies and the commandments of the Church

A high proportion of the propositions condemned in the edict of 1525 expressed contempt for the cult of the saints, the worship of images, and the ceremonies and commandments of the Church. Such charges had come to form part and parcel of a number of heresies over the centuries, and since the fifteenth century were associated with the more radical movements of reform. In Spain in the 1520s they could suggest the indifference to Christianity of the Judaizer or the hatred of Rome of the Lutheran. The *alumbrados* were accused of saying that it was not necessary to bow the head when the name of Jesus was mentioned, to stand up when the Gospel was read at mass or when the Holy Sacrament was carried through the streets, nor to take holy water and cross oneself on entering a church. Two of the propositions contained the statement that the cross was a piece of wood which was not entitled to be worshipped. Two were directed against the veneration of images and two against praying to the saints. Alcaraz was charged with describing ceremonies and fasts as *ataduras*, 'ties', and of denying the necessity of bulls for the salvation of souls from purgatory.[39]

In response to these charges the *alumbrados* managed to marshal an impressive number of witnesses who testified to their piety in church. They proved that they had purchased indulgences, even if Alcaraz admitted that he had been less and less attracted by images, fasts, vigils, prayers of supplication, and that he had indeed described them as *ataduras* for some people. He had been prepared to 'comply with the world' by attending the required ceremonies, but it is not difficult to see how easily a belief in *dejamiento* could exclude the greater part of external observances. Gaspar de Bedoya thus endeavoured to reduce the mass to its barest essentials. He was against the taking of holy water and all the gestures accompanying the elevation of the eucharist, maintaining that the most perfect state for a priest to be in was one of pure abandonment to the will of God.[40]

One might wonder what effect Alcaraz's teaching had on his younger followers. An answer is provided in the testimony of Pedro de

Marquina, working, like Alcaraz's son and Juan de Valdés, as a page at the castle of Escalona. When he was eighteen or nineteen, Marquina said, he had proposed to enter a religious order. He conceded that Alcaraz's doubts about whether he had a sufficient vocation and his advice that he should not go into a convent did have some influence on his decision to remain a layman. But Marquina was also interrogated about his behaviour at mass. He admitted that since his meeting with Alcaraz he had often failed to strike his breast at the elevation of the eucharist. Why? Marquina replied to the inquisitors that his devotion to the sacrament and his desire to commend himself to it were such that he forgot to perform purely ritual gestures. Before encountering Alcaraz he had always struck his breast. He had always prayed in silence during the prayers and the Epistle. Under the accountant's influence, however, he had started to pay attention to the words of the mass. Instead of praying during the Epistle and the Gospel he now listened.[41]

The Scriptures

One of the aspects of the *alumbrados* that most troubled Spanish churchmen in the sixteenth century was their use of the Scriptures. That laymen with no theological training, *idiotae et illiterati*, should dare to interpret the Bible of their own accord was viewed with increasing misgivings after the Lutheran schism of 1521 and the subsequent Protestant emphasis on the intelligibility of the Old and the New Testament. Alcaraz, Isabel de la Cruz and María de Cazalla had not only done this, but they had done it publicly and had tried to persuade other members of the laity to do so too. As the century drew on alarm grew greater. In 1537 the Franciscan Fray Luis de Maluenda wrote of the *alumbrados* that it was a sad day when 'men with little learning took advantage of Scripture but poorly understood to defend their opinions and pass as if they were learned and wise'; and it was a still sadder day when 'poor little women' left their distaffs and dared to read the Epistles of St Paul. All speculative and moral theology in the Epistles, the friar reminded his readers, was 'written in cipher' and could only be understood by a trained theologian.[42] Over twenty years later, in 1559, the Dominican Melchor Cano also pointed to the *alumbrados* and the Lutherans to illustrate the peril of the Scriptures in the vernacular.[43]

But how did the *alumbrados* believe the Scriptures should be read? Isabel de la Cruz held that they should be approached even without the desire for immediate or proper understanding. They should certainly be read without the sinful curiosity of the 'letter learned', but in the humble spirit in which they were written. As the reader progressed he would be enlightened.[44] Fray Diego de Barreda too said that he had taken from the *dejados* the idea that we should read the Scriptures in simplicity, without desiring anything but to please God.[45]

The dismissal of learning as a means of reaching God was another feature which the *dejados* shared with Francisco de Osuna and the approved writers on mysticism and *recogimiento*. When the inquisitors accused Alcaraz of despising the learned he replied that knowledge could be acquired and it could be infused. Both types were valid, but his own preference lay with the second. 'A saint says that he whose knowledge is infused speaks as a man with experience, like one who has tasted the honey and says it is sweet. He who has not tasted of it says that it is sweet, but he has only tasted of it through knowledge. This is the difference between men.'[46]

From such statements we see that Alcaraz held that only the inspired could truly understand the Bible. His quotation of Jn 3:8, *Spiritus ubi vult spirat*, his faith in the arbitrary distribution of the love of God, attest his belief in the existence of a group inspired with that same spirit which had blown on the simple Evangelists. Isabel de la Cruz and her followers referred to numerous Scriptural passages to confirm the privileges of the spiritual man and to emphasise the mysterious manner in which the Almighty might prefer the unlearned to the learned. Mt 11:25, 'Thou hast hid these things from the wise and prudent, and hast revealed them unto babes', was one of their favourite quotations. In his conversations with Doña Mencía de Mendoza's chaplain, Pedro de Rueda, Alcaraz never tired of asserting his claim to experience and of reminding Rueda that, however well acquainted he might be with Thomas Aquinas, he had advanced no further than the narrow confines of his own learning. Alcaraz quoted Heb 6:4-6, 'For it is impossible for those who were once enlightened, and have tasted of the heavenly gift, and were made partakers of the Holy Ghost, and have tasted the good word of God, and the powers of the world to come, if they shall fall away, to renew them again unto repentance . . . ' Rueda, he insisted, had 'fallen away' irrevocably - he was like Nebuchadnezzar in Dan 4:4, 'at rest in his house, and flourishing in his palace'. As one in the love of God who was most reluctant to have anything to do with someone who was not, Alcaraz also challenged the chaplain with 2 Jn 1:10, 'If there come any unto you, and bring not this doctrine, receive him not into your house, neither bid him God speed.' He advanced 1 Cor 13:8, 'Charity never faileth', as a proof of the sublime privileges the *dejados*, and they alone, enjoyed. In his first letter to the inquisitors written soon after his arrest Alcaraz was equally determined to assert the rights of the spiritual man. To Mt 11:25-26 he added 1 Cor 2:15, 'But he that is spiritual judgeth all things, yet he himself is judged of no man' and 1 Thess 5:19, 'Quench not the Spirit'.[47]

Mysticism or evangelism? Juan de Valdés

The impression of the *alumbrados* with which we are left is contradictory. To the inquisitors Isabel de la Cruz presented herself and her followers as mystics following the traditional stages leading from meditation to contemplation, from the asceticism of the *via purgativa* to the final state of union with the Deity, the hard-won *via unitiva*. Just as statements echoing those of María de Cazalla about the superiority of actions performed out of a disinterested love of God to fasts and penances performed for the sole purpose of reaching heaven can be found in such orthodox works as Alonso de Madrid's *Arte para servir a Dios*,[48] so we see again and again that the *alumbrados* echo or repeat the words of the approved mystics. The emphasis on experience, the hostility towards learning, the quest for permanent prayer, the insistence on the love of God, are all commonplaces which recur in the writings of Francisco de Osuna. Then there is the frequent confusion between *dejamiento* and *recogimiento* to which so many points of community inevitably led. Were the practitioners themselves, one wonders, always aware of the difference between the two?

None the less the teaching of the *alumbrados* does indeed differ from that of the orthodox mystics. Alcaraz's scepticism about ecstasies and trances goes hand in hand with a pessimism about human nature which is in contrast to the optimism of Osuna. Such pessimism extended, it appears, not only to the ritual gestures imposed by the Church but to any work preceding justification. Indeed, according to the inquisitors it even excluded activity at the time when the elect, secure in their attainment of grace, believed themselves beyond the reach of sin and free of all obligations.

Yet the complete passivity on which the inquisitors picked to discredit the movement must also be reconciled with the *alumbrados'* determination to study the Scriptures and with their disapproval of certain aspects of the Catholic Church which had more to it than an aversion to external works. Their criticism of the worship of images, the cult of the saints, the purchase of bulls and indulgences suggests a commitment to reform.

These last aspects of the *alumbrados'* doctrine have affinities with evangelism.[49] Evangelism implies the same pessimism about man, the same reliance on the will of God, the same concern with justification and the desire for a simple form of religion based on a study of the Scriptures, and the same interest in the Pauline Epistles. It existed before the Reformation, but was certainly redirected by Lutheranism, even if those who partook of it did not at first contemplate a break with the Church of Rome.

The similarity between the teaching of the *alumbrados* and evangelism brings us to the one man who can be regarded as a direct link between the two: Juan de Valdés. Because of his background and his career he was typical of the humanists who were to be pursued by the Inquisition in the 1530s. His father, a nobleman, was *regidor* of Cuenca, while his mother was of *converso* descent. One of his elder brothers, Alfonso, was to have a distinguished career at the court of Charles V to which he was attached as 'imperial secretary' for most of his adult life. Juan, as we saw, served for some years as page at the castle of Escalona. The date of his birth is uncertain, but he was probably about fifteen when he entered the service of the Marquess of Villena in the early 1520s and became a disciple of Alcaraz. By 1526 he had left the castle and was studying at the university of Alcalá where he remained until 1531.

In his years at university Juan de Valdés established his name as a writer. His brother Alfonso was a close friend of Erasmus, and Juan too corresponded with the Dutch humanist at the time when his reputation in Spain was at its height. In 1531, suspected by the Inquisition partly on account of his *Diálogo de doctrina christiana* which had been published in 1529, Juan de Valdés left Spain, making first for Rome where he worked at the papal court. In 1535 he settled in Naples, the owner of benefices accorded him by two popes, and remained there until his death in 1541.

By the time he moved to Naples Juan de Valdés was at the centre of a large and influential circle. It included members of the nobility - Giulia Gonzaga and the Marchioness of Pescara, Vittoria Colonna - and eminent churchmen such as Pietro Carnesecchi, Marcantonio Flaminio, Giovanni Morone and the English cardinal Reginald Pole. These distinguished men and women were enthusiastic readers of the elegant works which Valdés composed, finding in them a perfect compromise with Protestant teaching at a time when hopes of reconciliation between Catholics and Lutherans had not yet been abandoned.

The *Diálogo de doctrina christiana* was printed in Alcalá by Miguel de Eguía, Erasmus's Spanish publisher and a close friend of Rodrigo de Bivar and many of the more scholarly *alumbrados*. The book was dedicated to the Marquess of Villena. It was presented, and has often been accepted as, an 'Erasmian' dialogue. Recently, however, it has been shown to contain excerpts from the works of some of the leading Reformers, Luther, Oecolampadius and perhaps Melanchthon - a discovery the consequences of which will be discussed further.[50] Whether the work can also be seen as a reflection of the teaching of Alcaraz is a point which has long been debated.[51] Could ideas which resemble those of the Marquess of Villena's accountant not simply be the result of reading Erasmus? Does the incorporation of passages from early works by Luther not suggest that both Juan de Valdés and the *alumbrados* themselves may have derived their ideas from the great Reformer? Although it may never be possible to answer these questions to anybody's complete satisfaction it cannot be denied that certain parts of the *Diálogo*, which are neither paraphrases of, nor excerpts from, the works of the Protestant Reformers, do bear a strong resemblance to the views of Alcaraz.

Throughout the *Diálogo*, as in all Valdés's subsequent works, there is an overriding concern with justification by faith which could well be the consequence of his acquaintance with Luther. Far closer to the teaching of Alcaraz, on the other hand, is the definition of the 'spiritual man', 'he who tastes and feels spiritual things and rejoices and rests in them, and pays no heed to corporal and outer things, but despises them as inferior'.[52] The same applies to Valdés's words on how the Scriptures should be read: 'I approach them with the greatest devotion and reverence, humbling my spirit before the presence of God, and so I beg Him to enlighten my understanding, so that all I understand be for His glory, the edification of my soul and the benefit of my neighbours'.[53] The passage on conduct at mass, moreover, is reminiscent of the testimony of Pedro de Marquina. Valdés likewise attacks those 'who would not dream of paying attention to what is being said at mass' and who, on being asked after the service what part of the Gospels was sung or what was said in the Epistle, 'can no more tell you a word about it than if they had been in the Indies.'[54]

However many ideas in the *Diálogo de doctrina christiana* may have been derived from Alcaraz, the work shows few signs of mysticism. If it has taken elements from the teaching of the *alumbrados* it would seem to have taken the more evangelical ones. It is only in his later works that Juan de Valdés may have been trying to reconcile the apparent contradictions in the *alumbrados*' doctrine. In the products of his Neapolitan period, such as the *Cento e dieci divine considerazioni* which was to be published posthumously in Basel, we see that his concern with justification by faith is accompanied by an increasing insistence on the experience of a gradual revelation, a progressive enlightenment, which could indeed correspond to Isabel de la Cruz's statements about mystical progress.[55] By then, however, Juan de Valdés had embarked on a course of his own which also deviates from what we know of the views of the *alumbrados*. The Scriptures were to become less and less important for him and were to occupy a subsidiary place beside the work of the Spirit within the soul. Valdés thus exposed his works not only to the disapproval of the custodians of Catholic orthodoxy but also to the distaste of the more severe Protestants.

It may not be fully justifiable to take the writings, particularly the later ones, of a man as learned and as widely read as Juan de Valdés as evidence of where the teaching of the *alumbrados* was pointing, but what we know of the future of other individuals involved in the movement suggests that it may indeed have been one of the possible directions. Otherwise, we can conclude that the doctrine of the *alumbrados* had much in common with evangelism, but that Isabel de la Cruz and her followers also retained a mystical element which gave their teaching a flavour of its own. They did not, perhaps, have time to work out their ideas to the full. As they have been recorded they remain in a somewhat inchoate state. But this too can be said of certain expressions of evangelism elsewhere in Europe.[56]

Chapter III

Tradition and Discussion

Although the possibility of Lutheran influence on the *alumbrados* of Toledo by the time they were arrested in 1524 cannot be dismissed, Luther can hardly have had a part in the genesis of their ideas at an earlier period. It is thus necessary to look at other possible forerunners - at the great heretical movements of the Middle Ages with which the inquisitors so eagerly compared the *alumbrados*, at some of the works circulating among the *alumbrados*, and, finally, at ideas which had been, and were still being, discussed in the households of the Spanish aristocracy.

Medieval precedents
The doctrine of a passive surrender to the will of God (reminiscent of the *Gelassenheit* of the German mystics), the ensuing contempt for works and ceremonies, the claim to perfection to which it could lead and a faith in their own capacity to interpret the Scriptures, were all points which the *alumbrados* were said to share with the heresy of the Free Spirit or Beghards as it was described and condemned in the bull *Ad nostrum* of 1312. In the edict against the *alumbrados* two propositions, both concerning the possibility of attaining perfection on this earth, were equated with those attributed to the Beghards,[1] and one of Alcaraz's judges, the Dominican Domingo Pizarro, also believed the accountant to be in the same tradition.[2]

It is doubtful whether the Beghards and Beguines, those pious communities of lay men and women which proliferated in northern Europe in the early fourteenth century, ever really held the heterodox views ascribed to them.[3] But, guilty or not of the heresy of the Free Spirit, they did carry with them a spiritual vitality and a theological curiosity which did not leave those whom they encountered unaffected. They were highly mobile, travelling and forming groups throughout Europe north of the Alps and the Pyrenees, and assisting in the spread of the most diverse ideas, from justification by faith to the conviction of the approaching millennium and the mystical teachings elaborated in the Rhineland. A channel by which their views could have entered Spain can again be found in that indefatigable conveyor of ideas, the Order of St Francis, for there was a strong and reciprocal attraction between the Franciscan third order and the Beghards, especially after the latter had been condemned.

Franciscans were involved in the spread of a variety of more or less heterodox views. Throughout the fourteenth century friars cherishing Joachist prophecies had been detected in Majorca, Valencia, Aragon and Catalonia.[4] They were often also influenced by the first great schismatic movement within the order, the Fraticelli, determined to reimpose the rule of absolute poverty of the founder and condemned by the pope in 1317. At the same time, in central Italy and Provence, the effect can be charted of a movement among the conventual Franciscans known as the 'sect of the Spirit of Freedom', accused of denying the existence of hell and the freedom of the will and believing that, when a certain state of grace has been reached, man can do whatever he likes and whatever he does is perfect.[5] All these ideas were ascribed to the *alumbrados*. The denial of hell (to which we shall return in chapter V) was one of the propositions contained in the edict of 1525, while Alcaraz was accused of holding the concomitant view of universal salvation. Such a teaching, proclaimed in a modified form by the Greek Church Father Origen in the third century and revived in the ninth by Scotus Erigena, has a long history and could have any number of sources, but one of the only *alumbrados* to admit to having held it was a Franciscan, Diego de Barreda: the flames of hell, he had said, were in our own will and there was no hell other than offending God.[6]

Franciscans also made up the other significant heretical movement with which Fray Domingo Pizarro compared the *alumbrados*. This time it was purely Spanish, and its members were known as the 'heretics of Durango'. Its leader, Alfonso de Mella, was from a distinguished family in Zamora in Castile. One of his brothers was to be made a cardinal and another a bishop. Fray Alfonso's own orthodoxy, however, fell under suspicion after his first sermons in the early 1430s. As a punishment he was sentenced to ten years reclusion in a convent in Umbria, once the centre of Franciscan unrest. Returning to Castile with a papal absolution, he again visited Italy before settling in Durango, a small town in the hills behind Bilbao in the Basque region. There, in the 1440s, he and other Franciscans were accused of various misdemeanours which included inveighing against matrimony and indulging in fornication on a grand scale.[7]

According to Fray Alfonso himself his crime was simply to have preached the 'truth of the Holy Gospel as it has been disclosed by the holy doctors and decrees'. God, he continued in a letter addressed to the king of Castile from his place of refuge in the kingdom of Granada, had had the singular goodness to 'declare in my heart that His holy law and Gospels have never hitherto been explained satisfactorily by experts, according to the authentic truth which they contain, and therefore require a new and urgent exposition'. For revelation was a gradual process - Fray Alfonso recapitulated the phases of Biblical history - and it was not until the resurrection of Christ on the third day that the era of the Spirit alluded to by Joachim of Fiore had commenced, the reign of the Holy Ghost who had at last revealed all that had previously been hidden in proverbs and who 'has led us from the flames of legal servitude of man to the perfect liberty of divine law'. At this point Fray Alfonso quoted the ominous passage which had also been cited in the bull against the Beghards: 2 Cor 3:17, 'And where the Spirit of the Lord is, there is liberty'.

Despite the contrast between the accusations made against the so-called 'heretics of Durango' and Fray Alfonso's defence there is a discernible antinomianism in his beliefs. But whether and how his true convictions were transmitted within Spain remains as obscure as the passage of similar views from outside Iberia. All that can be concluded is that the Franciscans had distinguished themselves by their receptiveness and that, in their midst, Isabel de la Cruz could have assimilated a large number of the beliefs attributed to her.

Pedro de Osma

The other celebrated case of heresy in fifteenth-century Spain was set not in the Franciscan convents but at the greatest of the Spanish universities, Salamanca. It was there that Pedro de Osma (the teacher of one of the most distinguished scholars to work on Cisneros's polyglot Bible, Antonio de Nebrija) acted as reader of philosophy and professor of theology. Pedro de Osma's trial, which opened in 1478 in the kingdom of Aragon at the instigation of the vicar general of Saragossa, was caused by his book entitled *De confessione*. The theses which he sustained concerned the power of the clergy to grant absolution - a power which he regarded as severely limited. Contrition alone, he claimed, could bring about the forgiveness of sins: the Church had no power to remit or to impose the pains of purgatory. Setting out with this premise Osma went on to deny that the confession of sins was instituted by divine law, to repudiate the value of indulgences, and to challenge the concept of the infallibility of the Church. While the

Inquisition of Aragon decided that the book should be burnt, the archbishop of Toledo succeeded in persuading the pope to issue a bull condemning Osma's more scandalous ideas. Yet the discussion of the nine propositions attributed to Osma which the archbishop organised in Alcalá showed that the leading theologians in Spain were far from being in full agreement about the professor's condemnation. It was only after receiving attestations of the damage caused by his book and evidence that numerous readers had ceased going to confession that the archbishop declared the case closed, condemned Osma's doctrine as heretical, and ordered the book to be destroyed. Osma himself abjured his errors, accepted banishment from Salamanca for a year and retired to a convent in Alcalá where he died shortly after.[8]

Osma's followers were to be associated with a number of erroneous beliefs, including the denial of hell, but what remained a subject of intense discussion in Spain was the status of auricular confession. The proposition that confession was not instituted by divine law was contained in the 1525 edict against the *alumbrados* and was ascribed to Rodrigo de Bivar.[9] In the 1530s Pedro de Lerma, the chancellor of the university of Alcalá, was accused of proclaiming the same view from the pulpit, and it was also among the charges made against the humanist Juan de Vergara.[10]

Juan de Cazalla

Of the many Franciscans directly connected with the first *alumbrados* one of the most fascinating and tantalising is María de Cazalla's brother Juan. Although he is mentioned again and again in the trials, he was fortunate enough to die before being brought to trial himself. Since the proceedings being prepared against him at the time of his death in 1530 have been lost the true nature of his relationship with the *alumbrados*, when it started and how long it lasted, is still something of a mystery. This is all the more regrettable since Juan de Cazalla was perhaps the closest link not only between the *alumbrados* and Cardinal Cisneros but between the followers of Isabel de la Cruz and the world of learning.[11]

As Cisneros's chaplain, Juan de Cazalla had participated in the cardinal's reforming activities and had done so inspired by the prophecies so popular in the Franciscan order. In 1509 he had accompanied his superior to Oran where he wrote an account of the crusade in North Africa filled with references to the great mysteries and miracles marking the 'holy journey' and with faith in the divine power that guided the cardinal. It was Cazalla who provided Cisneros with one of the reports on the prophetic activities of Fray Melchor, but only after having fallen under the prophet's spell himself. Cazalla is even said to have set out with Diego López de Husillos (whom we shall encounter later as a protégé of the Admiral of Castile) in order to fulfil Cisneros's plan of converting the Muslims. The two advanced no further than Portugal, but the Franciscan undoubtedly foresaw for himself a part of outstanding importance in the reformation of Christendom.[12]

Attracted by Fray Melchor, Juan de Cazalla was also drawn by inspired *beatas*. He revered another of Cisneros's favourites, Madre Marta. Together with Fray Cristóbal de Tendilla he called on the woman who was to play such an infamous rôle in denouncing Isabel de la Cruz, Mari Núñez, in Guadalajara. He was briefly inveigled by Francisca Hernández, another source of denunciations, but in this case his reverence passed and he persuaded his sister to stop visiting her. The same may also have occurred with Isabel de la Cruz, for we know that he told Alcaraz that *dejamiento* savoured of heresy; that Alcaraz was subsequently to regard him as an enemy; and that Isabel de la Cruz accused him of preaching 'art rather than love'.[13]

Whether the fruit of art or of love, Juan de Cazalla's sermons seem to have been impressive. Alcaraz admired them, and the Countess of Saldaña had the deepest veneration for the preacher. Addressing congregations in Pastrana and Guadalajara, he explained the Pauline Epistles, elaborating on the need to worship Christ crucified rather than the mere wood of the cross (a proposition inserted in the *alumbrado* edict of 1525). The Church, he complained, was overburdened with commandments and cared more for bulls and excommunications than for souls. He insisted on the binding nature of the precepts of the Scriptures, and to pious groups of listeners he also read the New Testament in Greek.

Cazalla was an outspoken representative of the new learning encouraged by Cisneros. He was well versed in the works of Gabriel Biel, whose teaching was popular at the university of Alcalá. He knew the French prophet Charles de Bovelles, who stayed with Cisneros in 1506, and he imbibed the ideas of the two men Bovelles regarded as his masters, Nicholas of Cusa and Jacques Lefèvre d'Etaples. He was, finally, an enthusiastic reader of Erasmus.[14]

Whatever reservations Isabel de la Cruz and Alcaraz may have had about Cazalla, there was a time when they were close to him. Because of his learning, his experience and his international connections, he could have transmitted any number of sources including Luther and the early Reformers. Yet the association of the *alumbrados* with one particular proposition, that 'the love of God in man is God',[15] impels us to look at the only work of any substance which Cazalla is known to have published: *Lumbre del alma*, first printed in Valladolid in 1528. This is a Castilian version of the first work of piety issued under the patronage of Cardinal Cisneros at the very beginning of the century, the *Viola animae*, which, in its turn, was a summary, by the Carthusian Pierre Dorland, of the influential *Liber creaturarum sive Theologia Naturalis*, completed in 1436 by the Catalan theologian Raymond of Sebonde.[16]

The *Lumbre del alma* is a dialogue between a master and a disciple, and the question with which it opens is how man can repay God for His benefits. The master informs the disciple that the greatest gift he has received, and the most certain indication of the existence of God, is free will. From the free will proceeds the love of God in its purest and most disinterested form. This love produces all that is good and allows man to be transformed into the object of his love, whether superior or inferior to him. The highest object of love is God Himself. The emphasis is on the divinity of the love of God in man (contrasted with the impurity of self love). A divine gift, it unites the possessor with the giver.[17]

Troubadours and court poets

It was by no means only in the convents and at the universities that ideas which came to be regarded as heterodox had been discussed openly throughout the late Middle Ages: it was also in the courts of the Castilian nobility, in the poetry of the troubadours of the late fourteenth and early fifteenth centuries.[18] A work such as the *Cancionero de Baena* contains poems by men of different social origins and professions. There are Franciscans, like Fray Diego de Valencia, in whose poems we find strains of Joachist prophecies. There are Hieronymites, noblemen, *hidalgos* and *conversos*. Questions would be proposed as a subject of debate by one of the poets and were then discussed at the feudal courts. Among the most active in this respect was the court of Don Alvaro de Luna, the Marquess of Villena's grandfather, at his residence in the castle of Escalona.[19]

A problem which fascinated the troubadours and their protectors was predestination. Were works to any avail if God knew in advance who was to be saved and who was to be damned? So ran a question which Ferrán Sánchez Calavera put to the Chancellor of Castile, Pero López de Ayala, in the first years of the fifteenth century. Another recurrent theme was grace. Calavera had concluded that the grace of God assisted those who 'attained' it and was denied to those who were too careless to 'taste of its sweetness'. Although the importance of human effort was emphasised, grace was presented as an experience which the damned never enjoy and its distribution as altogether unpredictable. Like the *alumbrados*, the troubadours were sure that they possessed it. They had tasted its sweetness. In some cases the poets prided themselves on their lack of learning and harped on God's having bestowed grace on the simple and not on the learned. The Franciscan Fray Lope del Monte implied that the gift of grace was a licence to interpret the Scriptures. Others resigned themselves to accepting a chasm so great between creature and creator that very little understanding of the latter by the former was possible.[20]

The poets of Castile continued to express a type of spirituality which frequently comes close to that of the *alumbrados*. Alcaraz quoted extensively in his letters to the inquisitors from the Epistles of St John. A distinctive Johannine influence is also to be found in the letters of Juan Alvarez Gato, a *converso* poet living in Guadalajara in the 1460s and 1470s under the patronage of Don Iñigo López de Mendoza, the second Duke of Infantado.[21] To the study of the Scriptures Juan Alvarez added a devotion to Seneca and preached a Stoical abandonment of the will to God, which has been interpreted as a reaction to the dangers facing all the New Christians after the establishment of the Inquisition. In one of his last letters he maintained that the object of our existence should be 'renunciation of the love of the world, of the flesh, of one's own will, and the abandonment of free will for the love of God until we are transformed in Him and He is made one with us'. He supported this idea not only with quotations from the Gospel of St John, Jn 14:23 and 17:11, but also with 1 Jn 4:16: 'God is love, and he that dwelleth in love dwelleth in God and God in him'[22]

The tradition of the troubadours persisted in Castile well into the sixteenth century. While various members of the Mendoza family - the Countess of Coruña, the Duke of Infantado's daughter Doña Marina, and others - were addressed in the religious poetry of Ambrosio Montesino,[23] another Franciscan, Fray Luis de Escobar, was preparing his *Quinquagenas*, first published in 1526 and subsequently reissued in a revised version with the title *Quatrocientas Respuestas*.[24] Luis de Escobar lived in Medina de Ríoseco in the Franciscan convent built by the Admiral of Castile. The work is dedicated to Don Fadrique Enríquez who used to call on the friar as he lay ill in bed to challenge him with successive theological problems. The dialogue between the admiral and the Franciscan shows how concerned the two men were about the state of the Church and of their country. They lamented the absenteeism of prelates and the unchristian behaviour of the nobility, justly punished by the rise of 'Luther and other heretics'.[25] To the admiral's questions Fray Luis replied both in prose and in verse. He gave answers about the sale of indulgences and the literal interpretation of the Scriptures, and returned repeatedly to the theme with which the admiral seems to have been most preoccupied: freedom of the will.[26]

Theological speculation and discussion thus formed an important part of life in those households and courts with which the *alumbrados* were connected. An episode described in the trial of Alcaraz shows how deep ran the tradition of medieval debate. In his residence in Almorox, not far from the castle of Escalona, the Marquess of Villena once summoned his Mercederian confessor, Fray Alonso de Figueroa, together with Alcaraz, and 'put a question' to them: what did they mean by the love of God and how can we know that charitable works are performed for the love of God? The two men discussed the point in the presence of the marquess and his wife.[27] Fray Alonso later reported Alcaraz's heterodox replies to the Inquisition. The marquess, like the other high-ranking noblemen protecting the *alumbrados*, the Admiral of Castile and the Duke of Infantado, was never questioned by the Holy Office,[28] but he appears to have attended the debate in a spirit of the utmost tolerance.

Such a spirit, however, was not to last. Gradually it was decided, sometimes by men who can hardly be said to have represented an official attitude of the Church, that certain ideas were orthodox and others heretical. This tendency started surreptitiously, and the *alumbrados* of Toledo were among its first victims.

Chapter IV

The First Arrests

For about seven years the *alumbrados* of Toledo seem to have been free to proselytise. Only in 1519 did they fall under suspicion, and it was not until 1524 that the leaders were arrested. To shed light on this change of fortune, the events leading up to their imprisonment by the Inquisition and the conduct of their trials must now be examined.

The first denunciations

The Spanish Inquisition began to acquire information about the heresy of the *alumbrados* in 1519. On 13 May the inquisitor Sancho Vélez of the tribunal of Toledo received a somewhat sinister trio - the *beata* Mari Núñez, attended by her maidservant and a priest, Hernando Díaz. Together they denounced Isabel de la Cruz, Pedro Ruiz de Alcaraz and María de Cazalla.[1] Although there was still no telling where these denunciations would lead nor that the new heresy which had been revealed would, in years to come, be detected even among the highest ranks of Spanish society, the inquisitors cannot have been unaware of the utility of an embittered woman whose reputation was declining. They had recently had to cope with the drunken and incontinent María González who had denounced enough suspected Judaizers to keep the tribunal of Toledo occupied for many years.[2] At first, however, the matter brought to their attention by Mari Núñez appeared to be largely domestic. The denunciations were prompted by squabbles in the households of the Mendozas. Mari Núñez was protected by Doña Juana de Valencia, the second wife of Alcaraz's first patron, Don Pedro Hurtado de Mendoza, *adelantado* of Cazorla. With the priest Hernando Díaz (whose brother was the accountant of the Duke of Infantado's eldest son, the Count of Saldaña), Mari Núñez exercised a strong spiritual influence on the retinue of the Count of Priego, by whom Alcaraz was also employed. Yet Isabel de la Cruz, too, was favoured by Doña Juana de Valencia: to Mari Núñez's indignation Doña Juana granted the tertiary a pittance. And Isabel was menacingly influential in the Priego household.

The two *beatas*, Mari Núñez and Isabel de la Cruz, were thus rivals contending for power, and by 1519 Mari Núñez was losing. Alcaraz had once been a follower of hers and later said that it was she and Hernando Díaz who had first aroused his interest in spiritual matters.[3] But he left her circle for that of Isabel de la Cruz. María de Cazalla experienced a similar evolution. Soon after her arrival in Castile she had grown devoted to Mari Núñez, but had then abandoned her on the advice of Isabel de la Cruz and had left Guadalajara to settle in the nearby village of Horche.[4]

When Mari Núñez appeared in Toledo in May 1519 she was both jealous and frightened. Alcaraz had threatened to spread information which would destroy her claim to virtue. Her relationship with Hernando Díaz, whom she affectionately nicknamed 'the priest of the ladies', was apparently by no means chaste; she was also known to have been the paramour of the Duke of Infantado's cousin, Don Bernardino Suárez de Figueroa y Mendoza, Count of Coruña, whom she had taunted with impotence. Increasingly vexed by her worldliness, her fondness for food and clothes, and her lavish treatment of Isabel de la Cruz's former maid (whom she had suborned to obtain slanderous details about her rival's life), Alcaraz and his friends did all they could to remove her followers from her society. They too had been gathering evidence and the vicar of Alcalá had opened proceedings against the *beata*. It was in an effort to be the first party to engage the support of the Inquisition that Mari Núñez and her companions set off for Toledo.[5]

Also in 1519 another tribunal, the tribunal of Valladolid, had its first encounter with a *beata* who was to play a major part in the prosecution of the *alumbrados*: Francisca Hernández was summoned by the inquisitors in December.[6] She had been living in the university city of Salamanca where she was reputed for her beauty, her holiness and her miraculous powers of healing. Although she had never studied she was said to provide brilliant expositions of the Scriptures. She was an object of special veneration for members of the Franciscan order, with the 'guardian' of the local convent, Fray Antonio de Sahagún, sending his novices to her for religious instruction.[7]

The inquisitors wished to investigate rumours concerning Francisca Hernández's relationship with her male disciples, and she arrived in Valladolid accompanied by three admirers suspected of improper dealings with her: Bernardino de Tovar (a distinguished Greek scholar), Diego de Villareal and Antonio de Medrano.[8] Nothing resulted from the first meeting of Francisca Hernández with the Inquisition other than that she was thenceforth to be kept under surveillance in Valladolid, where she was to lodge in the house of the royal accountant, Pedro de Cazalla, a cousin of María de Cazalla. The impression she made on her interrogators seems to have been favourable. The inquisitor general, Adrian of Utrecht, had doubts about her sanctity, but when he was elected pope three years later he allegedly instructed his confessor to ask her to pray for him and the entire Church. Slightly less indulgence was shown to her three companions. The inquisitors forbade them to have any further direct communication with her - an order which they ignored.

The case against Francisca Hernández and her circle was not pursued immediately. In the years to come her followers were to mix with those of Isabel de la Cruz. To the rivalry between Isabel de la Cruz and Mari Núñez was added competition with Francisca Hernández, whose vindictiveness was to prove particularly redoubtable. The area of the *alumbrados* thus expanded far beyond the region around Guadalajara and the university of Alcalá. It stretched to the city which frequently housed the Spanish court, Valladolid, and to the city with the most illustrious university in Castile, Salamanca. But this was a later development. At first the groups were separate and the denunciations supplied were different.

In May 1519 Mari Núñez denounced a number of unorthodox propositions and acts which, from the inquisitors' point of view, could lead in various directions. Some of the more damaging - the denial of hell, feasting on Maundy Thursday, contempt for the sacraments - were commonly associated with Judaizers, and Mari Núñez reminded the inquisitors that Isabel de la Crux, Alcaraz and María de Cazalla were of *converso* descent. Judaizing (which is examined further in the next chapter) was a sufficiently serious heresy to warrant immediate prosecution by the Inquisition, but although a representative of the tribunal of Toledo, Juan de Mendoza, hastened to Guadalajara to interrogate Mari Núñez's associates and also questioned Alcaraz,[9] no action was taken against the accused. In the spring of 1520 the investigation seems to have been all but completely abandoned and was interrupted for nearly five years. Why?

The revolt of the comuneros

One of the more obvious reasons that have been suggested for the interruption of the investigation into the *alumbrados*[10] is the unrest in Spain in the early 1520s when the country seemed about to revert to that state of interfactional warfare that had characterised it in the fifteenth century. Dissatisfaction had been increasing with the new ruler, Ferdinand of Aragon's grandson, Charles of Ghent. He had arrived from Flanders in 1517, a foreigner surrounded by Flemish and Aragonese advisers, and prone to be distracted from Spain by his concern for his foreign possessions. He had inherited Sardinia, Sicily and Naples. He was the ruler of the Netherlands, Franche-Comté and what remained of the kingdom of Burgundy and, after the death of his paternal grandfather and his own election as Holy Roman Emperor in the summer of 1519, of the territories of Maximilian of Austria. Charles I of Spain, now the emperor Charles V, was incapable of devoting to the Castilians the care which they expected, but needed their money to pursue his foreign policy and to look after his foreign domains. Within days of his departure for northern Europe in May 1520 the revolt of the *comuneros* broke out.[11]

The immediate cause of the revolt was the attempt on the part of the imperial advisers to force the Castilian parliament or *Cortes* to vote a subsidy large enough to cover the emperor's travelling expenses; but the demands of the various rebel movements which formed in the towns of Castile went far beyond resentment at Charles's treatment of the *Cortes*. Their first aim was, arguably, to secure the cities from any infringement of their traditional rights by the Crown. The first victims were consequently the royal officials, the *corregidores*. By and by royal authority became associated with anything found distasteful and some of the more radical rebels began calling equally for the abolition of the Holy Office and freedom from the oppression of the landowners.

For Charles the decisive moment in the *comunero* revolt was when the nobles decided to combat it. In September 1520 the vassals of Dueñas had rebelled against their overlord, the Count of Buendía. Few aristocrats continued to support the rebels. Even the most cautious, such as the Duke of Infantado, came down on the side of the royalist government presided over by Adrian of Utrecht, and by the Admiral and Constable of Castile. The rebel army was finally defeated by the constable in April 1521, and when Charles returned to his Spanish possessions in July 1522 royal authority had been restored.

It would hardly be surprising if disturbances of such magnitude had prevented the inquisitors from pursuing the investigation of what had all the appearances of a mere quarrel among the Mendozas' servants. For almost a year the territory of their jurisdiction was in arms. Toledo, where the inquisitors resided, had been the first city to rebel and the last to surrender. The very existence of the Inquisition had been threatened and Adrian of Utrecht, both regent and inquisitor general, was obviously distracted from the Holy Office by other, more demanding duties. Guadalajara too had been in turmoil. The *comuneros* had been supported by the Duke of Infantado's son, the Count of Saldaña, and, after an unsatisfactory parley with the duke in June 1520, had burnt and devastated the houses of the local authorities.[12]

Yet, notwithstanding these difficulties, the inquisitors did find time to follow up other cases in the diocese of Toledo, and even in the town of Guadalajara, in this period.[13] The revolt of the *comuneros* cannot therefore have been the only reason for the interval between the first denunciations and the first arrests of the *alumbrados*. It is even questionable whether the revolt had anything to do with it. When the inquisitors at last arrested Alcaraz and Isabel de la Cruz a major religious change in the Holy Roman Empire had taken place. Charles's northern territories were threatened by the spread of Lutheranism, and the Spaniards were taking precautions not to be affected by it.

Proselytism and expansion

Exactly what was said when Alcaraz was questioned by the inquisitor Juan de Mendoza in 1519 is not known.[14] All we know is that Mendoza reprimanded him. There are two possible reasons for such lenience. The first is that the protection of Alcaraz by his aristocratic employers was still effectual against the Holy Office. But references in Alcaraz's trial also suggest another, more likely reason: that the accountant managed to persuade Mendoza that his opinions were so innocuous as not to be worth proceeding against. It seems probable that Mendoza led Alcaraz to believe that the case was closed, and closed to the inquisitor's satisfaction, since, although Alcaraz was well aware of the charges against him, he made no attempt to modify his views or alter his behaviour. Nor did either Isabel de la Cruz or María de Cazalla. The time of their greatest success, when they started to proselytise intensively and to gain an impressive number of supporters, was in fact after Mendoza's visit to Guadalajara. Mari Núñez's denunciations to the Inquisition would seem only to have increased the local popularity of the *dejados*. A sizeable group of Franciscans ranged themselves behind Isabel de la Cruz. The tertiary's confessor told Mari Núñez to beware of attacking Isabel since 'the whole order of St Francis' would come forward in her defence.[15] The matter was placed briefly in the hands of the civil governor of the archbishopric of Toledo,[16] but, owing to the protection of the Count of Coruña, Mari Núñez managed to escape the ploys of her enemies. Either, as Alcaraz claimed, driven by shame, or, according to her own testimony, for family reasons, she left for Seville.

Hernando Díaz remained for a short while in Guadalajara but, having lost the favour of the Duke of Infantado, he soon joined Mari Núñez in Andalusia and obtained a chaplaincy in Puerto de Santa María.

It was after May 1519 that the first *alumbrados* visited the towns in the neighbourhood of Guadalajara, Cifuentes and Pastrana, and made numerous converts both among the friars in the local Franciscan *recolectorios* and among the town dwellers. In Cifuentes, Isabel de la Cruz obtained the devotion of Fray Diego de Barreda and Fray Antonio de Pastrana. In Pastrana, where María de Cazalla had also been particularly active, Isabel de la Cruz's faction won over the priests Gaspar de Bedoya and Graviel Sánchez, and laymen such as Francisco Jiménez and his wife Elvira González, Mencía Jiménez, Bachiller Juan López and his wife Agueda Jiménez, and Alonso López Sebastián.

In Guadalajara, too, the *dejados* extended their influence in the period after the first denunciations, winning the support of Rodrigo de Bivar, chaplain and cantor of the Duke of Infantado's choir; Diego de Espinosa, a flageolet player in the duke's orchestra; Campuzano *el mozo*, a member of the duke's guard; the wife and daughter of García de Buytrago, the duchess's treasurer; Gabriel de Vega, steward to the Count of Saldaña; and, of course, Alcaraz's own kinsmen: his brother Hernando and his nephew Pedro de Albadán, son of the duke's groom.

These names give an idea of the social categories most attracted by the new doctrine: members of the clergy, educated (or semi-educated) laymen, and a strikingly high proportion of women. This impression is confirmed by the list of 'alumbrado correspondents' submitted to the Inquisition in 1527: of forty-six names thirteen are of women, eleven of friars and at least five of ordained priests.[17] Although the correspondents were by no means solely devoted to *dejamiento* they made up a large group of men and women searching for spiritual advice and methods of meditation, and surveying all the possible paths to perfection.

Alcaraz had to travel for professional reasons and supervise the administration of his employers' estates. As he did so he spread his spiritual message. On his journeys he encountered members of rival factions far more numerous than that of Mari Núñez and, in his view, in every way as distasteful. The most menacing was the one gathered round Francisca Hernández in Valladolid. On a couple of occasions Alcaraz came across her gifted and celebrated admirer, the Franciscan preacher Francisco Ortiz. They met in Pastrana in 1523 and, although Alcaraz was one of the first people to denounce Ortiz, the preacher seems to have been favourably impressed by their encounter. Alcaraz and Ortiz met again at Ortiz's convent in Alcalá, and this time the accountant was appalled by the terms in which Fray Francisco praised Francisca Hernández. He set out for Valladolid in the hope of converting her, but she refused to receive him. This was a slight he never forgave.[18]

In 1522 the Count of Priego had died and Alcaraz departed for Madrid in the service of Don Benito Cisneros. There he first attended the spectacle provided by one of the men for whom he was to develop such contempt some months later. The Franciscan Juan de Olmillos satisfied the expectations of an enthusiastic congregation with physical displays of his divine inspiration. Alcaraz was horrified by what he referred to as '*tales visajes*', such grimaces, and he warned Olmillos that his ecstasies might well be temptations of the devil. Alcaraz knew about these temptations. He had had experience of them shortly before his arrival in Madrid. Not only had he observed the devil at work in Hernando Díaz, Mari Núñez and her maid, but he had also seen the effects of Satan on María de Tejeda, an ecstatic *beata* whom the Franciscans had entrusted to Isabel de la Cruz. When the tertiary had accepted the *beata* (whom she and Alcaraz were later to abandon) she had quarrelled with María de Cazalla who had withdrawn her children from her care and had ceased visiting her.[19]

The final phase of Alcaraz's activity as a proselytiser lasted for just over a year, from the beginning of 1523 to April 1524. It took place mainly in the castle of Escalona, where the Marquess of Villena seems to have been delighted with his new employee. Since neither the marquess nor his wife were ever interrogated we can only infer their reactions to Alcaraz's views from statements by Alcaraz himself and witnesses at his trial. According to a prejudiced source, the Mercedarian Fray Alonso de Figueroa, the marquess and his wife were '*angustiados*', anguished, by Alcaraz's words about God's indifference to works.[20] But spiritual anguish was a sentiment which they clearly enjoyed and the affection which the marquess developed for Alcaraz is indicated by his efforts to secure his release after his arrest. It is also demonstrated by the jealousy which other members of the marquess's household felt towards the accountant. Fray Alonso de Figueroa, who believed that Alcaraz threatened his power as the marquess's confessor, and various servants in the Pacheco retinue, were obviously disgruntled by this novel influence.

Alcaraz, for his part, regarded it as his mission to deliver the marquess from the hold of the apocalyptic Franciscans. In Escalona he found Fray Juan de Olmillos, whose behaviour had incensed him in

Madrid, acting as guardian of the convent the marquess had founded thirty years previously. He also encountered another visionary living with Olmillos, Fray Francisco de Ocaña. At first Alcaraz had no quarrel with Ocaña. He praised his sermons and the Franciscan spoke highly of the accountant, commending the spirituality he taught and pronouncing himself in full agreement with Alcaraz's doctrine on love and with his words on the superiority of the spirit over the letter and on the importance of denying one's own will.[21] Ocaña's approval of Alcaraz is of interest since it illustrates once more the considerable area which Alcaraz shared with men generally represented as his opponents. Where Alcaraz and Ocaña clashed, where Alcaraz found himself in conflict with Francisco Ortiz and Francisco de Osuna was on the question of trances, visions and certain prophecies which Alcaraz put on the same level as those external observances he had stigmatised as *ataduras*.

The substance of Francisco de Ocaña's prophecies was disclosed to Alcaraz in February 1524 when he returned to Escalona after visiting his wife and children in Guadalajara. Ocaña had already informed the bishop of Utica, Pedro del Campo, that reform of the Church was impending and that the current ecclesiastical hierarchy would be cast out 'like swine'. Ocaña then delivered a sermon on Lk 18:31, 'Behold, we go up to Jerusalem, and all things that are written by the prophets concerning the Son of man shall be accomplished', in which he elaborated on the theme of the New Jerusalem on earth. After his sermon he made further revelations to Alcaraz. 1524 was to be the fatal year. The king of France was to be dispossessed of his kingdom by the emperor, and Olmillos and Ocaña himself were to go to Rome in order to accomplish the reform of the Church. They were to act in close collaboration with Francisca Hernández, who was to revise the Scriptures, and '*este buen viejo*', 'this good old man' the Marquess of Villena, was to install the new pope. Alcaraz was dismayed by the plan and scolded Ocaña for distorting the text.[22] He was not alone in his concern. The chapter of Toledo met; the bishop of Utica conferred with the canon Alonso Mejía; inquiries were again opened into the various circles of '*dejados y alumbrados y perfectos*' in Pastrana, Guadalajara, Madrid, Escalona and the nearby convents. Mejía summoned Alcaraz and wrote to the Marquess of Villena. The *fiscal* or prosecutor of the tribunal of Toledo pressed the inquisitors to collect further evidence and the plans were made for Alcaraz's arrest.[23]

In the meantime Alcaraz had resolved to act independently. He went to the Franciscan convent of San Juan de los Reyes in Toledo to speak to the vicar about the 'illusions' of the friars in Escalona. The vicar called the guardian and they accompanied Alcaraz to the provincial, Andrés de Ecija. To the three friars Alcaraz expatiated on all he knew of Olmillos and Ocaña. The friars listened. They even invited Alcaraz to stay for dinner. But Fray Andrés gave him some advice: he reminded the accountant that it was as well not to inform the Inquisition about what had occurred since the Franciscans were bound by obedience solely to their superiors. The Order of St Francis was still outside the jurisdiction of the Holy Office.[24]

Alcaraz did what Fray Andrés had told him to do. When Pedro del Campo and Alonso Mejía summoned him he did not inform the chapter of Toledo about the exact nature of the Franciscans' activities in Escalona. He simply said that he regarded Ocaña as mentally unstable, a '*persona desconcertada*'. According to him his interlocutors shared his amusement at the episode, dismissing it lightly, and indeed it is quite possible that Pedro del Campo, a friend of the humanists and readers of Erasmus who were to be implicated in the trials of the 1530s, gave little weight to the information about the *alumbrados*.

At this point the Franciscan provincial himself decided to visit Escalona in order to remedy any cause of scandal. Ecija's visit and its consequences illustrate the attitude prevailing in the Franciscan order. Shortly after his arrival, on Maundy Thursday, Ecija said mass in the Franciscan convent. When communion was celebrated Olmillos knelt, received the eucharist from the provincial, and fell into a trance. Ecija ordered the friars to interrupt the plainsong so that he could hear what Olmillos was saying. The words of the visionary were so moving that the provincial's face was soon wet with tears. How could he proceed against a man so obviously inspired with the spirit of sanctity as Fray Juan de Olmillos? The disciplinary measures he imposed were slight. He decreed that Olmillos was only to say mass in the cloister (and not in the chapter house) and that Ocaña was to preach exclusively to the Marquess of Villena.[25] The penance was brief. Soon afterwards Olmillos was again preaching in public. In 1527 he was elected provincial of Castile, and when he died in Madrid in 1529 the chronicler of the order described him as '*virum . . . religiosissimum et obedientiae virtute insignem*' who died '*magna pietatis opinione*'.[26]

Instead of inflicting a stricter punishment on the visionaries Ecija chose to look into the activities of Alcaraz and Isabel de la Cruz. This time the conclusions he reached were far from favourable. Isabel's influence had expanded not only in Guadalajara, Cifuentes and Pastrana, but also among the Franciscans themselves and at the university of Alcalá. Andrés de Ecija promptly set out for Guadalajara and defrocked the tertiary.

Alcaraz continued to engineer his own downfall. He made no secret of his disapproval of those numerous individuals who had fallen under the spell of Ocaña and Olmillos or who had been duped by Francisca Hernández. He tried to enlist the marquess's support against the Franciscan visionaries, but Don Diego simply replied that their behaviour was regrettable and that their superiors should be informed.[27] Villena's household in Escalona seems to have been divided between the followers and the opponents of Alcaraz. Grooms, pages, secretaries, stewards, ladies- and gentlemen-in-waiting, preachers, confessors - when the inquisitors arrived in the marquess's demesnes there was hardly a member of the retinue who did not put in a good word, or a bad one, for the accountant. The *alcalde* Antonio de Baeza and his family (his wife, brother and sister-in-law) supported Alcaraz. The accountant had devoted followers among the marchioness's maids. The marquess's chaplain Sebastián Gutiérrez and the nurse of the *corregidor* Pedro de Barrios hung on his lips. Noguerol, Pedro de Marquina and Juan de Valdés, the marquess's pages, were constantly in his society.

But for every adherent Alcaraz made at least one enemy. His denunciations to the Franciscan provincial had the opposite effect to that which he had intended. In May 1524 the general of the order, Francisco de Quiñones, arrived. After holding the chapter of Toledo in Escalona he issued a decree on 22 May[28] condemning the practices of Isabel de la Cruz and Alcaraz, both of whom had been arrested by the Holy Office some four weeks earlier.[29] The Marquess of Villena protested. He dispatched Sebastián Gutiérrez to plead with the inquisitor general in Burgos and sent him to confer with Gaspar Dávalos, bishop of Guadix, whom the inquisitor general had appointed to investigate the *alumbrados* before dispatching him to Valencia to deal with the converted Muslims. But the marquess's intercession had no effect.[30] Antonio de Baeza was equally unsuccessful.[31] Alcaraz's trial was to last until 1529.

Imprisonment

The apprehension in the spring of 1524 of Alcaraz, Isabel de la Cruz and Gaspar de Bedoya set into motion a series of arrests which went on for almost fifteen years. Fray Diego de Barreda, from the *recolectorio* of Cifuentes, was imprisoned by his superiors in the convent of San Juan de los Reyes in February 1526. Alonso López de la Palomera from

Pastrana was also arrested. The denunciations provided by Francisca Hernández, who was herself arrested in 1529, yielded further material which the inquisitors could use against the circle of Isabel de la Cruz, and also led to the incarceration of Francisca Hernández's own followers - Antonio de Melrano, Bernardino de Tovar, Fray Francisco Ortiz and several others. By then the charges, like the social and geographical area, had expanded. Those captured, often attached to the universities or the court, were frequently suspected of Lutheranism. In nearly all the trials, however, at least one charge was connected with the 'heresy of the *alumbrados*'.

Treatment of the prisoners varied. Recent studies on the Spanish Inquisition have shown that the inquisitors were generally reluctant to resort to torture. Nevertheless it was applied on a number of occasions in the *alumbrado* trials - to Alcaraz, to María de Cazalla, and, in her old age when she was living in Seville, to Mari Núñez to prompt her fading memory.[32] Shortly after his incarceration Alcaraz, who seems to have been treated with greater severity than anyone else, complained of being kept in chains.[33] Most of the accused were handled more leniently. The women prisoners could often keep a maid servant. The secrecy on which the Holy Office insisted was frequently infringed. Prisoners corresponded with one another and with the outside world, and María de Cazalla's trial shows how statements could be agreed upon and defences co-ordinated.[34]

The heaviest sentences were those passed on the first members of the movement, Alcaraz and Isabel de la Cruz. In 1529 Alcaraz was flogged, and Isabel de la Cruz led, through the streets of the towns where they had proselytised, Toledo, Guadalajara, Escalona and Pastrana.[35] Their property was confiscated and they were condemned to 'perpetual reclusion' and 'perpetual habit'. Reclusion meant confinement in some religious house or institution and the 'habit' was the penitential garment or San Benito. 'Perpetuity', however, was always limited in practice. Alcaraz was an obstinate man - hence his ill treatment in prison - and his insistence that he had been sentenced unjustly induced the inquisitors to prolong his confinement until February 1539. Even then it was modified in the course of the decade. By 1537 he was sharing lodgings with his wife and one of his daughters, and in 1539 he was allowed freedom of movement within the precincts of Toledo, relieved of his San Benito, and given some light spiritual penances.[36] Isabel de la Cruz shared his sentence to 'perpetual reclusion' until 24 December 1538. She was then released, given spiritual penances to perform, and obliged to remain in the town of Guadalajara.[37]

The other sentences were more moderate. Gaspar de Bedoya was generally agreed to have been a follower rather than a leader. He does not appear to have been flogged, but was confined in the same building as Isabel de la Cruz and Alcaraz in 1530. By 1533 he was free.[38] María de Cazalla was made to abjure *de levi*, the mildest form of publicly disavowing the heretical statements she was said to have pronounced, and was fined 100 ducats.[39] Luis de Beteta, tried in 1538 on various charges, one of which was showing sympathy with Isabel de la Cruz when she was wearing her penitential habit, also had to abjure *de levi* and perform certain spiritual penances.[40] Rodrigo de Bivar was sentenced in the following year to the more serious form of abjuration, *de vehementi*, to pay 200 ducats, and to confinement in a monastery. The last part of his sentence was subsequently commuted to a fine of 30 ducats.[41]

The inquisitors divided

The attitude of the inquisitors to the heresy of the *alumbrados* can be assessed by their reactions to the trial of Alcaraz. In the summer of 1527 a quarrel broke out among them which suggests a disagreement between the tribunal of Toledo and the *Suprema*. Towards the end of June Diego Ortiz de Angulo, the *fiscal*, presented the inquisitors with a letter in which he accused one of them, Antón González Francés, of partiality towards the accused. During an interrogation of Isabel de la Cruz Francés had allegedly prevented the defendant from making a full confession - an error for which he was later reprimanded by his colleague Mariana - and on another occasion he had expressed the view that 'all the evidence against the *alumbrados* was of little or no importance'.[42] Francés appears to have been especially delegated as a judge by the inquisitor general, Alonso Manrique. The extent to which he was actually representing the archbishop remains unclear, but the *fiscal*'s reaction is reminiscent of other earlier incidents when the tribunal of Toledo had attempted to pursue a course independent of that set by the inquisitor general.[43] As it was, Francés said that he would willingly withdraw from the tribunal if Manrique ordered him to do so but that the *fiscal* was lying about his partiality. Ortiz de Angulo failed to discredit him and Francés remained.

Later in the same year the inquisitors and judges first voted on the sentence (which was later modified). Seven voted in favour of the stake, 'relaxation to the secular arm', and six for a more merciful punishment. When they justified their views the Dominican Fray Domingo Pizarro alone compared the *alumbrado* errors to those of

Luther, but he added that they were in the tradition of Jan Hus, the Beghards, Amalric of Bena and of Fray Alfonso de Mella and the 'heretics of Durango'. He also associated the *alumbrados* with the *comunero* revolt and with the political crime of *lèse majesté*. Alonso de Mariana, another judge to vote for relaxation, said that the defendants 'were all the more suspicious since they were *conversos*'. It was generally concluded that the prisoners had interpreted the Scriptures freely and that, by preaching *dejamiento*, they had encouraged the total quiet of the senses, denying the freedom of will and repudiating the benefit of works.[44]

Antón González Francés, who voted for mercy, did all he could to mitigate the importance of the heresy, presenting Alcaraz, Isabel de la Cruz and Gaspar de Bedoya as Catholics who had been misled but whose intentions remained good. The Franciscan Antonio de la Cruz, too, regarded the 'root of these errors' as 'a zealous desire to come closer to God, however senseless, proud and foolhardy and unsuitable it might be'. Even Alonso Mejía admitted that Alcaraz might have believed his errors to be 'a shorter way of reaching God'.[45] By and large this more moderate attitude was to prevail in Spain. Fray Luis de Maluenda published his *Tratado llamado Excelencias de la fe* in Burgos in 1537, before the last *alumbrado* trials had taken place. 'If certain dangers of errors have occurred in this kingdom,' he wrote, 'such as the *dejados* and *alumbrados* and *beatos*, they sprung from a desire for fervent faith and devotion'.[46]

The judgements of Alcaraz suggest some uncertainty about the importance and the origin of the heresy. This same uncertainty was reflected in the edict of 1525 in which the propositions were subjected to very diverse qualifications. Some, as we saw, were qualified as heretical, some as false, rash, erroneous and scandalous. Three, to which we shall return, were qualified as Lutheran, two as proceeding from the Beghards. But despite the attempt to link the *alumbrados* with other heretics the inquisitors tended to agree that what they were judging was something new. For them, indeed, it was novel for, by the very nature of their institution, they were above all accustomed to a heresy of a very different sort: Judaizing.

Chapter V

The *Alumbrados* between two Heresies

Numerically the trials of the *alumbrados* are of little significance in the history of the Spanish Inquisition. By the time the *alumbrados* of Toledo were being properly investigated the inquisitors in Castile were dealing with more and more cases of blasphemy and of utterers of 'scandalous words'. The trials were brief and the sentences light, but the culprits, who often appeared spontaneously, were numerous.[1] The *alumbrado* trials are important for a different reason. They occurred when the tribunals of Castile had almost finished with the first wave of Judaizers and before they had got to grips with the other heresy which seemed to threaten sixteenth-century Spain, Protestantism. The trials thus present hybrid traits. They form a passage between two heresies, and in them we see inquisitors accustomed to one type of heretic preparing to face another. As the fear of Lutheranism increased, moreover, a second feature emerged: in their efforts to trap potential Protestants the inquisitors would include one or more of the propositions condemned in the edict against the *alumbrados* in a bill of indictment largely composed of different charges. *Alumbradismo* consequently acquired a broader significance.

Judaizers and conversos

The Spanish Inquisition was founded in order to deal with Judaizers, and for a few years, until about 1488, the Castilian tribunals treated the accused with a severity which was rarely repeated during the long life of the Holy Office. Some idea of the extent of the inquisitors' activity can be gathered from the trials of the *converso* community of Ciudad Real where there appear to have been approximately fifty New Christian households.[2] At least one member of each of these was tried and condemned. After 1488, however, the victims diminished. There was a brief revival of ferocity, albeit on a smaller scale, in the first four years of the sixteenth century. Thereafter, even if they remained the principal objects of the inquisitors' attention during the first two decades of the century, the converted Jews could expect to be handled more leniently. Death sentences, so common at first, decreased. In 1507, after the atrocities of the inquisitor of Cordova, Diego Rodríguez Lucero, Cardinal Cisneros succeeded the *converso* Diego de Deza as inquisitor general. The policy of the Holy Office grew more clement as the inquisitors found themselves trying a dwindling number of suspected Judaizers ever more advanced in years and innocuous in behaviour.

Just how widespread Judaizing really was among the *conversos* is difficult to estimate. Nor do we know much about the form it took. It probably varied from sincere attempts to revive the old religion to the more or less superstitious observance of ritual gestures and customs. Occasionally, too, there seem to have been efforts to combine Judaism with Christianity in a third, syncretistic and supposedly perfect faith.[3]

The degree of assimilation of the New Christians and their descendants in the fifteenth and sixteenth centuries also varied. Throughout the fifteenth century *conversos* tended to distinguish themselves in commerce, in the liberal professions and in the arts, 'accumulating,' as H.C. Lea wrote, 'honours, wealth and popular hatred.'[4] They were appointed to high posts at court and intermarried with the Old Christian aristocracy. By the end of the century many aristocrats had Jewish ancestors. The Mendoza family and the Pachecos, Marquesses of Villena and Dukes of Escalona, the Enríquez family, Admirals of Castile and future Dukes of Medina de Ríoseco, even King Ferdinand of Aragon had Jewish blood. It was also among the nobility that the *conversos* met with least prejudice. A great many New Christians joined the Marquess of Villena's uprising against the Catholic Kings in 1474,[5] while others entered the service of the aristocracy as bailiffs, stewards and accountants, secretaries and treasurers, and in a variety of humbler professions.

In such positions the New Christians became the repositories of great confidence on the part of their employers. An example is Juan Ramírez, whose posthumous trial extended from 1512 to 1524.[6] Although Ramírez had confessed to Judaizing before the tribunal of Cordova in 1487 and had been sentenced to payment of a substantial fine, he entered the household of Cardinal Cisneros in Ciudad Real in the early 1490s and became the cardinal's major-domo. The cardinal was aware of his precedents but never ceased to trust him and, on his death, he was succeeded in his office by his son Diego.

The resentment the Old Christians felt for the *conversos* increased in proportion to their success. They were resented by the impoverished gentry, the *hidalgos* whose chief claim to nobility was a mythical racial purity; by the peasants who associated the *conversos* either with a sybaritic urban way of life or with the demands of a landowner; and by all those whose rents, taxes and debts were collected by New Christians.[7] In the late fourteenth century the Old Christians had released their anger in pogroms. By 1500 the practising Jews had been expelled, but the Old Christians had two new weapons against their descendants. The first was the Inquisition. The second was the *estatuto de limpieza*, the statute of purity of blood on which all sorts of religious and secular institutions could insist as a condition for preferment, or even acceptance. The statutes, first devised and imposed in the fifteenth century, were a matter of controversy over many years. Besides military and other secular foundations, religious orders too had endeavoured to apply them. They had been accepted by the Spanish Hieronymites, despite severe opposition, in 1486. Although they were not always imposed consistently for any length of time and were liable to papal revocation, other orders tried to introduce them into certain convents, the Dominicans in 1496 and again in 1531, and the Franciscans in 1525. The purpose was usually to close the hierarchy to New Christians, and the statutes remained a constant threat which grew in prominence after 1547 when the archbishop of Toledo, Juan Martínez Silíceo, imposed an *estatuto de limpieza* on the entire chapter of Toledo, a large organisation in which numerous *conversos* were employed.[8] Thereafter even the rumour of Jewish ancestry could be an insurmountable obstacle to a career in every sort of field for a man not protected by a patent of nobility.

In the first part of the sixteenth century the *conversos* who were most vulnerable were those whose ancestors or relations had been denounced to the Inquisition as Judaizers and few descendants from the more recent converts to Christianity could claim to have no forefather or relative who had been penalised. Such a precedent could dishonour a family for anything up to three generations. The defendants of the *alumbrado* trials were nearly all affected by arrests among their ancestors. The parents of María de Cazalla had been tried and subsequently reconciled by the Holy Office. Alcaraz's maternal grandfather had been imprisoned and his paternal grandmother condemned. Both of Luis de Beteta's parents and his mother's sister had been tried and reconciled. Old Christians were so exceptional that Rodrigo de Bivar urgently stressed his racial purity as a point in his defence.[9]

That Alcaraz, Isabel de la Cruz and María de Cazalla were New Christians was emphasised by the more malignant witnesses. But even if they had not done so the inquisitors would soon have discovered it from the books of genealogies so frequently referred to in the trials of the Holy Office which contained details about *converso* families. There were also the lists and the catalogues. In Toledo in 1503 a list was drawn up of all the parishioners who had not taken communion at Easter. A few years later a catalogue was produced in Segovia of all the New Christians, descendants of Jews and Muslims, listed by parish, together with particulars concerning their families and other members of their households.[10]

In the Middle Ages Guadalajara had been an important centre of Judaism. It was thus rigorously supervised after the establishment of the Holy Office. A conspicuous number of *conversos* had entered the service of the Mendoza family, and the gossip and jealousy which thrived among the various retinues guaranteed for the inquisitors a regular flow of denunciations. In 1520 proceedings were opened against Guiomar Fernández who was employed as cook by Doña Brianda de Mendoza, the Duke of Infantado's sister.[11] Both Guiomar and her husband, Luis Alvarez who acted as Doña Brianda's accountant, had been converted to Christianity in 1492 and had subsequently spent some time in Portugal. Like Alcaraz they were denounced by their fellow servants - in this case by the wife of Doña Brianda's muleteer - and were charged with observing the Sabbath and a traditional Jewish diet. In the same period Mayor Meléndez, employed with her husband in the Duke of Infantado's pantry, faced similar charges made by the wife of the Count of Coruña's steward and the daughter of the duke's steward out of the pettiest vindictiveness.[12] Ten years later Antonio Meléndez, the Count of Saldaña's accountant, was also charged with Judaizing and abjured, together with his wife, in the summer of 1531.[13]

The pattern which emerges from the trials is monotonous. The delations tended to be motivated by revenge of the basest kind, and the vengeance the denouncers gained must have been satisfying. Even if the charges were never wholly substantiated the victims were frequently arrested and had their property confiscated during the time of their imprisonment.

The Inquisition was not only a weapon used by Old Christians against New. It was used among the *conversos* themselves, by one New Christian against another and by New Christians against Old. The *alumbrado* trials are full of such cases and also indicate the faith which some *conversos* had in the Holy Office. Even if he did not actually do so, Alcaraz seems to have been just as ready to denounce the Franciscan visionaries to the Inquisition before his arrest as they were to denounce him. Francisco Ortiz, of *converso* descent, was convinced that Christendom was indebted to the Holy Office for the extirpation of Judaism.[14] When it became evident that the Holy Office was being used to stifle ideas which were by no means unorthodox, during the trials of the humanists in the 1530s, men who had once had faith in it turned against it. But to start with, in the early years of the *alumbrado* trials, we can still discern that eagerness to use it as a means of purifying Christianity which had contributed to the Inquisition's foundation some forty years earlier.

Alcaraz as a Judaizer

The inquisitors who filed the evidence against the first *alumbrados* and who conducted the interrogations were therefore accustomed to trying Judaizers. It was in the trials of the Judaizers that they had acquired their experience and it was to detect Judaizers that they had been trained. They had developed an extreme perceptiveness for all the propositions or habits that smacked of Judaism, and the heretic with whom they were most familiar was a *converso* who had reverted to the faith of his ancestors.

In the Judaizing trials of the early sixteenth century the same charges, the same propositions recur again and again. formulated in the same words. And so a type of man was created - a man who had reneged on the religion of his fathers and denied the faith he acquired. He was prone to both political and religious treachery. Gathering in conventicles with his fellow culprits, he elaborated plans to subvert the Church of Rome and undermine the state of Spain, allying himself with the Turks or the Protestants, inspired by ancient Jewish prophecies predicting the return of the Mosaic law.[15] From a Christian point of view he had no religious belief. He was a materialist, a 'libertine', and had become the mouthpiece of a number of current blasphemies characteristic of heresy at all times.[16] Not only did he break Christian feastdays, observe Jewish feasts, eat Jewish food and wear Jewish clothes, but, when obliged to go to mass, he turned his head away in disgust at the elevation of the eucharist. He denied the Trinity, mocked the sacraments and the commandments of the Church, and denied the existence of an after-life.[17] This last charge was perhaps the most recurrent in Judaizing trials. One victim after another was accused of the atheistic conviction that life on earth consisted of birth and death alone, *'que en este mundo no avía otra cosa syno nacer y morir'*, and that there were no such things as heaven and hell.

The denial of hell was a common charge against early and medieval heresies. In Spain a similar proposition had been attributed to the readers of Pedro de Osma in the fifteenth century and it was one to which the inquisitors were sensitive. This emerges from the trial not of a *converso* but of an Old Christian, Don Juan Gastón, in 1522.[18] Gastón was arrested for what was soon to be the commonest of crimes, 'scandalous words'. He admitted to the inquisitors that he used to regale the local chaplain with a joke: hell, he told him, was between a woman's legs and the devil behind a man's codpiece. The joke was clearly derived from a popular anecdote, a version of which is to be found in Boccaccio's *Decameron*,[19] but the inquisitors were not satisfied as to its harmlessness. Did the defendant's statement, they asked, mean that he did not believe in hell? Don Juan Gastón protested his orthodoxy, but was nevertheless sentenced to temporary banishment. The inquisitors were Alonso de Mariana, a veteran investigator of Judaizers whose theological ignorance amused Francisco Ortiz,[20] and Sancho Vélez, the men who received some of the earliest denunciations made against the *alumbrados*.

Denial of hell was one of the first propositions attributed to Alcaraz and there were times in his trial when his accusers contrived to provide a picture of him which the inquisitors would have associated with that of the Judaizer. If Alcaraz and his fellow sectarians did not look away at the elevation of the eucharist they behaved almost as badly: they had the insolence to stand motionless, their hands at their sides, and to stare at it. Every gesture they made in church was given a sacrilegious interpretation by hostile witnesses. Even Alcaraz's somewhat slovenly way of dressing was taken as a sign of mockery.

Six months after his arrest Alcaraz was presented with his first bill of indictment.[21] Of the twenty-two charges the first eight centred on the denial of hell, disrespect for the sacraments and contempt for indulgences. The next ten concerned impeccability, *dejamiento*, and suspicious interpretations of the Scriptures; and the last charge was that 'the said Pedro de Alcaraz and other people ate *adafina* cooked in the Jewish manner on the Sabbath as a Jewish ceremony and with the intention of observing the Mosaic law.' To this Alcaraz replied that he had never eaten *adafina* (a form of stew) and did not even know what it was.[22] The inquisitors then ordered him to do something which suspected Judaizers were frequently made to do: to recite the Pater Noster, the Ave Maria, the Credo and the Salve Regina, and to cross himself. Alcaraz did so perfectly. Nevertheless other accusations aimed at the traditional image of the Judaizer followed. In 1526 Alcaraz was accused of having rejoiced at Barbarossa's recent victory over the Spaniards - he would thus have been a supporter of his country's most redoubtable enemy, the Turk. Alcaraz replied that he could not possibly have been gladdened by Barbarossa's triumph since he had lost both a cousin and a brother-in-law in the battle.[23] In 1527 the prosecutor again referred to Judaism; for what, he asked, was the purpose of *dejamiento* if not to subvert the Catholic Church and to conduct the whole of Castile to the observance of the Mosaic law?[24]

The actual accusation of Judaizing soon disappeared from the *alumbrado* trials. However, the heresy itself continued to be associated with *conversos* until the end of the century, while many of the accusers of the followers of both Isabel de la Cruz and Francisca Hernández expressed strong feelings of antisemitism. One of the maids of the Marchioness of Villena referred to Alcaraz's habit of talking in private to other servants of her mistress's and added how shocking she regarded it 'since he was a layman, married, and of *converso* descent'.[25] To imply that Fray Francisco Ortiz, one of the emperor's favourite preachers and the pride of the Friars Minor in Castile, was guilty of Judaizing would have been rash. Yet that Ortiz remained a Jew 'at heart' was indeed suggested, while some of his fellow friars expressed their dislike of the 'rapacious little Jew', as the new provincial, Fray Juan de Olmillos, described Ortiz after his arrest.[26]

The tentative use by the inquisitors of charges associated with Judaism reflects above all the uncertainty with which they approached the new heresy. They were no doubt tempted to shift the trial of Alcaraz onto ground that was familiar to them, but they soon realised they were dealing with something new - with something resembling the other new heresy, Lutheranism.

Lutheranism in Spain

The first stages of the Reformation, from the composition of Luther's ninety-five theses attacking indulgences in 1517 to the issue of the papal bull *Exsurge Domine* in June 1520, seem to have had little impact on Spain.[27] The official attitude was initially divided. At the end of 1519 Adrian of Utrecht pronounced himself against Luther, but many of Charles V's courtiers were more favourably disposed. In May 1520 the court moved from Spain to Flanders where there was a considerable tolerance of Luther's views. In the months following the bull *Exsurge Domine* condemning forty-one of Luther's propositions as heretical, this conciliatory approach altered. The papal legate Jerome Aleander acquired the assurance of the emperor's full support against the Reformer. On 8 October he succeeded in having Luther's books burnt in Louvain; on 29 December he obtained a decree banishing Luther and his followers from the entire empire; and on 3 January 1521 Luther was excommunicated.

There is little information about the circulation of Luther's early writings in Spain. No doubt, some of them were accessible in Latin to a small number of theologians in the universities as early as 1519, but it does not seem to have been until 1521 that the first works of Luther to be translated into Castilian were brought into the peninsula. The initiative was taken by *conversos* living in Antwerp who regarded them as an excellent weapon against the Inquisition, but what these works were, and who read them, is unknown. On 21 March 1521 the pope urged the Constable and the Admiral of Castile to prevent the spread of Luther's writings. On 7 April Adrian of Utrecht issued orders that all books by Luther should be handed over to the Inquisition and burnt, and that anyone possessing or selling them three days after the decree should be punished. A week later the royal council announced serious penalties for those who sold or kept Luther's works or who discussed his errors in public or in private.

The inquisitors, the bishops and the various governors of Spain were now unanimous in calling for the strictest measures against the new heresy. They associated it both with the *conversos*, responsible for circulating Lutheran literature, and with the rebellious *comuneros* who had disrupted the life of the country for eleven months and whose demands had included the abolition of the Inquisition and tithes. Lutheranism was thus widely connected with civil disorder.

Yet this view was still not shared by some of the more enlightened members of the emperor's peripatetic court. April 1521 was the month of the Diet of Worms at which Luther had to defend his teaching before the emperor. Courtiers such as Juan de Vergara and Alfonso de Valdés attended the diet in the eirenic spirit characteristic of many humanists at the time. Juan de Vergara said later that 'His Majesty's entire court' was full of Luther's books and that '*todo el mundo*' approved of Luther's ideas on the necessity of reforming the Church and putting an end to the corruption of the clergy.[28] There was, moreover, a wide interest, particularly evident in Italy, in Luther's teaching on justification by faith, and the persuasion that Catholic acceptance of such a doctrine might lead to reconciliation between the Lutherans and Rome. These hopes were to remain alive for twenty years to come and had a deep effect on the thought of a number of loyal Catholics.

Luther's enemies, in the meantime, did his cause almost as much good in Spain as those who admired him. Within a few months of the Diet of Worms there appeared some invaluable vehicles for the propagation of his ideas: the attacks by Jaime Olesa and Cipriano Benet, detailed confutations of Lutheranism containing equally detailed analyses of it. Written in Latin, these and other polemical works were admittedly only accessible to the educated, but the inquisitors considered some of them dangerous enough to forbid their circulation in 1540.

In the middle of July 1522 the emperor and his court returned to Spain. Luther's works were easily available in the imperial retinue, among Charles V's cosmopolitan staff, Flemings, Italians, and Spanish *conversos*. Even if the inquisitors seem at first to have been successful in preventing the infiltration of Lutheran writings in the peninsula beyond the court and the universities, an alarming discovery was made in May 1523. This was a consignment of Lutheran literature smuggled from the Low Countries into the Basque lands and distributed among 'bachelors of arts, priests and other persons of that area'. The books were apparently intended to reach Valencia.

What effect did these events have on the *alumbrados*? The first explicit evidence of their knowledge of Luther is of a later date: Alonso López de la Palomera said he had heard the Reformer referred to as Antichrist in 1523 or 1524.[29] Certainly the *alumbrados* had received information about the developments in Germany well before then, but we can only speculate about what they knew. Pedro Ruiz de Alcaraz and Isabel de la Cruz can hardly have had enough Latin to read Luther's early writings, yet these must have been accessible to their more learned friends, scholars and theologians at the university of Alcalá and in the Franciscan convents. Juan de Cazalla, for example, would have read them. Juan de Valdés, whose brother was at Worms, was acquainted with works by Luther dating from 1518 and 1520, though this can only be documented in 1529. It may therefore be surmised that Luther's views were first transmitted to the leading *dejados* orally. In the early 1520s, however, they might have come across Castilian translations, and any works effectively smuggled from the Basque area to Valencia would probably have passed through Guadalajara. These, however, all remain hypotheses, and the inquisitors never managed to prove that the *alumbrados* arrested in 1524 had direct knowledge of Protestant writings.

What does emerge from the investigation into the early *alumbrados* is the fear of Lutheranism. That the decision to prosecute them was connected with the advance of Protestantism is virtually certain, and a concern with Lutheranism is evident in the conduct of the trials. The edict of faith of 1525 qualified three of the propositions as Lutheran - that confession was not instituted by divine law, contempt for indulgences, and mockery of the cult of the saints. The bill of indictment presented against Alcaraz in October of the previous year contained the last two charges besides accusations of having denied transubstantiation and of having asserted that good works were performed out of self interest and were of no avail for salvation.[30] At a later stage Alcaraz was interrogated about the infusion of grace by God independently of any works.[31]

The last occasion on which Alcaraz's interrogators seem again to have been trying to gauge whether or not he was a Lutheran was shortly before the final sentence was passed. The interrogation took place in March 1529 before the *Suprema*,[32] and is of particular interest since those present included the inquisitor general, Alonso Manrique, and an official, Fernando de Valdés, who had been appointed to the *Suprema* in 1524, had followed the *alumbrado* trials closely and was himself to become inquisitor general many years later.[33]

Alcaraz was first questioned about his interpretation of Ps 118:22: 'The stone which the builders refused is become the head stone of the corner'. Those who refused the stone, said Alcaraz, were the Pharisees, and the builders were the men who wanted to establish their own doctrine against the Christian Church. The stone was Christ. The way not to refuse the stone was humility. Originally, the inquisitors reminded him, he had said that the builders were those who struggled against temptations and refused the stone which was the love of God. Now, however, Alcaraz stood by the more orthodox interpretation. Then he was asked about his interpretation of 1 Cor 13:8, 'Charity never faileth'. This was a passage now closely associated with the *alumbrados* and about which a blind beggar who laid a momentary claim to carnal impeccability, Martín Cota, was interrogated a year later by the tribunal of Toledo.[34] But Alcaraz's reply was orthodox. Man, he said, could fall if God dropped him from His hold, but charity never. Alcaraz was also questioned about whether he had indeed maintained that man's salvation lies more in God's mercy than in works, and he admitted he had. He believed it, he added, and regarded good works simply as a 'means' to obtain salvation.

Two days later Alcaraz was summoned again.[35] This time he was asked about the hundred and ninety-nine letters submitted to the tribunal by the prosecutor. To start with he was examined about the cryptic language used. Then the questions turned to faith. What did Alcaraz mean by those who were sustained by faith? In what way were they different from others? Alcaraz said he had never intended to draw a distinction. He was interrogated about the phrase 'living in silence' and what he meant by the word '*pospuesto*', subordinated. Those, he replied, who subordinated everything that was contrary to the service of God. Had Alcaraz introduced a form of obedience among his followers? No, he answered. Obedience was due only to God or to ecclesiastical prelates.

The insistence of Alcaraz's interrogators on the security of grace, God's mercy and good works, faith, obedience and the existence of conventicles, suggests that the inquisitors may, in a circuitous manner, have been trying to establish whether Alcaraz was a Lutheran. Yet they never broached the matter directly. Their approach, Fernando de Valdés was to write thirty years later, was the result of inexperience.[36] They were still unfamiliar with the new heresy, but they were to acquire a better idea of it in the course of the next decade and learn to recognise it under the various guises it assumed.

Chapter VI

Humanism Attacked

The uncertain and tentative approach of the inquisitors in the trial of Alcaraz may have been partly due to their inexperience of Lutheranism, as Fernando de Valdés was later to claim, but it was also a reflection of the continuing dogmatic uncertainty of the Catholic Church which continued, throughout the 1530s, to admit a wide range of views. On one side there was a variety of evangelical positions extending from more or less strong sympathies for Lutheranism to that of individuals who would have agreed with the words later ascribed by Thomas Starkey to Cardinal Pole in the fictitious *Dialogue* with Thomas Lupset: 'I will not follow the steps of Luther, whose judgement I esteem very little; and yet he and his disciples be not so wicked and foolish that in all things they err. Heretics be not in all things heretics. Therefore I will not so abhor their heresy that for the hate thereof I will fly from the truth.'[1] On the other side there were those who would accept no form of compromise with Lutheranism or with anything resembling it.

In Spain the conflict between the two extremes was characterised both by the accusation of *alumbradismo* and by resentment of the *conversos*. It turned into a campaign against a certain type of man, a *converso* who had studied at the university of Alcalá and who either remained at the university or who travelled with the court and would in both cases have had access to Protestant literature. One of the features these men often had in common was an admiration for the Dutch humanist Desiderius Erasmus and it is his fortunes in Spain that best illustrate the development which took place.

Erasmus and Spain

By 1516, the year of his appointment as councillor at the court of the future Charles V in Brussels, Erasmus was a celebrity. He had published some of his best-known works: the *Adagia*, the vast collection of proverbs to which he added over the years and which was to obtain enduring popularity; his *Moriae encomium* or *Praise of Folly*, the satirical masterpiece which, with its mockery of the absurdity of scholastic theologians, the superstition and ignorance of friars and monks, and the abuses by prelates, gained him both admirers and enemies; and his *Enchiridion militis christiani*, the *Handbook of a Christian Soldier*, with the best definition of his *philosophia Christi*, a simple piety based on the precepts of the Scriptures and free of superfluous ceremonies and devotions. In 1516, moreover, he published his book on the education of the Christian prince, the *Institutio principis christiani* for the benefit of Charles of Ghent, and his edition of the New Testament. The intention of this last work, one of the most controversial of his publications, was in many respects similar to that of Cardinal Cisneros's polyglot Bible. In an effort to improve on Jerome's Vulgate which, he believed, had been corrupted over the centuries, Erasmus provided a new Latin translation of the New Testament printed beside the Greek original, and a large apparatus of notes. Despite the many criticisms drawn by the edition, it was widely greeted as a monument of scholarship and contributed still further to Erasmus's swiftly growing reputation in Spain. Patronised by Charles's chancellor, Jean Le Sauvage, he was offered a bishopric there. He was also invited to the country by Cisneros in 1517, and he was urged by the royal courtiers to accompany them to their sovereign's new kingdom. Erasmus declined all these invitations.[2]

Three years later the Spaniards started to attack Erasmus. In 1520 Diego López de Zúñiga published his first criticism of Erasmus's edition of the New Testament. Zúñiga regarded himself as the defender of the Biblical scholarship at the university of Alcalá. Insofar as his book was a cry of indignant patriotism it was relatively harmless, but this was no longer true of his far more brutal attack of 1522. The Lutheran schism had taken place and Zúñiga now emphasised Erasmus's attacks on the cult of the saints, on the sacraments of matrimony and penance, on indulgences, pilgrimages, miracles, ceremonies and monastic orders, to prove that the humanist was 'not only a Lutheran but the standard-bearer and prince of Lutherans'.[3]

These accusations coincided with the beginning of Erasmus's true success in Spain. The court had returned to the peninsula, and it included personal friends and admirers of the Dutch humanist: the new chancellor Mercurino Gattinara; the future imperial secretary Alfonso de Valdés; the secretary of the archbishop of Toledo, Juan de Vergara; Alonso de Fonseca, archbishop of Compostela and future archbishop of Toledo, and others. At the Complutensian university, moreover, there was the highest esteem for Erasmus as a Biblical scholar despite Zúñiga's attack. But even beyond the court and the universities a vast number of educated Spaniards saw Erasmus and his *philosophia Christi*, as synonymous with a Catholic reformation.

In Alcalá in 1525 the printer Miguel de Eguía started to produce editions of Erasmus's principal works in Latin, and in the following year he printed the Castilian version of the *Enchiridion militis christiani*, translated some time earlier and at last approved by the inquisitor general. It was amazingly popular. 'In the court of the emperor, in the cities, in the churches, in the convents, even in the inns and in the streets', wrote the translator, 'there is no one without a copy of Erasmus's *Enchiridion* in Spanish.'[4] But for all the support of Alonso Manrique, the imperial court and the professors at Alcalá, the Spanish translation of the *Enchiridion* was received with distaste in certain monastic circles. Although Erasmus's attacks on monks and friars were modified in the Castilian version, his spirit remained. His contempt for the tyranny of the convent, for hollow rites and for the parasitism of the mendicant orders was clearly perceptible.

The men offended by Erasmus protested and in 1527 Manrique organised a conference in Valladolid to decide on whether or not Erasmus should continue to be read. For the event the mendicant orders prepared a list of objections to Erasmus's views on twenty-two points, including the Trinity, the sacraments, the freedom of the will, ecclesiastical authority, the commandments of the Church, and the cult of the saints and the Virgin Mary.[5] Erasmus defended himself against the charges and at the conference his supporters triumphed. Between 1527 and 1531 the Spanish presses produced one translation of his works after another.

Yet hostility to Erasmus was mounting fast. Attacks started to appear which showed that it was not only the more bigoted friars who opposed him. The *Apologia monasticae religionis* of 1528, for instance, was written by Fray Luis de Carvajal, a Franciscan with a humanist education who truly believed that scholasticism and monasticism had been maligned. The suspicion was also growing that the Dutchman's works were being used as a cover behind which to cultivate Protestant ideas. Such a view was not altogether unjustified. In Italy in 1526 Erasmus's name had, after all, actually been put to a work by Luther. That the approval of the *Enchiridion* could have practical uses in the defense of those accused of heresy in Spain is shown by an episode in the trial of Alcaraz. In maintaining that he had always believed it was the intention with which a charitable deed was performed that counted, Alcaraz referred to the Castilian translation of the work. He did so in June 1527, after he had been in prison for over three years. He is thus most unlikely to have consulted the book - he even misquoted the Castilian title, giving it as *Arma* rather than *Manual del caballero cristiano*, and the reference was probably suggested to him by his counsel, Fray Reginaldo de Esquina.[6] The case of Juan de Valdés's *Diálogo de doctrina christiana* is even more relevant. The book, published by Miguel de Eguía in 1529, was presented as an Erasmian catechism. In reality, however, it contains excerpts from Luther's *Decem Praecepta Wittenbergensi praedicata populo* of 1518 and from his *Explanatio dominicae orationis pro simplicioribus laicis* of 1520. Valdés also paraphrases Oecolampadius's *In Iesaiam Prophetam Hypomnemata* of 1525 on the vanity of human knowledge and probably Melanchthon's *Enchiridion elementorum puerilium* of 1524.[7]

Whether they were right or not in seeing Erasmianism as a cover for Lutheranism and despite Erasmus's own refusal ever to leave the Church of Rome, Erasmus's Spanish enemies could undermine the official approval and protection accorded to the humanist's works even by the inquisitor general. They did so by applying to the local tribunals of the Inquisition which could still operate with a considerable measure of independence of the *Suprema*.

Again we find the Holy Office being used as an outlet for personal bitterness and vindictiveness. The rôle of Mari Núñez, her maidservant and Hernando Díaz in denouncing the first *alumbrados* was now to be filled by Francisca Hernández, her maid and her confessor. Playing on the inquisitors' fears of Lutheranism, they supplied them with the denunciations behind the second wave of *alumbrado* trials which included those of courtiers and humanists. This was preceded, however, by an experiment in religious reform to the failure of which Francisca Hernández also contributed: the attempt to evangelise the territories near Medina de Ríoseco of the Marquess of Villena's brother-in-law Don Fadrique Enríquez.

An experiment in evangelisation

The experiment was suggested to Don Fadrique in the summer of 1525 by the Basque priest of *converso* descent Juan López de Celain.[8] Juan López had been in the service of the Duke of Infantado's chaplain Alonso del Castillo since about 1523. In Guadalajara he had encountered the followers of Alcaraz and Isabel de la Cruz. His name appears as one of the *alumbrado* correspondents, and Antonio de Baeza introduced him to the Admiral of Castile.

At first Don Fadrique adopted Juan López's proposals which aimed, he informed the admiral in a letter of 30 July 1525, at 'la reformación de la verdadera cristianidad'. Furnished with a certificate from his protector, Juan López set out to find twelve apostles to assist him in his mission - apostles whom Don Fadrique undertook to pay 20,000 maravedís a year and to house in the vicinity of Medina de Ríoseco while more appropriate lodgings, in the form of a convent, were being found. Juan López was accompanied by Diego López de Husillos, a priest from Toledo, the friend of Juan de Cazalla and a former follower of Francisca Hernández. Together they sought out their disciples in the humanist circles of Alcalá. Those they approached included scholars and theologians of distinction, such as Fray Francisco Ortiz and Alejo de Venegas. There was also a woman, the Fleming Ana del Valle.[9] To start with, however, only three of the twelve accepted the admiral's offer: Gaspar de Villafaña, Luis de Beteta and Juan del Castillo, the last a professor of Greek attached to the retinue of the inquisitor general who had met Juan López through Juan de Vergara's half-brother Bernardino de Tovar.

The apostles' arrival at Medina de Ríoseco was a disappointment. They found no money, no lodgings, no employment. Don Fadrique showed no inclination even to receive them and, one after another, they departed. Juan López was left alone with his protector who suddenly displayed a renewed interest in the project and lodged the priest in a house near the town. Three other candidates now arrived: the canon of Palencia Pedro Hernández, the printer Miguel de Eguía, and Fray Tomás de Guzmán, a Dominican related to the Mendozas. They soon left, however, and when Juan del Castillo returned from Valladolid, where he had visited Francisca Hernández, he found Juan López on his own. By this time he had abandoned the entire idea and, towards the end of 1526, he agreed to accompany the professor of Greek back to Valladolid. Don Fadrique, it appears, had heard from Francisca Hernández that his protégés had expressed a favourable opinion of Luther and had decided to have nothing further to do with them.[10]

What were their opinions? The plan to evangelise an estate certainly had a Protestant ring and recalls Caspar Schwenckfeld's slightly earlier projects in his own Silesian lands.[11] Juan López, at all events, was arrested by the Holy Office two years after his departure from Medina de Ríoseco after having stayed in Valladolid, Alcalá and, finally, Granada, where he had been appointed chaplain of the Royal Chapel. In the prisons of the tribunal of Granada he found himself together with another aspirant apostle, Diego López de Husillos, and was accused of having defended sixty-five erroneous propositions. These he alternately acknowledged and denied, interrupting the investigation with two successful escapes. In the course of the second of these he went to Alcalá where he dined with Miguel de Eguía and Rodrigo de Bivar, and discussed Erasmus's paraphrase of the New Testament.[12]

A number of the propositions attributed to Juan López resemble those imputed to the *alumbrados*, but could equally well have been taken from Luther. He was alleged to have maintained that it was sufficient to love God fervently without performing any work, that the advice of theologians was unnecessary for understanding the Scriptures, that the true spiritual exercise was contemplation of God. He was charged too with saying that perfect peace could be attained on this earth, that the 'spiritual man' was not bound by common laws, that the man reborn with the divine will cannot sin and that God was indifferent to man's attitude towards Him. He was suspected of defending predestination and claiming that, since Christ had died for our sins, nothing further could be done by man to obtain forgiveness.[13] Too little information about Juan López has survived to show how many of these propositions he had actually upheld and whether he really did maintain that 'Luther was no heretic but a good Christian'. The books which he said he had written on 'the true nature of the soul' have disappeared. The inquisitors certainly believed him to have been a Lutheran; his escapes weighed heavily against him; and he is one of the very few defendants of these trials to have been burnt at the stake.

Slightly more information is available about Juan del Castillo. After studying at the university of Louvain in 1523 he entered the service of Alonso Manrique in Seville. He then came to Toledo where he obtained a master's degree in theology and a post as teacher of Greek in the Colegio de Santa Catalina. At the university of Alcalá he encountered Bernardino de Tovar and the men who were to involve him in the apostolate of Medina de Ríoseco. He conferred with María de Cazalla in Guadalajara and with Francisca Hernández in Valladolid. To the inquisitors Juan del Castillo, despite his attachment to the inquisitor general, was doubly suspicious: he had studied in the Low Countries and was therefore likely to have developed Lutheran sympathies, and he was a New Christian. It is uncertain whether, at the time of his association with Juan López de Celain, he had already acquired the high regard for Luther which was to bring him too to the stake ten years later. Certainly he admired Erasmus and the five letters he wrote to his sister Petronila de Lucena from Valladolid at the time of the apostolate are filled with a belief in spiritual renewal. He refers to the ties between the believer and Jesus Christ who dwells 'in our souls for ever', to the total abandonment to God who 'commands us to appear empty and in reverence before Him'. He writes of works as 'pertaining to death' and begs 'our Lord, in His infinite goodness' to 'number us all among His chosen people'. Above all he emphasises the importance of attaining 'that peace of God which passeth all understanding' (Phil 4:1).[14]

Scholars and courtiers

The first sign of an official association between *alumbrados* and Lutherans was an order from the *Suprema* to the inquisitors of Aragon, Castile, Majorca and Navarre, dated 11 August 1530, proposing that to all edicts issued by the Holy Office be added 'those who know about the books and doctrine of Luther and his followers or about the *alumbrados* and *dejados* and others'.[15] This was a convenient clause for proceeding against the friends and admirers of Erasmus. Their enemies at last had the chance for which they had been waiting since their defeat in Valladolid in 1527. The court had left for Italy and Germany in 1529 and was to stay away for four years. Manrique was disgraced in the emperor's absence; the other great protector of Erasmus at court, the chancellor Mercurino Gattinara, died in 1530. Now, with the assistance of Francisca Hernández and her confessor, the lecherous and fanciful Diego Hernández, some revenge could be taken.

Francisca Hérnández had been placed under arrest in March 1529.[16] Attended by her maid and cosseted by her warders, her imprisonment was of the most comfortable kind, and her readiness to collaborate with the Holy Office ensured the continuation of her privileges. She started to denounce her numerous acquaintances in July 1530 and her evidence was corroborated and elaborated on by her confessor two years later. Her interrogator, the inquisitor Vaguer, interrupted her examination by reading to her the edict against the *alumbrados*. This enabled her to attribute the propositions it contained to those she denounced without any further effort of memorising.[17]

The charge of *alumbradismo* in the trials of Francisca Hernández's followers both altered and expanded the image of the *alumbrado*. This is particularly evident in the case of one of her first admirers, Antonio de Medrano.[18] A *converso* from the Rioja area where his family had long been in the service of the Dukes of Nájera, Medrano had been tried on various occasions by the Holy Office on account of his behaviour with his female penitents and his claim that he had reached such a state of grace that he could not sin. A lover of good food and drink, he had also maintained that God was as much present in the eucharist as He was in a fatted capon - an idea which he said he had taken from a sermon by Juan de Cazalla.[19] After having been arrested again in 1530 he admitted under torture that his relationship with Francisca Hernández had indeed been 'carnal', although, as the physician who established her virginity confirmed, it had stopped short of sexual intercourse.[20] Medrano's misdemeanours contributed to the ascetic piety of Isabel de la Cruz, Alcaraz and María de Cazalla being transformed into the orgiastic antinomianism encountered in the *alumbrado* movements of the later sixteenth century.

But was Medrano an *alumbrado*? He was indeed accused of saying 'love God, for love instructs us, as the so-called *alumbrados* had said', but when questioned about the movement in Guadalajara he replied that he had no idea who the *alumbrados* were or what their errors were.[21] This denial seems to have been accepted by the majority of his judges. Only one out of nine, the inquisitor Yáñez, associated him with the *alumbrados* and recommended he be sent to the stake. The others were far more moderate, and three of them did not even regard him as a heretic.[22]

If Medrano is at one end of the spectrum which *alumbradismo* now started to present, the scholars and preachers arrested are at the other. Fray Francisco Ortiz, admired by the emperor and the court and highly esteemed within the Franciscan order, occupies, admittedly, a somewhat exceptional position. He caused his own arrest by publicly attacking the Inquisition for having imprisoned Francisca Hernández in a sermon delivered in San Juan de los Reyes. His principal crime was his overriding devotion to the *beata* and not the thoroughly orthodox form of mysticism which he practised. With other of Francisca Hernández's victims the matter was different. Unlike Ortiz they were open to the charge of Lutheranism and it is in their trials that we find *alumbradismo* and Lutheranism linked.

The first of these, and the longest, for it was still going on in 1541, was of a man at the centre of Castilian intellectual life. Bernardino de Tovar had accompanied Francisca Hernández to the tribunal of Valladolid in 1519 and had long been in the *beata*'s thrall. Subsequently, he was involved in the apostolate of Medina de Ríoseco. He came from a powerful New Christian family. One of his half-brothers, Francisco de Vergara, was professor of Greek at the university of Alcalá, and another was the versatile humanist Juan de Vergara. The brothers - above all Juan - were close friends of Erasmus, and Bernardino de Tovar endeavoured to propagate the Dutch scholar's ideas from his residence in Alcalá. He also possessed works by Luther and other Reformers.[23] These were compromising items of evidence. First interrogated in December 1529, he was arrested ten months later.

Tovar's trial has been lost, but that of his brother Juan de Vergara survives and allows us to see how a humanist of distinction dealt with the charge of *alumbradismo*. It also shows how the protection accorded to the admirers of Erasmus broke down.

Juan de Vergara had studied at Alcalá and had worked on the Complutensian polyglot Bible. In about 1516 he had been appointed secretary to Cardinal Cisneros and then passed into the service of Cisneros's successor as archbishop of Toledo, Guillaume de Croy. He travelled in 1520 to the Low Countries where his friendship with Erasmus began, and in the following year attended the Diet of Worms. After the archbishop's death Vergara became imperial chaplain. In 1524 he accepted an appointment as secretary to yet another archbishop of Toledo, Alonso de Fonseca.[24] Widely respected at the court and at the universities, Vergara believed that his friendship with the inquisitor general and his post as secretary to Fonseca placed him beyond the reach of the Holy Office. Yet he had blatantly flouted its rule of secrecy. Promising favours and money to the notaries, bestowing gifts on the warders, he sustained a long correspondence with Bernardino de Tovar, whom he was determined to rescue. The letters were only discovered almost three years after he had started writing them.

Vergara's main offence when he was imprisoned in June 1533 was his contempt for the Inquisition, and he was accused of insulting the Holy Office. But there were also other charges. He was accused of being a Lutheran and of 'knowing, teaching and believing the errors of those called *alumbrados* which almost coincide with the said Lutheran errors'. Besides possessing books by Luther and defending his doctrine, he was charged with denying the necessity of religious ceremonies and good works, with preferring mental to vocal prayer, with denying that confession was ordained by divine law, and with supporting certain views of Erasmus which had been proscribed. To this Vergara replied that he had approved of some of Luther's ideas before he had been condemned by the pope, and that Erasmus, far from having been anathematised, was protected by the pope, the emperor and the inquisitor general. To the charge of being an *alumbrado* he answered with one of those bursts of sarcasm which make his defences such a pleasure to read:

I have always kept my shoulders in their place without raising them to my ears . . . My dress has always been extravagant rather than shabby. I have always shared the company and pastimes of all, shunning nobody and displaying no particular eccentricity. My conversation is never about prayers and saints; if anything I am, according to some, slightly given to gossip. I believe that these vanities of poor little women have no greater enemy than I in the whole world, nor one who is more suspicious of them.[25]

The arrest of Bernardino de Tovar in 1530 was a sign of warning for all those who had associated with the *alumbrados* as well as for courtiers and scholars who had admired Erasmus. The imprisonment of Juan de Vergara confirmed what might happen to anyone who did not heed the warning. The intercession of Vergara's highly placed friends had no effect and his greatest patron, Alonso de Fonseca, on whose help he had counted most, died in 1534. By then, moreover, the campaign was well underway. Trials had been prepared against Juan de Cazalla, who died in 1530, and against the Valdés brothers, Juan and Alfonso. Juan del Castillo had fled to France but was arrested in Bologna in 1533 and brought back to Spain. His brother, Gaspar de Lucena, had been imprisoned in the previous year and his sister, Petronila de Lucena, was to be incarcerated in 1534. In the course of the decade nearly all those involved in the apostolate of Medina de Ríoseco were apprehended: Juan López de Celain, Diego López de Husillos, Gaspar de Villafaña, Diego del Castillo, Luis de Beteta, and, as late as 1540, Ana del Valle. Miguel de Eguía was captured in November 1531. Mateo Pascual, the rector of the university of Alcalá, left Spain but was tricked into returning from Rome in the summer of 1533 and kept in the prisons of Toledo for thirty-six months. Late in 1534 the arrest was made of the Benedictine Alfonso de Virués who had translated Erasmus's *Colloquia* into Castilian and was a particular favourite of the emperor. The aged chancellor of the Complutensian university, Pedro de Lerma, was imprisoned in 1537. The Portuguese priest Manuel de Miona and Miguel de Torres, the vice-rector of the Trilingual College of Alcalá, were, together with the Valdés brothers, among the few to make a successful escape abroad.[26]

Shortly after the incarceration of Juan de Vergara Rodrigo Manrique, the illegitimate son of the disgraced inquisitor general, wrote from Paris to his former tutor, the humanist Juan Luis Vives, that Vergara had fallen into the hands of

worthless . . . boors who hate men of value and think they are performing a fine and pious work by eliminating scholars on account of a mere word or joke . . . You are right, ours is an envious, proud land - and a barbarous one. It appears increasingly evident that no one can practise good letters in Spain without their being charged with heresies, errors and Judaism. In such a way silence has been imposed on learning, and those attracted by erudition have, as you say, been terrorised.[27]

An atmosphere of terror had indeed been created. Otherwise, however, the official measures against the readers of Erasmus were surprisingly mild: the only book by the Dutch scholar actually to be prohibited in this period was the *Colloquia*, the reading of which, either in the vernacular or in Latin, was forbidden by the inquisitors in 1536 and 1537 respectively.[28]

The last alumbrados of Toledo

Not all the victims of the great wave of arrests were scholars. María de Cazalla was imprisoned in April 1532, her late apprehension being due, as we saw, to her response to an edict proclaimed in February 1525. But further evidence had been provided against her by Francisca Hernández and Diego Hernández, and she was charged with 'believing the Lutheran errors and [the errors] of those who called themselves *alumbrados* but who should rather be called blind, and other types of heresy.'[29]

Since 1525 María de Cazalla had continued to attract individuals in search of spiritual guidance. Her influence was especially strong in Alcalá. From there Bernardino de Tovar, Juan López de Celain and Juan del Castillo set forth to converse with her, and in their company she would occasionally utter a word in favour of Luther and came across Juan de Valdés's *Diálogo de doctrina christiana*. She also read Erasmus, and in her trial, perhaps disingenuously, she placed great emphasis on him as a writer who had been officially approved. 'There is not a single word in Erasmus which she does not believe and quote,' said her confessor, 'reaching the point of regarding him as the Gospel and not wishing any other author to be read, preached or translated into Castilian'. The *Enchiridion* was presented as her favourite reading matter.[30] What attracted her most about it was Erasmus's treatment of the struggle between the flesh and the spirit. She too, she admitted to the inquisitors, was tormented by the same conflict, and the words of Erasmus, after those of St Paul, were the most consoling she had read.

Courageous even under torture, María de Cazalla managed to convince the inquisitors that she was not the Lutheran described by the prosecutor. She denied having justified Luther, but admitted that she had initially heard people say he was right about certain points and that she had repeated what she had heard. She confessed to having regarded Isabel de la Cruz 'as a good woman and a servant of God until she saw her condemned as the contrary'. She had, she said, admired Juan de Valdés's *Diálogo de doctrina christiana* although she put it in a chest and forbade her daughters to read it after hearing Bernardino de Tovar upbraid Valdés for publishing it without correcting certain points.[31] She accounted satisfactorily for the other charges and submitted herself to the mercy of the Church.

María de Cazalla's sentence was light: abjuration *de levi* and a fine of a hundred ducats. Light, too, were most of the other sentences of the 1530s. Antonio de Medrano was sentenced to abjuration and 'perpetual reclusion', but his behaviour in 'perpetual reclusion' is a further indication of the manner in which the punishments of the Holy Office were imposed. Despite his request to be imprisoned in his home town of Navarrete he was originally recluded in a convent in Toledo. Here he pestered the friars with his complaints about the food, would leave the convent grounds only to return late at night, and insisted on bringing women to his quarters. He was therefore transferred to a hospital where he was supposed to work as a guard. He repeated his offences and soon the inquisitors agreed to send him to a convent in Navarrete. In 1537, five years after his sentence, he was released, partly as a result of a plea by the Duke of Nájera.[32]

The sentences did not necessarily even affect the reputation or the careers of those who had been arrested. After having to retract his more offensive statements Fray Francisco Ortiz was sentenced to confinement in the convent of Torrelaguna for two years, during which time he was to perform various spiritual penances. He resolved never to leave the convent again, but he was respected by his fellow friars, venerated by all who heard about him, and his superiors vainly implored him to relinquish his seclusion, resume his functions and return to the pulpit. Don Fadrique Enríquez, with whom he corresponded, repeatedly but unsuccessfully invited him to his estates near Medina de Ríoseco.[33]

Some two years after his arrest in 1531, Miguel de Eguía returned to his birthplace, Estella in Navarre. There he was appointed *alcalde* in 1535, *regidor* in 1537 and 1539, and *alcalde* once more in 1541. By 1546 he had set up a printing press in Estella (the second to be introduced into Navarre) and when he died in the same year he was buried, in accordance with his last wishes, in a Franciscan habit.[34]

Juan de Vergara's sentence was one of the heaviest: abjuration *de vehementi*, a fine of a thousand ducats and a year's reclusion in a monastery. Within four months the inquisitor general agreed to modify the punishment to confinement within the precincts of the cathedral of Toledo, but Vergara was soon accused of breaking the rules by attending a chapter meeting and was again imprisoned for a few days. The inquisitor general prevented the local tribunal from doing more than sending him back to the cloister for a month, after which he was once more confined to the cathedral grounds. In February 1537, just over two years after his original sentence, he was set at liberty and returned to his intellectual activities, compiling an attack on the *estatutos de limpieza* as well as a brief tract in reply to certain questions put to him by the fourth Duke of Infantado.[35]

Only three of the many defendants of the 1530s seem to have been sent to the stake: Juan López de Celain, Juan del Castillo, and Tovar's disciple Alonso Garzón.[36] The clemency shown otherwise suggests that the equation between Lutheranism and *alumbradismo* proposed by the prosecutor in the bills of indictment was not accepted. Even if the inquisitors were gathering experience in the treatment of Lutheran views they still hesitated to condemn defendants guilty of little more than evangelism. Their relative clemency suggests that they considered imprisonment a sufficient penalty for the type of man at whom the campaign was aimed: a courtier or a scholar of *converso* descent who availed himself of his privileged position to read works attacking the Church of Rome. It can also be concluded that the local tribunals were satisfied with showing their strength to the emperor. That they did so effectively is demonstrated by the trial of Alonso de Virués. The emperor followed the proceedings attentively. He ordered Manrique to supervise the trial in person, but the inquisitor general, either unwittingly or deliberately, proved dilatory. During the two years of the Benedictine's imprisonment the inquisitor general received letter after letter from the emperor and the empress urging him to accelerate the trial. By April 1536 the emperor's secretary had written to the *Suprema* to obtain an explanation for the delay. In October of the following year, after Virués had abjured *de levi* and had been sentenced to two years reclusion during which time he was not allowed to preach, the imperial secretary beseeched the inquisitors to modify the sentence. The emperor finally managed to obtain a papal brief of absolution and, later in 1538, boldly confirmed his devotion to the Benedictine by appointing him bishop of the Canaries.[37]

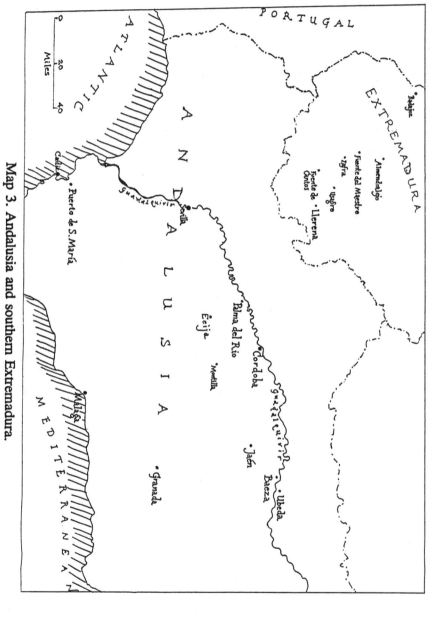

Map 3. Andalusia and southern Extremadura.

Chapter VII

The Fear of Novelty

The association between *alumbradismo* and Lutheranism evident in the 1530s was accompanied by a tendency, which persisted until late in the century, to use the charge of *alumbradismo* against various forms of novelty, not only against Protestantism and evangelism but also against the carriers of a revived Catholicism. Certainly, as we shall see in this chapter, some of the latter had once been attracted by evangelism and had been acquainted with the victims of the campaign of the 1530s. They often had a similar background. Former students of Alcalá, they had connections with the court and were sometimes of *converso* descent. For these and other reasons they were easy targets.

Conventicles

One of the features which made the Catholic reformers vulnerable was the formation of prayer groups in which the laity took part. The spirit behind such movements, it could be argued, was to have a glorious future in the confraternities founded by the Jesuits from the late sixteenth century onwards, one of the more successful achievements of the Counter-Reformation. At first, however, assemblies of pious men and women who met in order to pray, frequently in private houses, evoked the image of the *alumbrados*.

The *Suprema* had displayed its concern at the discovery of the hundred and ninety-nine letters found in the possession of the *alumbrado* leaders in 1529.[1] The cryptic language, recurrent terms such as 'living in silence', 'subjection', 'subordination' and 'sustaining oneself in faith', the correspondents' custom of calling one another 'brother' and 'sister' and of not referring to each other by name - all this, besides the habit of Isabel de la Cruz's followers of meeting in order to discuss the Scriptures, suggested the existence of a secret sect whose members formed conventicles.

The somewhat obsessive idea among the inquisitors that any movement or group which displayed extreme piety smacked of *alumbradismo* is demonstrated by an episode involving Juan de Valdés's brother Alfonso, the imperial secretary. In 1529 he completed his *Diálogo de Mercurio y Carón* which has long been regarded as one of the great products of Spanish 'Erasmianism'. In 1531 the manuscript was submitted to the Inquisition and judged by a censor, Dr Vélez. Most of the passages Vélez found unacceptable contained echoes of Erasmus, and sometimes of Luther - mockery of bulls, indulgences and jubilees; jibes at the pope and the friars, bishops and ecclesiastical ceremonies; a reiterated claim for the superiority of mental prayer; and a belief in the importance of faith. But there were other passages which also aroused suspicion. Mercurio is telling Carón about his recent visit to earth. There, he says, he found lamentably few good Christians - a single group of truly devout men mercilessly persecuted by a far larger group 'usurping the name of perfection'. Vélez was in no doubt as to who made up these groups. The smaller one, he said, referred to the *alumbrados*, persecuted by a large throng of inquisitors and friars.[2]

There is no evidence to suggest that this interpretation was correct. Alfonso de Valdés may equally well have been describing the admirers of Erasmus who, in 1529, were beginning to feel the effects of the surreptitious but widespread dislike of all the Dutch scholar represented. But that the censor should have leapt with such alacrity to the conclusion that a small and pious group could only be the *alumbrados* is an instance of a prejudice which will be further illustrated in other cases.

Ignatius Loyola

Later in the century the Jesuits were especially open to charges of *alumbradismo* both because of the many links between Ignatius Loyola and those implicated in the *alumbrado* trials before and after the foundation of the Society of Jesus in 1540, and because of Loyola's own experiences in Spain.

Loyola, who came from an aristocratic family of Old Christians, had served as a page in the household of the second Duke of Nájera, Don Antonio Manrique de Lara, and probably encountered Antonio de Medrano, who was also protected by the duke and had a friend in common with Loyola in the duke's half-brother, Don Francisco Manrique de Lara, future bishop of Salamanca.[3] By 1522 Loyola had renounced the secular life he had been expected to lead as a young nobleman. After recovering from a wound received at the siege of Pamplona he had gone to Montserrat, had exchanged his clothes with a beggar, and made his way to Manresa, north-west of Barcelona. Here, influenced by the meditational treatises of the Devotio Moderna, he wrote a first draft of what was later to become a manual of Jesuit instruction, the *Ejercicios espirituales*. From Manresa he made a pilgrimage to Jerusalem, passing through Rome. When he returned to Spain in 1524 he studied theology first in Barcelona and then at the university of Alcalá.

Loyola arrived in Alcalá in February 1526 and was followed shortly after by three companions.[4] In the university town he became acquainted with some of the most prominent individuals later to be pursued by the Inquisition. He and his companions were given hospitality by the printer Miguel de Eguía and his brother Diego. As his confessor Loyola chose the Portuguese priest Manuel de Miona, who introduced him to the works of Erasmus. Miona, a friend of Bernardino de Tovar and Alonso Garzón, was to be denounced as an *alumbrado* by Diego Hernández in 1532 after he had left for Paris.

Within a few months of his arrival Loyola found himself at the head of a group desiring spiritual instruction. The majority were women - two gentlewomen, the widow María del Vado and her daughter Luisa Velázquez, and a number of young maidservants and wives of craftsmen. Here too there were some who were involved, albeit marginally, with the *alumbrados*. Beatriz Ramírez, Luisa Velázquez and Luisa Arenas (whose maid and sister were implicated in Loyola's trial) all knew both Manuel de Miona and Bernardino de Tovar. They were later to take Diego Hernández as their confessor and, like so many of his penitents, to be denounced by him. Such acquaintances make it likely that Loyola himself encountered Tovar and possibly even Juan del Castillo and the Lucenas.[5]

Loyola, the three young men who had followed him from Barcelona, and a fourth who had joined him more recently, were obtrusive for the eccentric manner in which they dressed, their long grey habit with a grey hood. The meetings they held savoured of the secret conventicle. Loyola's disciples would assemble either in his rooms or in their own houses where they would hear him preach about the commandments, sin and the power of the Spirit. He persuaded his congregation to go to confession and communion once a week, to examine their consciences twice a day and to meditate according to the instructions in the early draft of his *Ejercicios espirituales*. Such meditation probably consisted in the identification of the subject's sins, followed by the rendering of thanks to God, a request for further grace and for forgiveness, and the resolution to improve. This exercise would have been succeeded by three types of prayer: a preparatory prayer connected with meditation on the commandments and an analysis of sin; a prayer pronounced aloud attended by meditation on each word; and a prayer recited in the mind with the same system of meditation.[6] Mystical union with God, if Loyola touched on it at all, occupied no place of significance in his exercises. He himself, as we see in his *Diario espiritual* composed many years later, did indeed experience it, but he made no attempt to inculcate the need of it in his followers. Nevertheless, by concentrating on the technique of meditation, Loyola can be said to have placed the practitioners of his exercises in a position to proceed to higher forms of prayer. He provided the means for acquiring a mental discipline which, in the *Ejercicios* as it stands, ends in meditation on scenes from the Gospel, but such a basis could be, and was, used to advance further.[7] There would thus seem to have been a certain ambivalence in the exercises which accounts for the developments at the early prayer meetings.

The younger and more impressionable of Loyola's female followers were soon subject to curious fits. Some broke out in sweat and fainted, some vomited, some writhed on the ground claiming to have visions of the devil. The more lucid participants attributed this behaviour to hysteria. It was pointed out that, with the exception of two widows given to swooning, only the very young were affected. The married women retained their senses throughout.

In November 1526 Alonso Mejía, acting as the inquisitorial visitor of the university of Alcalá engaged in a general enquiry into the *alumbrados*, decided to investigate the matter.[8] Loyola was warned that he was under suspicion of being an *alumbrado*. Mejía interrogated his disciples, but the evidence was inconclusive. The Holy Office abandoned the case. Loyola and his four male companions were ordered to relinquish their grey habit and to dress more conventionally. Just before Christmas the vicar general summoned Loyola and forbade him to go barefoot or to hold meetings. Loyola took no notice and in March of the following year the case was reopened, not by the Holy Office but by the episcopal tribunal. Once more the investigation was suspended. The matter might have rested there had it not been for the sudden disappearance in the middle of April of María del Vado, her daughter and her maid. Pedro de Ciruelo, former professor of Thomism at the university of Alcalá who is better known for his important work on mathematics and astrology and was distinguished from his more liberal colleagues by his opposition to Erasmus, denounced Loyola as being responsible.

Loyola was arrested on 21 April. His followers were interrogated yet again. The most damaging evidence was now provided by a reformed prostitute, María de la Flor. Loyola, she said, was in the habit of establishing which sins were mortal and which not, and of advising his disciples not to reveal certain matters to their confessor. Both he and his companion Calixto de Saa, she continued, claimed to have taken a vow of chastity and said that if they were to lie in the same bed with a young woman they would not be committing a sin.[9] Further witnesses told the vicar general about their fainting fits. Loyola was gravely incriminated, but his position was improved by the unexpected return of the three women, who had been on a pilgrimage. Absolved on the score of having engineered their disappearance, Loyola was nevertheless still under suspicion because of the utterances of María de la Flor. On 1 June, after again forbidding him to wear his grey habit, the vicar general prohibited him from preaching publicly or privately for the next three years, after which he was only to do so with the permission of the bishop or his vicar.

The sentence would have put an end to Loyola's activity as a preacher. He therefore left Alcalá and, having vainly tried to persuade the archbishop of Toledo to revise his sentence, settled in Salamanca. Here, after being questioned and even imprisoned by the friars in the Dominican convent of San Esteban,[10] Loyola and Calixto de Saa were transferred to the town prison and again came before the episcopal tribunal. Martín Frías, vicar general of the bishop of Salamanca, asked Loyola for a copy of his *Ejercicios espirituales*. Finding that the most suspicious aspect of his teaching was that someone who was not a trained theologian should decide on what was mortal and what venial sin, Frías released him, telling him to refrain from such definitions until he had studied theology for at least four years. Otherwise Loyola was free to discuss spiritual matters. Although the sentence of the episcopal tribunal of Toledo appeared to have been reversed by this verdict, Loyola realised that the vicar general had in fact stifled the essence of his teaching. At the end of September 1527 he left for Barcelona and thence for Paris.

Having obtained a degree in Paris in 1534 Loyola, with nine companions, took the 'vow of Montmartre' by which they undertook to lead lives of absolute poverty and chastity and to travel to Palestine. The latter plan proved impossible so, after ordination in Venice, they made their way to Rome. Encouraged by some of the leading figures in Italian evangelism, such as the cardinals Reginald Pole and Gasparo Contarini, Loyola founded the Society of Jesus. It was finally sanctioned by the pope in 1540, a society of clerks regular devoted to works of charity and to education, to the propagation of the principles of Catholicism throughout the world, and totally obedient to the papacy. Its members took vows of poverty and chastity, and Loyola's *Ejercicios espirituales* was, after its approval by the pope in 1548, a widely used manual. It had, however, been heavily revised since the founder's experiences in Alcalá and Salamanca, and the final passages concerning the Church militant, eighteen rules on the observance of the commandments of the Church, had been added.[11]

From the outset the Society of Jesus had a number of features striking for their novelty. It had abolished the choir office to which the earlier orders attached such importance. This was a sign of the subordination of tradition to practical purposes. Certain passages in the first constitutions against excessive external observances such as fasts and disciplines seemed a deliberate attack on monasticism. Answerable solely to the pope, finally, the Society was both international and mobile.

A powerful group of Spanish Dominicans resented the new order directed from abroad and, despite Loyola's declared disapproval of Erasmus, saw the Society as a continuation of the movement against which the Inquisition had struggled in the 1530s. Loyola, they believed, had rightly been accused of being an *alumbrado*. He had, after all, fallen under the suspicion of the ecclesiastical authorities twice in Paris, once in Rome and once in Venice. In 1538 his orthodoxy had been established after a revision of his former trials,[12] but his Dominican enemies chose to ignore this. Their suspicions found further confirmation in the number of men who had once been implicated, directly or indirectly, in the *alumbrado* trials and who either helped or joined the Society. Pedro Ortiz, the brother of Fray Francisco and former professor of theology in Salamanca, was of immense assistance to Loyola when he arrived in Rome. Miguel de Eguía's brother Diego was one of the very first members of the Society of Jesus and became Loyola's confessor. Manuel de Miona, who had fled from Spain in 1530, joined the Society in 1544, while Miguel de Torres, another distinguished fugitive, joined it in 1547 after passing through Paris and Basel.[13]

The Society clearly attracted the liberally educated humanists who had admired Erasmus. At a time when the *estatutos de limpieza* were being applied with increasing rigour, moreover, it was still open to men of *converso* descent. Loyola's successor as general of the Society, Diego Laínez, had Jewish blood. Although, as the case of John of Avila showed, there was sometimes a marked reluctance to accept New

Christian members, it was not until 1592 that the general Claudio
Acquaviva agreed officially to exclude *conversos*.[14]

The Dominicans therefore had even more cause to distrust an
organisation which insinuated its way into the hearts of kings, which
abolished the more traditional customs of the Church, and which was
not bound by any conventual rule. One of the most celebrated
Dominican theologians, Melchor Cano, recalled that the founder of the
Society had fled from Spain under suspicion of being an *alumbrado*.
The new Society, he said, 'would corrupt the simplicity and Christianity of Spain.'[15] In 1553 Fray Tomás de Pedroche was nominated by the
archbishop of Toledo to preside over a committee examining Loyola's
Ejercicios espirituales. Pedroche also pointed out that Loyola was an
alumbrado who had fled to Rome to save himself from the Inquisition.
The traces of *alumbradismo* in the *Ejercicios espirituales* were manifest. The work was originally written in the vernacular; there was no
place in it for preaching; the method recommended led to perfection-
ism.[16] Years later, as we shall see, Fray Alonso de la Fuente identified
the Society with the *alumbrados* of Llerena - Theatines, *alumbrados*,
Jesuits, to him they were all the same thing. In 1587 yet another
Dominican, Fray Alonso de Avendaño, accused the Jesuits of being
alumbrados. The Society retorted by denouncing him to the Inquisition
in 1594 and claimed that if there was an *alumbrado* who imperilled
Christendom it was surely Alonso de Avendaño himself.[17]

John of Avila

Another future saint whose teaching was associated with that of the
alumbrados was John of Avila.[18] Born near Toledo in the last years of
the fifteenth century, he was of *converso* descent on his father's side.
He attended the universities of Salamanca and Alcalá, and was at the
Complutensian university at the time when the *alumbrados* were
proselytising. There he studied philosophy and theology, and was
ordained in 1525. In 1526 he arrived in Seville, intending to set sail for
the Indies in order to act as a missionary. Such was the name he gained
as a preacher, however, and such his reputation among the aristocracy,
that the archbishop, Alonso Manrique, forbade him to leave. The
'apostle of Andalusia', as he was later to be called, preached in the city
and its neighbourhood, sometimes even out of doors, to congregations
so numerous that other priests found themselves addressing empty
churches. His sermons were on the importance of spiritual renewal to
be acquired by the study of the Scriptures and the Church Fathers, and
by the regular practice of meditation. At the same time he organised

smaller prayer meetings in private houses where he would continue his spiritual instruction.

Within five years of John of Avila's arrival in Andalusia a large enough number of statements, made in his sermons and at his meetings, had been assembled for the prosecutor of the Inquisition to present a case against him. In 1531 he was arrested.

Although he spent about two years in prison John of Avila either denied or succeeded in justifying the propositions imputed to him and was absolved. Yet the charges do give us an idea of his beliefs at the time.[19] One was that he had claimed that the victims of the Inquisition were martyrs. Avila managed to prove that this was based on a misunderstanding, but he does seem to have insisted on the importance of not hating those condemned by the Holy Office and to have said that those who truly regretted their sins and displayed fortitude at the stake might go to heaven. He was accused too of saying that heaven was reserved for the poor and the peasants (a stricture which might have dismayed his aristocratic patrons, but which could reflect his taste for a literal interpretation of the Gospels), and of maintaining that he could explain the Scriptures better than Augustine (perhaps an expression of his distaste for the exegesis of the past).

The charge that he had described the state of matrimony as superior to that of virginity could be associated with John of Avila's admiration for Erasmus and his opposition to forced entries into convents, but it also leads on to that aspect of his activity which, more than any other, had laid him open to suspicion: his prayer meetings. The ones which were found most offensive were held in a house in Ecija at dusk, when the absence of light was particularly conducive to meditation. As in the cases of Loyola and of John of Avila's later disciples, the gatherings were criticised largely because of the women who attended them. For their benefit, apparently, John of Avila had stressed the divine favour accorded to simple women, and had advised his followers to confess to him alone. He was said, moreover, to have been persistent in his attentions to a *beata* given to fainting fits and trances. All these charges, together with the complaint that he had upheld the superiority of mental to vocal prayer, had come to form part and parcel of the image the inquisitors had created of the *alumbrado* - the false mystic organising conventicles attended by the laity where, behind the back of the Church, immoral deeds could be performed with impunity and hetero-dox methods of meditation be put into practice.

Such a view of John of Avila was hardly justified. Undoubtedly, after his early experiences with the Inquisition, he learnt to be cautious, and this caution is evident in his writings on meditation of a slightly later date. All we know of his religious instructions shows that they varied according to the condition of the individual he addressed. Although he admired Bernabé de Palma and Francisco de Osuna, he told Fray Luis de Granada, the Dominican mystic who so revered the 'apostle of Andalusia', that while the second and the fifth of Osuna's *Abecedarios* were always edifying, the third should not be read too 'generally'.[20] He warned against excessive frequency in taking communion: the common people, *el vulgo*, he said, need only do so three or four times a year; those more interested in spiritual matters nine or ten times; those truly dedicated to religion once a fortnight, or, if they were married, once a month. The meditational method he recommended was traditional: he advised that certain times of day be reserved for meditating, for praying, for reading and for attending mass; he suggested subjects of meditation; and he dwelt on the need to accompany its practice with works of charity. Here too his advice was always adapted to the circumstances of the individual. Members of the clergy were expected to spend more time on their spiritual training than the laity, and to priests he recommended greater rigour and strenuousness in the practice of prayer.[21]

In contrast with the Franciscan mystics, John of Avila was not primarily concerned with the attainment of perfection or a mystical union with the Almighty: these privileges were reserved for the few and, in the letters he was later to write to Teresa of Avila, he expresses to the full his doubts about whether such experiences should even be divulged.[22] Like Loyola he set meditation on Christ's passion at the centre of his exercises, a large part of which was devoted to the examination of conscience. In his counsel about virtuous living, the image of Christ crucified, the need to follow Him in the path of suffering, was stressed repeatedly. The place of the Church, although not overlooked, was accorded less emphasis than a more direct relationship with the Saviour, and, in the 1530s, we can detect in John of Avila's work another element which was bound to displease the investigators of his orthodoxy: the supreme importance of faith.

Just over a year after his absolution by the Holy Office John of Avila was preaching in Cordova and, at the end of 1536, in Granada. At the same time he continued to work on the book he had started to write during his imprisonment, *Audi, filia*. The first version was completed between 1545 and 1548 and dedicated to one of his aristocratic patrons, Don Luis Fernández de Portocarrero, Count of Palma. The book did not appear until 1556, however, when John of Avila had withdrawn to

Montilla where he was protected by the Marquess of Priego, and it was promptly condemned by the Inquisition.

The first version of *Audi, filia* contains various unguarded statements about the trust we must have in God's mercy and in Christ's having died for us on the cross which, in spite of the author's emphasis on the necessity of a good confessor, of a spiritual adviser within the Church, and of prudence and humility, prevented the book from being approved until 1565. By then, Avila had added passages on the sacraments of baptism and penance and attacking Lutheranism. But we have only to look at the original version of the work, and at certain letters written when he was composing it, to understand the anxiety of the Inquisition. In a letter to one of his earliest followers in Ecija, Doña Leonor de Inestrosa, he wrote:

> Here our foundation and support is the mercy of God who wishes to save us through the merits of Jesus Christ His Son, giving us the means so that, even if our works are lacking, even if God's commandments are broken, we can, if we wish and if He helps us to wish it, obtain forgiveness, and recover the lost grace, and find salvation in Jesus Christ our Lord, whose merits obtain for us the mercy we do not deserve.[23]

A further aspect of John of Avila's teaching in those years which savoured of evangelism was his attitude to the Bible. This emerges in a letter written in 1538 to another of his early followers, García Arias, the prior of the Hieronymite convent of San Isidro del Campo in Seville, who was to be executed for Lutheranism in 1559. Arias was a priest and John of Avila adapted his advice to his superior spiritual condition, making suggestions he would have hesitated to make to a layman. He counselled him to study the New Testament 'raising his heart to the Lord, reading the text without any other gloss'. Only if doubts arise about the meaning of the words does John of Avila suggest that certain commentators be consulted: John Chrysostom, Nicholas of Lyra, and Erasmus, or someone else 'who only explains the letter: he is likely to examine the real sense which the Lord intended.'[24] In the same year John of Avila repeated his advice to a different disciple, but urged a certain caution in reading Erasmus's paraphrases of the New Testament.[25]

In all the editions of *Audi, filia*, as well as in his epistles, John of Avila warned his readers about the heresy of the *alumbrados*, and he did so with ever greater urgency when his own followers were being accused.

There has been no lack in our days of persons who were sure they were going to reform the Christian Church and bring it to the perfection it had at the beginning or even to a greater one . . . Others wished to seek new paths which seemed to them a very short cut to reaching God quickly. They thought that once they had given themselves to Him perfectly and had abandoned themselves in His hands, they were so well loved of God and ruled by the Holy Ghost that all that came into their heart was nothing but light and the inspiration of God. And their illusion reached such a point that, if that interior movement did not take place, they refused to proceed to any work, however pious. And if their heart moved them to perform any work, they had to do it, even if it was against the commandment of God, thinking that the desire which they felt in their heart was the inspiration and freedom of the Holy Ghost which liberated them from any obligation towards the commandments of God whom, they said, they loved so truly that they could not forfeit His love even if they broke His commandments.[26]

With his austere emphasis on ascetic preparation rather than on mystical union with God, Avila was opposed to the visions and trances which could so easily be the work of the devil. Even on his deathbed he expressed his concern about the turn the prayer meetings of his disciples were taking, and ordered them to guard against treacherous feelings of sweetness *'las dulzuras y sentimientos espirituales'*.[27]

Yet the stigma of heterodoxy continued to cling to John of Avila as well as to his followers. His arrest in the 1530s was never forgotten. He could still be remembered as an organiser of conventicles, and his association with men later charged with Lutheranism served to confirm the danger of his statements about faith. *Alumbradismo* remained a convenient term with which to express this combination of suspicions, and John of Avila's enemies, who were principally Dominicans, were further able to attack the 'apostle of Andalusia' and his school on account of their relations with the Jesuits.

For years there was talk of John of Avila entering the Society of Jesus himself, and he expressed the desire to make over his educational foundations to the Jesuits. His own *converso* descent seems to have been one of the main reasons for his not joining the new order at a time when it might have embarrassed its leadership. Consequently he gave up the idea. The Jesuits retained the greatest esteem for him, however, and a number of his disciples did join them.[28] Such close connections put into relief the affinities between the two movements, whose founders had had similar experiences at the start of their careers.

The indignation which the Dominicans felt about John of Avila was due, at least in part, to the position of power he and his followers acquired in southern Spain. In the large cities and in relatively neglected areas of Andalusia and southern Extremadura they succeeded in creating an atmosphere of religious revival and excitement. Of the various establishments for lower and higher education whose foundation John of Avila encouraged, the most influential was to be the university of Baeza which developed in the 1540s. One of the main objects of the institution was to equip its students with the knowledge necessary for the study of the Scriptures. Besides two chairs of philosophy, two of scholastic theology, and a chair of grammar, it revealed the marks of humanism in the provisions for chairs in rhetoric and Greek. At the same time John of Avila sponsored the publication, also in Baeza, of a number of devotional works in the vernacular which included texts on mysticism.[29]

Like the Complutensian university before it, the university of Baeza was bound to attract the attention of the Inquisition. Staffed largely by New Christians, it taught the study and the exposition of the Scriptures. Following the example of their master, moreover, John of Avila's disciples had congregations of their own in which the devotional methods devised by the 'apostle of Andalusia' were practised. These congregations were joined by numbers of *beatas* and these pious women were to pose a growing problem for the ecclesiastical authorities in the second half of the century.

The inquisitors seem to have started investigating the university of Baeza in 1549. Two prominent members of the staff, Gaspar Loarte and Bernardino de Carleval, were arrested in the early 1550s, but soon released. Both were *conversos*. Carleval was the first rector of the university, and Loarte, who had a chair of theology, was later to join the Society of Jesus. The more systematic prosecution of John of Avila's disciples began some twenty years later - after the master's death in 1569.[30] But by then there had been considerable changes in Spain. Illustrious churchmen had been charged with *alumbradismo*, and guilt, usually by association, could be found in a wider range of individuals than ever.

Protestantism

After the late 1540s many Spanish churchmen again saw dangers in innovation and reform. These were of two kinds. One has already been discussed: the establishment of the Society of Jesus. Its aims were closely linked with the decisions taken between 1545 and 1563 at the

Council of Trent to reform the Catholic Church, and the arrival of members of the Society in Spain was followed by further efforts to reform other religious orders. In the Iberian peninsula the reformers found friends and powerful protectors, but also enemies. Their enemies regarded the piety which they spread as an imported faith which menaced a national tradition. They distrusted them as they had distrusted *conversos* and readers of Erasmus in the past.

The other danger was Protestantism. This, however, was different from the evangelism of the 1520s and 1530s, and to understand its development we must glance briefly at the events which had occurred in Italy. Throughout the 1530s there was a far more tolerant climate in much of Italy than in Spain. It was there that various fugitives from the Spanish Inquisition sought refuge, and Juan de Valdés could live unmolested in Naples at the centre of a circle of scholarly aristocrats and churchmen who assisted him in spreading views he would certainly have been unable to express in his homeland. In Italy, where Protestant works could be obtained without too much difficulty,[31] interest in the Lutheran doctrine of justification by faith was wide even among the prelates, and the belief persisted throughout the decade that an agreement with the Protestants might be reached.

Hopes were raised at the Conference of Regensburg in 1541 when the Venetian cardinal Gasparo Contarini, acting as papal legate, seemed to have come to terms with Philip Melanchthon, one of the most humanistic of Protestants. But they were dashed by the ultimate failure of the ensuing meeting and the opposition to compromise of the faction of Cardinal Gian Pietro Carafa in Italy and of Luther himself in Germany. As a result of the collapse of the conference, the pope, Paul III, founded the Roman Inquisition in 1542, its first purpose being to combat Lutheranism. Three years later the Council of Trent opened and, in January 1547, a Catholic doctrine of justification was defined and the Lutheran teaching condemned once and for all.[32]

There followed a polarisation of beliefs. Some of the men who had been close to Valdés in the 1530s left the Catholic Church, thereby committing themselves to Protestantism. This was the course taken by the Capuchin Bernardino Ochino and the Augustinian Pietro Martire Vermigli, who fled north of the Alps in 1542. Others, with the two cardinals Giovanni Morone and Reginald Pole, remained within the Church of Rome. Yet eager though such men were to serve the Counter-Reformation they remained under suspicion on account of the concili-atory ideas they had once held and of their approach to justification. For many years they were able to demonstrate their loyalty to the

Church. Pole and Morone attended the Council of Trent and, however disappointed they were by its decisions, they obediently bowed to its decrees.[33] Their enemies awaited their chance which came in 1555 when Gian Pietro Carafa was elected pope. No churchman was out of Paul IV's reach. He arrested Morone and was preparing a trial against Pole. Pole died just in time and Morone, after a long imprisonment, was only acquitted by Carafa's successor, Pius IV, in 1560.

The hardening of papal policy had its effect on Spain, even if the Spanish Inquisition was hardly in step with the Roman one. In Spain, too, a vigilant eye was kept on statements about justification by faith and it was often on their authors that the term *alumbrado* was bestowed. Although the inquisitors could claim that, with their campaign against the readers of Erasmus in the 1530s, they had purged their country of any potential sympathy with Luther, they had formed, by the 1550s, a far clearer idea than before of what Protestantism was. They saw it as a combination of seven main errors, some of which had been discovered among the Judaizers and the *alumbrados*: the denial of purgatory; opposition to the worship of the saints and the Virgin Mary; contempt for the authority of the pope and his bulls; the rejection of clerical celibacy; the refusal to confess to a priest; the refusal to fast in periods prescribed by the Catholic Church; and denial of the real presence of Christ in the eucharist.[34]

By far the greater part of the Protestants tried by the Holy Office in Spain was made up of foreigners - French immigrants (especially in Catalonia), but also merchants, sailors and travelling scholars from other parts of Europe. It was not until the late 1550s, in Valladolid and Seville, that the inquisitors detected two large groups of Spanish Protestants, the intellectual and social distinction of whose members made them particularly alarming.

The Valladolid group seems to have been converted to Protestantism by an Italian nobleman who had emigrated to Spain and had close connections with Protestants in his country of origin: Don Carlos de Seso.[35] His wife was related to the royal house and he had been appointed *corregidor* of the town of Toro in about 1554. Another prominent figure in the group was the Dominican Fray Domingo de Rojas, a son of the Marquess of Poza. In the company of the future archbishop of Toledo, Bartolomé Carranza, he had attended the Council of Trent and appears to have made at least one visit to Germany before settling in Palencia. Together with his brother, his sister, his nephew and his sister-in-law, Fray Domingo represented, among the Valladolid Protestants, a family both ancient and powerful.

But the family with the greatest number of adherents suggested a continuity flowing from the *alumbrados* of Toledo: the Cazallas. María's cousin[36] Pedro, the royal accountant, had had Francisca Hernández to stay with him in Valladolid many years earlier and had been denounced by her. He had died in 1543, leaving his wife, Doña Leonor de Bivero, and a number of sons and daughters who were all to display varying degrees of commitment to the new doctrine. The most distinguished was Agustín de Cazalla who had studied at Alcalá in the late 1520s and had been appointed imperial chaplain in 1542. He travelled with the court in Flanders and Germany and returned to Spain in 1552, but he does not seem to have been truly converted to Protestantism until the late 1550s. Then there were Agustín's younger brothers, two of them priests, Pedro de Cazalla who served in Pedrosa and Francisco de Bivero who lived in Valladolid, and one of them, Juan de Bivero, a layman. Finally, there were the royal accountant's two daughters, Beatriz and Costanza de Bivero. The Inquisition was alerted to the activities of the group in 1557 and their habit of assembling to pray and discuss religious topics does not seem to have started very much earlier, despite the efforts of Carlos de Seso.

In Seville, on the other hand, sympathy for the Reformation had a longer history. It can be traced back to the Biblical sermons of Juan Gil or Dr Egidio, the Alcalá-educated cathedral preacher in the 1540s. It was sustained in the following decade by Dr Egidio's fellow-student at Alcalá, the imperial confessor and chaplain Constantino Ponce de la Fuente who, after accompanying the court to the Netherlands in 1548, returned to Seville in 1553 and succeeded Dr Egidio as cathedral preacher. As in Valladolid conventicles were formed at which prayers were said and theological matters discussed. Prohibited Bibles, both Protestant and in the vernacular, together with the works of a number of the northern European Reformers and Spanish and Italian dissidents, seem to have been circulated still more widely in Seville than in Valladolid in the 1550s.[37] Besides a scholar of distinction such as Ponce de la Fuente, the prayer groups included members of the higher nobility - Don Juan Ponce de León, for example, second son of the Count of Bailén and cousin of the Duke of Arcos. Nor was it only the laity and the secular clergy who were affected in Seville: Protestantism was also popular in certain local convents. One of the most zealous members of the group was a nun from the convent of Santa Isabel, Francisca de Chaves, and a profound Protestant influence was detected in the Hieronymite convent of San Isidro del Campo. Among the friars who fled from San Isidro in the summer of 1557, before the Inquisition had started fully to investigate the Protestant conventicles, were three men who were to play a prominent part in Reformed circles in Northern Europe: Antonio del Corro, Cipriano de Valera and Casiodoro de Reina.

That the men and women tried both in Valladolid and Seville did not remain evangelical Catholics but were actually converted to Protestantism seems certain.[38] What is less certain is the type of Protestantism to which they were converted. They have gone down to history as Lutherans. They read works by Luther, but also by Calvin and other Reformers such as Bucer, Bullinger, Oecolampadius and Melanchthon and by more spiritual writers such as Juan de Valdés. The beliefs to which they confessed hardly correspond to those of any of the Protestant Churches north of the Alps. They were, rather, an amalgamation of various creeds in which the influence of Calvin may have prevailed over that of Luther, even if their ideas on the eucharist prevent them from ranking as Calvinists. Those of the Spanish Protestants who managed to flee to northern Europe tended to be bewildered by the Reformed communities they met. This is clearly illustrated by Casiodoro de Reina who joined a succession of Protestant Churches.[39] Hoping to find harmony, simplicity and tolerance, he found squabbles, acrimony and attempts to impose a doctrinal discipline he could never accept.

The presence of scholars, some of whom were *conversos* and who had studied at Alcalá and attended the court, the popularity of Juan de Valdés, and the prominence of the Cazalla family made it possible to regard the Protestants of the 1550s as the spiritual heirs of the first *alumbrados* of Toledo. The inquisitor general responsible for their trials and the exceptional severity of their sentences - fifty-nine of the accused in Seville and Valladolid were burnt at the stake - was Fernando de Valdés who, as we saw, had followed the *alumbrado* trials and attended the interrogations of Alcaraz. In a report on the Protestants which he dispatched to Paul IV, Valdés stated that their origins were to be found in the heresies of the past. 'The errors held by those called *alumbrados* or *dejados*, natives of Guadalajara and other parts of the Kingdom of Toledo and elsewhere,' he wrote, 'were of the same seed as these Lutheran heresies, but the inquisitors dealing with those cases were not well enough acquainted with the Lutheran errors to act with sufficient rigour'.[40]

The Protestant centres of Valladolid and Seville were given particular consideration because of the presence of citizens of distinction - theologians, scholars, officials and members of the nobility. But the elevated connections of the accused also facilitated the implication of personal enemies of the inquisitor general and of the spiritual innovations some of his allies had come to suspect.

Carranza

Besides the works of the northern European Reformers, the educated Protestants of Valladolid and Seville possessed writings by Luis de Granada, Thomas of Villanova, John of Avila and Bartolomé Carranza.[41] They had, in their cosmopolitan careers, known some of these men. John of Avila had acted as spiritual adviser to García Arias, the prior of the convent of San Isidro del Campo executed in September 1559. He was also a close friend of the Jesuit Don Diego de Guzmán, the brother of Don Juan Ponce de León executed at the same *auto de fé*. One of Avila's most distinguished disciples, Diego Pérez de Valdivia who is examined in more detail later, shared the common admiration for Constantino Ponce de la Fuente, went to hear him preach and called on him at his house after the sermon.[42] While John of Avila's name was also mentioned by witnesses in the trials of the Valladolid Protestants, he was further incriminated by his connections with the recently appointed archbishop of Toledo, Bartolomé Carranza, who had been consulting his *Audi, filia* and with whom he had a common friend and disciple in Luis de Granada.

Bartolomé Carranza was connected still more firmly with the Protestants of Valladolid.[43] He had once been Augustín de Cazalla's confessor. He had known Juan de Valdés in Alcalá and, on his travels, had met Carlos de Seso. His fellow Dominican Domingo de Rojas constantly reminded the inquisitors of his own intimacy with the archbishop. Such charges gave Fernando de Valdés the chance he had awaited. He had long hated Carranza for personal reasons and he could count on the support, in impeaching him, of some of his Dominican enemies. Carranza was consequently arrested in August 1559.

From a humble but Old Christian family, Carranza, who had once studied at Alcalá, had had a career of distinction in the Dominican order and the service of the Church. Few Spaniards had done more than he to combat Protestantism. After participating in the Council of Trent he accompanied the future king Philip II to England in 1554 in order to attend his marriage to Mary Tudor. In England he actively supervised the reintroduction of Catholicism and the punishment of its opponents. Yet even in his struggle against heresy Carranza betrayed a sympathy for some of the churchmen who had been drawn by Juan de Valdés and justification by faith. Both at Trent and in England he had had much to do with Reginald Pole. This was to be held against him and to be interpreted as a confirmation of the evangelical views detected in his writings.

From England Carranza went to Flanders where he was equally zealous in defending the Catholic faith. In the summer of 1558 he returned to Spain after his elevation to the see of Toledo, and was arrested soon after. During his long trial, in which he fell victim to the contention between the Spanish Crown and the papacy, Carranza appealed to the pope. In 1567 he was transported to Rome. The death of Pius V, who believed in his innocence, led to further protraction of the proceedings. In the end Carranza was sentenced to abjure sixteen propositions in the presence of Pius's successor, Gregory XIII. He died shortly after his release in 1576, having spent seventeen years in prison.

In 1558, some little time before his arrest, Carranza had preached a sermon to the court in Valladolid. Thirty years ago, he told the congregation, 'there arose a sect of *alumbrados* and the kingdom fell into such perdition that if a Christian was seen kneeling before a crucifix he was called to justice and accused. This shows how, in the course of time, names lose their decorum and reputation.' A few days later, on entering Toledo, the archbishop returned to the same theme. 'People call prayer, church-going, communion and confession *alumbrado*,' he said. 'They will soon call them Lutheran.'[44] Certainly this is what happened in his own case.

Earlier in the same year Carranza had published in Antwerp his *Comentarios sobre el catechismo christiano*. The work contains a stirring appeal for the reform of the Catholic Church. It attacks every kind of abuse, argues for the improvement of the clergy, insists on the importance of punishing heresy, and contains numerous confutations of Luther. It was published hurriedly, however; many statements were somewhat unguarded and, especially if taken out of context, could be exposed to censorship. When Carranza arrived in Spain the book was being read attentively by a board of theologians, members, like himself, of the Order of Preachers. The most decisive condemnation was provided by Melchor Cano, a scholar of impressive erudition, able to detect the forgeries of Annius of Viterbo[45] but always ready to condemn attempts at introducing novelty in the Church. From Carranza's book Cano, supported by his fellow censor Fray Juan de la Peña,[46] managed to extract a sufficient number of careless passages to associate the archbishop with the Lutherans and the *alumbrados*.[47]

Cano's criticisms of Carranza's *Comentarios* begin with its being written in the vernacular: it was accessible to 'women and the

ignorant', the same people who made up the movement of the
alumbrados of Toledo. To encourage them to read the whole, or part
of the Scriptures, Cano claimed, was dangerous and had led to the
alumbrado heresy. It was equally rash to reveal to them 'the mysteries'
of the faith and to publicise Luther's errors, even if only for the sake
of refuting them. Cano was deeply concerned about the traces of
evangelism he could find in the book. Carranza had maintained that a
Christian should give up the use of reason and 'navigate according to
faith'.[48] Besides smacking of Lutheranism this reminded Cano of the
alumbrados who 'let themselves be ruled in all, or nearly all, things by
revelations and divine enlightenment.' He thought that Carranza had
derived the idea from 'some Lutheran or *alumbrado* book' which
emphasised the prerogatives of the spiritual man, dismissed the
benefits of reason, and undermined both the structure and theology of
the Church. The importance of faith also led Carranza to underestimate
the importance of works - another idea Cano associated with the
alumbrados - and to stress the certainty of grace. Here too Cano
referred to the peril, which had emerged among both the Lutherans and
the *alumbrados*, of knowing who had grace and who had not, the peril
of using personal experience as a criterion. He quoted Alcaraz's claim
that 'the love of God in man is God' and traced the conviction of
impeccability from the Pelagians to the Beghards and the *alumbrados*.
The reliance on the love of God, Cano continued, led to complete
passivity 'which always savours of *alumbramiento*': 'these *alumbrados*,
the sons of Beghards and Beguines, are troubled by nothing so as not
to lose the quiet and inner peace of their abandonment (*dejamiento*)'.[49]

A further point which Cano regarded as *alumbrado* was the idea of
the spiritual sabbath. Carranza had said that 'spiritual men and perfect
Christians do not have to distinguish between days. All days are
feastdays, since they always have joy in God and perform a true and
perpetual sabbath'. 'The *alumbrados*', countered Cano, 'convinced
that they were spiritual men, considered themselves freed from this law
of the external sabbath . . . They would withdraw for twenty or thirty
days at a time in order to practise their secret exercises and fail to go
to mass on feastdays when this would not cause a scandal'. Yet, said
Cano, 'the people (*los populares*) must all, or most of them, take part
in the active life, otherwise the Republic will be ruined'. He here
connected the *alumbrados* with Calvin and pointed to the disastrous
effects of a doctrine of perpetual rest.[50] He drew the same conclusions
from Carranza's statements on the benefits of prayer since 'some
alumbrados of our days have placed the goal of Christian life in prayer

and contemplation'. In order to condemn Carranza's emphasis on the superiority of mental to vocal prayer Cano again argued that the *alumbrados* had used prayer as an excuse for neglecting all outward actions and duties.

Cano even saw *alumbrado* errors in Carranza's pleas for reforming the clergy. To Carranza's insistence that the clergy should lead irreproachable lives he objected that 'some of our *alumbrados*, the Lutherans of Spain,' wanted to 'revive the impeccability of the baptised, particularly of the spiritual men and the perfect'.[51]

It was not only Carranza who was attacked in Cano's report. The Dominican extended his censorship to a man who had been Carranza's pupil in Valladolid and had remained one of the archbishop's closest friends: Fray Luis de Granada. Recently appointed provincial of the Portuguese Dominicans, he had hastened from Lisbon to Valladolid to intercede for his former teacher. Luis de Granada was in too strong a position to be implicated in Carranza's fall, but the inquisitor general could not forgive his interference and Cano acted according to his wishes.[52]

Fray Luis's newly published *Libro de la oración* was censored on a variety of points. These, we shall see, were to become a standard part of Dominican criticism and were taken up by Alonso de la Fuente later in the century. Like Carranza's work, the *Libro de la oración* was in the vernacular. It was generally accessible and the devotional method recommended could be practised by anyone, irrespective of condition. The method itself was claimed to lead to perfection. But, Cano reminded his readers, such instruction should in fact be restricted. Luis de Granada, moreover, bestowed lavish praise on mental prayer. To do so at the expense of vocal prayer was, according to Cano, a direct outcome of the teaching of the *alumbrados*.[53]

The Index

To confirm the severity of his policy and in emulation of the new Roman Index of prohibited books issued by Paul IV in 1558, Fernando de Valdés published an index of his own in 1559.[54] Valid only for Spain (where the Roman indexes were of no effect), it contained the works of the inquisitor general's enemies: Carranza's *Comentarios*, Luis de Granada's *Libro de la oración*, *Guía de pecadores* and *Manual de diversas oraciones*, and *Audi, fila* by John of Avila. Besides various works of Erasmus, in Latin and Castilian (the *Enchiridion*, the *Colloquia*, the *Praise of Folly*, and others), it included a number of the earliest devotional writings to have been published in the vernacular:

Savonarola's commentary on the Lord's Prayer, Jiménez de Préjano's
Luzero de la vida christiana, Hernando de Talavera's *Católica
impugnación*, Juan de Cazalla's *Lumbre del alma*, and the widely read
Flos sanctorum. There were several mystical works: Herp's *Theologia
mystica* in Latin and Castilian, Bernabé de Palma's *Via Spiritus*, and,
by Francisco de Osuna, the *Gracioso convite* on the eucharist, suspicious
because of its insistence on frequent communion.

The first object of the Index of 1559 was to eliminate the circulation
of anything resembling Protestant doctrine. In addition to the writings
of the northern European Reformers which had already been prohibited in the first years of the Reformation, books by Italian Protestants
(Bernardino Ochino), by Spanish Protestants (Juan Pérez de Pineda
and Juan del Encina), and by writers whose sympathies were less
overtly declared (Juan and Alfonso de Valdés and Constantino Ponce
de la Fuente) were all included. The second object was to curb
devotional literature in Castilian. The Index was stringent in the
prohibition of the Scriptures in the vernacular - more so than ever
before. Besides the devotional works already mentioned, it listed
books by authors whose orthodoxy had never been questioned, such as
Fray Luis de Maluenda, Francis Borgia and Jorge de Montemayor.

Coinciding as it did with the trials of the Protestants in Seville and
Valladolid, the Index was interpreted as a gesture of uncompromising
strictness. If not the first of its kind - indexes had been published since
1551, while, ever since the 1520s, the Inquisition had issued numerous
orders forbidding individual publications - it was by far the most
rigorous. Valdés revoked the permissions accorded to a large number
of theologians to read prohibited works, and made provisions for a
sharp control of printers, bookshops and libraries. By forbidding so
many books published with the approval of Cisneros, the Index could
also be regarded as the first official statement condemning his spirituality, the coronation of the trials which had started in the 1520s and of
which the *alumbrados* had been the first victims. Teresa of Avila
reminds us in her autobiography what a shock it was for a pious admirer
of mystical writings to encounter in the Index the names of so many
authors she had been reading with devotion.[55]

In fact Valdés's Index was less oppressive than it seemed at the time.
In its condemnation of the works of Erasmus it did not go nearly as far
as earlier indexes issued in Milan and Venice. Most of Erasmus's works
on the New Testament, as well as other polemical tracts, could thus still
be read in Spain.[56] The same can be said about mysticism. Many works
remained uncensored. The writings of Alonso de Madrid and Bernardino

de Laredo were not condemned. Even if, with the exception of the third, Francisco de Osuna's numerous *Abecedarios* were to be expurgated in subsequent indexes, they were not even mentioned in the one of 1559 and were a rich source for later writers on the subject. Finally, we should keep in mind that the austere policies of Paul IV in Rome and Fernando de Valdés in Spain ended with their devisers. Already in 1559 Paul IV was succeeded by a more moderate man, while Valdés died within seven years of the publication of his Index.

Nevertheless, both the Index and the discovery of the Protestant conventicles, particularly in the south of Spain, help to account for the attention the inquisitors dedicated to the disciples of John of Avila after the death of the 'apostle of Andalusia' in 1569. It was prompted more immediately, however, by the discovery, in the vicinity of places where John of Avila had taught, of the antinomian groups of enthusiasts whose significance is discussed in the next chapter. Their detector, the Dominican Fray Alonso de la Fuente, was determined to associate them with John of Avila and could indeed show that they read his works and often practised the devotional methods he recommended.

John of Avila's disciples

Many of John of Avila's disciples who held high posts in his educational establishments were, as we have seen, *conversos* - Bernardino de Carleval, rector of the university of Baeza, Hernando de Herrera, canon of the *Colegial* of Ubeda, the Dominicans Domingo de Valtanás and Alonso de Vergara, possibly Pedro de Hojeda, also rector of the university of Baeza, and certainly Diego Pérez de Valdivia, professor at the university. The campaign against them - for so it must be considered - continued into the final decade of the century. The last victim, Pedro de Hojeda, was arrested in 1590 and sentenced to abjure and perform various minor penances in April 1593.

One of the most recurrent charges against these men was their opposition to the *estatutos de limpieza*, which Domingo de Valtanás had attacked in 1556.[57] Another was the persuasion that, in the present corrupt state of the Church, New Christians were worthier in the eyes of the Almighty than Old. But while such accusations were connected with their suspicious ancestry, their descent from converted Jews, the trials against them were almost invariably prompted by information about the prayer groups which they formed. Obedience was supposed to be due solely to the organiser; there was allegedly no esteem for religious orders; and mental prayer and meditation were said to have replaced vocal prayer. The prayer groups were reminiscent of the circles of Protestants in Seville and Valladolid, but above all they evoked the image of the first *alumbrados* and it was as *alumbrados* that John of Avila's disciples accordingly became known.

One reason for anxiety about the prayer groups is familiar to us - the presence of *beatas*, a feature of significance in the prosecution of both Ignatius Loyola and John of Avila himself. By the 1570s the inquisitors were more alarmed than ever by the immense rapidity with which the number of pious females was increasing. In Baeza alone there were said to be between one and two thousand *beatas*, a sizeable proportion of the population, and there were still more in the region of Jaén.[58] The Church was making ever more endeavours to control this group so attracted by mysticism and open to hysteria and imposture, but was hardly successful.

It was to the *beatas* that one of the Inquisition's many victims, Diego Pérez de Valdivia, devoted an extensive work. The professor at the university of Baeza wrote his *Aviso de gente recogida* after his release from the prisons of the Inquisition where he had spent almost two years and published it in Barcelona in 1585. The book is striking for its humanity and for the enlightened and empirical manner in which the author attributes what was commonly diagnosed as diabolical possession to hysteria.

At the outset of his work Pérez de Valdivia emphasises the importance of charity and good works in the lives of the *beatas* and provides a definition of faith deliberately formulated so as to avoid any suspicion of Lutheranism. Aware of the other groups of *alumbrados* in Andalusia and Extremadura, he also stresses the necessity of chastity, cautions the *beatas* not to confess too frequently, to exercise prudence in their choice of a spiritual adviser and to avoid, whenever possible, the society of men (since women, he reminds us, act as 'fire' and men as 'straw'). Finally he assures his readers that the Church of Rome is the custodian of the truth and that *beatas* never cease to be under obligation to observe the conciliar decrees and accept the instructions of the ecclesiastical hierarchy.[59]

In his scepticism about spiritual consolations and the outer manifestations of grace Pérez de Valdivia comes far closer to Pedro Ruiz de Alcaraz than to the great Franciscan mystics. In order to put his readers on their guard he not only refers frequently to Vincent Ferrer's strictures but he also reproduces in the appendix that very section of the Dominican's *Tractatus de vita spirituali* which Cisneros had removed from the edition published during his primacy.[60]

The *Aviso de gente recogida* is manifestly the book of a man wishing to make his peace with the Church. The charges made against Pérez de Valdivia during his trial, many of which he admitted, suggest that his sobriety was a recent acquisition. He was accused of claiming that the eucharist sustains the body as much as the spirit, of having persuaded a woman not to enter a convent, of saying that anyone who was not in a state of mortal sin could take communion as often as he or she wished without confessing, and with prophesying the imminent end of the world.[61] Such ideas were current among the groups of *alumbrados* to be discussed in the next chapter and the effect of their detection was twofold. That the antinomian *alumbrados* of Extremadura and Andalusia should have shared certain views with scholars as respectable as Pérez de Valdivia damaged the disciples of John of Avila, but it also allowed the *alumbrados* to claim an intellectual respectability to which they hardly seem to have been entitled.

Chapter VIII

The *Alumbrados* of Llerena and Seville

As a term of abuse the word *alúmbrado* had various meanings from the outset. One of the first, even before the word was applied to Isabel de la Cruz and her followers, was hypocrisy, piety which was ostentatious but assumed. In the second half of the sixteenth century the term was applied more and more frequently to religious impostors. Although it is hard to ascertain whether cases of imposture were really increasing, undoubtedly they were being investigated with ever greater severity. During the primacy of Cardinal Cisneros few of the visionaries were examined attentively, but within years of his death the situation had changed.

Imposture and enthusiasm

One of the most celebrated episodes of imposture was that of Magdalena de la Cruz, prioress of the Franciscan convent of Santa Isabel de los Angeles in Cordova. Like earlier prophetesses she was venerated by the aristocracy and the court, but she confessed in 1543 that her inspiration came from the devil. Magdalena's example affected Teresa of Avila, inducing her to inspect her own sources of grace more thoroughly, and was one of the reasons for her to compose her confessions, the *Libro de su vida*, in the early 1560s. Another case which acquired much publicity concerned the Dominican María de la Visitación in Lisbon, whose miraculous powers had been approved and sanctioned by Luis de Granada. She too confessed to engineering her own levitations and to producing her stigmata artificially. In 1588 she was heavily sentenced, and efforts were made to involve Fray Luis in her fall.[1]

Magdalena de la Cruz and María de la Visitación are perhaps the best-known illustrations of imposture and its detection. Their notoriety made them useful instruments for discrediting mysticism in general. But they were two of many. Throughout the sixteenth century, all over Spain as well as in Spanish territories in the New World, prominent political or ecclesiastical events would throw into action a legion of visionaries and dreamers, sometimes in good faith, sometimes disingenuous, and frequently manipulated by a faction at court or in the Church. The protagonists were often described as *alumbrados*, even if they had nothing to do either with the original movement or with the later groups whose detection was followed by other edicts of faith.[2]

If, by the end of the sixteenth century, the term *alumbrado* had assumed the meaning of imposture, it also had another significance difficult to reconcile with the piety of Alcaraz, but certainly applicable to the *beatas* and the friars whom he censored. It meant enthusiasm, exaggerated displays of emotion in church and at prayer, and a propensity to ecstasies. That is the association in the description of the *alumbrados* provided by one of Teresa of Avila's most trusted followers, Jerónimo Gracián, in the early seventeenth century. After his participation in the reform of the Carmelite order in Spain and Portugal, followed by persecution and adventurous journeys which brought him to Italy and North Africa, Gracián arrived in the Low Countries. Horrified and fascinated by the variety of heresies he encountered there, he composed his *Diez lamentaciones del miserable estado de los ateistas de nuestros tiempos*, which appeared in 1611. The proximity of Protestants and Anabaptists in Flanders, one of the homelands of the Beghards, reminded him of the *alumbrados* about whom he had heard so much when he had first professed in the Carmelite order in Pastrana. The word *dejado*, he explained, was used because the early *alumbrados* abandoned themselves in the hands of God and refused to perform any activity, but also because they surrendered themselves to raptures and ecstasies ('*porque se dejaban caer diciendo que tenían éxtasis y raptos*'). He then recalled that, over thirty years earlier, a nonagenarian penitent in Pastrana had told him of an uncle of his who had witnessed the arrival from Guadalajara of 'a cleric and certain women' spreading the doctrine of the *alumbrados*. One day, during the elevation of the host at mass, they all fell 'with their mouth on the floor and howled and trembled'. Enraged by such a spectacle the nonagenarian's uncle seized the aspergill and started flogging the *alumbrados*, saying: 'Raise your eyes, watch and adore the Holy Sacrament, rather than howl like animals'.[3]

Although there is nothing in the edict of 1525 which warrants such an interpretation of the *alumbrados* of Toledo, they had certainly acquired the reputation at an early stage for a behaviour Alcaraz and Isabel de la Cruz condemned. Gradually this was to be considered one of their characteristics - a development due, certainly in part, to the last groups of *alumbrados* discussed in this chapter.

Fray Alonso de la Fuente

The first substantial movement of *alumbrados* after that of Toledo, the *alumbrados* of Llerena, is named after the town in southern Extremadura where the participants were sentenced by the local tribunal of the Inquisition. The best-known protagonist of the episode is the man who detected it and who persistently urged the Holy Office to act: Fray Alonso de la Fuente.[4] Born in Extremadura in 1533, he studied at the Colegio de Santo Tomás in Seville and entered the Order of Preachers in 1557. Subsequently he taught at his former college and was elected rector. In 1570 he returned to Extremadura, where he was appointed preacher at the Dominican convent in Badajoz. In what was one of the poorest areas in Spain, he started his campaign against the *alumbrados* which was to obsess him until his death over twenty years later.

Alonso de la Fuente was infected by the prejudice so frequent among the Spanish Dominicans. He regarded himself as an heir of the medieval inquisitors, a guardian of orthodoxy as it was defined by the schoolmen - a perfectly ordered system in which there was no place for the widespread practice of mysticism and in which divine favours were bestowed with increasing scarcity over the centuries. In the Catholic reformers he saw almost as great a threat to this system as in the Protestants. He was suspicious of the entire Society of Jesus and of innovators such as John of Avila, Juan de Ribera, Teresa of Avila and Luis de Granada. He resented the idea, recurrent in John of Avila's epistles and in his *Audi, filia*, that man must actually experience the cross of Christ, and he was appalled by the promise he found in Luis de Granada's *Libro de la oración* and in other mystical writings that the result of prayer would be to feel the effect of grace.[5] But what he deplored most, as shown by his attacks on Teresa of Avila, was the universal accessibility of mysticism, the claims to composing a shortcut to a perfect method of prayer. Ultimately Alonso de la Fuente paid a high price for his obsessions. His determination to carry his campaign against Luis de Granada and the Jesuits into Portugal incensed the Portuguese ruler and severely damaged Fray Alonso's reputation. It led to his being tried himself in 1577.

Not always an objective source, Fray Alonso is not, however, an entirely unreliable one. He was a man with a sound theological training and his description of the religious situation in Extremadura remains of value. Besides, although Fray Alonso's passion drove him to extreme positions, his opinions, which frequently echo those of Melchor Cano, were widely shared and respected within the Order of Preachers both by his contemporaries and by later generations.

The spiritual climate described by Fray Alonso in Extremadura in the 1570s is reminiscent of that created by Cardinal Cisneros in Castile. Piety of a mystical kind had been encouraged on an unprecedented scale. It had been fomented by two successive bishops of Badajoz, Cristóbal de Rojas and Juan de Ribera; it had been spread by John of Avila, by his disciples, and by Luis de Granada during the years he spent in western Andalusia; and it had been supported throughout by Jesuit preachers. By the time Fray Alonso returned to Extremadura in 1570 Rojas and Ribera had been translated to other sees, Luis de Granada had moved to Portugal, and John of Avila was dead. What remained were the writings of these men, conveniently available in the vernacular, and thus read in circles of men and above all women with little theological training.[6]

The Alumbrados of Llerena

The existence of *alumbrados* became apparent to Fray Alonso on his travels and preaching missions in the south and south-west of Extremadura. He first came across them in his birthplace, Fuente del Maestre. His disgust was heightened by finding, early in 1571, that his own niece had become a member of what he described as 'the sect'. He made further discoveries above all in Zafra, but also in Fuente de Cantos, Usagre, Almendralejo and in numerous other towns and villages. Thereupon he started to draw up a series of reports which, he trusted, would prompt the Inquisition to proceed.

According to Fray Alonso's reports the 'sect', befriended and protected by the Jesuit preacher Diego de Santa Cruz,[7] was headed by three priests, Hernando Alvarez, Gaspar Sánchez and Francisco Zamora. While the last two died in prison just over a year after their arrest and do not appear to have made a full confession, more information has survived about Hernando Alvarez, who was generally considered to be the leader.

Alvarez had assembled a group of clerics and female followers, *beatas* and widows, and imposed on them a rule of obedience and secrecy. Once he was confident of their obedience to himself alone, he absolved them of any further obligation to parents or prelates and freed them from observing the commandments of the Church. They thus ceased from fasting and abstinence in Lent or other prescribed periods. Refusing to perform any manual labour, spurning vocal prayer as a mark of imperfection, their only duty was to devote their lives to mental prayer and meditation. The women, who had their hair cropped ritually, were assured by Alvarez and his male companions that their state as *beatas* and members of his community was far superior to that of nuns or married women. From Alvarez or his fellow priests they received communion almost every day. Besides attending the ecstasies and trances of their leader, they too were encouraged to experience such manifest proofs of the grace and sanctity they had acquired. Some claimed to have seen 'the essence of God'; others indulged in sexual relations with Alvarez and his male followers in the certainty that this was 'no mortal sin but rather what God orders and desires'.[8]

Hernando Alvarez's persuasions seem to have been shared by his male and female followers alike. A few added idiosyncrasies of their own. Juan García, who said he could lead his disciples to perfection within three days, had his female devotees adore him as he posed in a crucified position. Francisco de Mesa, a priest in Zafra, told his penitents they should never say '*non sum digna*' when they received the eucharist since such words were reserved for the imperfect. Cristóbal Chamizo, also from Zafra, maintained that he could restore the virginity of those of his penitents he had seduced and practise miraculous abortions.

The main heresy of the *alumbrados* of Extremadura was antinomianism. They were convinced they had attained such a state of perfection that they could not sin. They also believed in the miraculous qualities of mental prayer which led to raptures and trances. They found their views confirmed in the works on meditation which they read eclectically and passionately: Loyola's *Ejercicios espirituales*, John of Avila's epistles and his *Audi, filia*, Luis de Granada's *Guía de pecadores* and *Libro de la oración*, the writings of Juan de Ribera and the life of St Catherine of Genoa.[9] They were so enamoured of this last work, which they read in the Portuguese translation issued in Lisbon in 1575, that the Holy Office ordered its suppression.[10] Indeed, it is not difficult to understand the appeal which the hagiology of Caterina Adorno, composed soon after her death by her disciples and first published in 1547, must have had for them. The Genoese saint was married, and, although she devoted her life to works of charity, lived in the world rather than in a convent. When a Dominican claimed greater superiority in the eyes of God than herself on account of his monastic vows she expatiated convincingly on her own capacity to love God as well as he. Such passages must have been appreciated in circles which expressed their contempt for conventual life. Catherine of Genoa, moreover, stressed the speed with which she received divine revelations. Her followers gave details of the miraculous effects on her of grace - her trances, visions and stigmata, the state of perfection in which she had no sins to confess and could never receive any temptation of the senses, and her claim to be able to tell whether a host had been consecrated by its taste.[11]

In his reports Alonso de la Fuente insisted that the *alumbrados* were inspired, and in some cases possessed, by the devil. He compared their doctrine to that of the Beghards,[12] but he also referred to their similarity to the *alumbrados* of Toledo. Originally this comparison does not seem to have been an idea of his own. He owed it to a fellow Dominican, Fray Juan de Ochoa, to whom he showed one of his reports when he called on the provincial of the order in Seville in 1572.[13] Juan de Ochoa, was an old man and was to die in Rome two years later. He had taken an active part in the investigations into the humanists in the 1530s. Ordered to qualify the propositions attributed to Juan de Vergara, he was later summoned to Madrid, in 1570, to judge the writings of Carranza. As a result of his part in the trial of Juan de Vergara he was well acquainted with the accusations against the *alumbrados* of Toledo and suggested the comparison to Alonso de la Fuente.

Despite Fray Alonso's urgent reports, the Holy Office was slow to act against the *alumbrados* of Extremadura. Only after Fray Alonso had paid a personal visit to the *Suprema* in Madrid did the tribunal of Llerena receive orders to proceed against the suspects. The first arrests were made in November 1573. The *Suprema* subsequently dispatched a visitor to Extremadura, and in July 1574 an edict of faith was issued condemning the errors contained in the accusations.[14] Although the edict of 1574 was directed specifically against the *alumbrados*, its difference from that issued in Toledo in 1525 is obvious. *Alumbradismo* had officially acquired another significance. While the ideas of antinomianism, passivity, abandonment and sectarianism were retained, there was now a clear emphasis on mystical extravagance, imposture and licentiousness.

The principal members of the movement were sentenced at an *auto de fé* in Llerena in June 1579, but the arrests and trials of the *alumbrados* of Extremadura continued for just under ten years. By the standards of the Inquisition both the treatment and the sentences of the accused were severe. Torture was applied in a number of cases - and resisted. The culprits had to abjure their errors *de levi* and forfeited their clerical offices and benefices. Hernando Alvarez and most of his male followers were sentenced to the galleys - Cristóbal Chamizo to six years, Hernando Alvarez himself, Juan García, Francisco de Mesa, Cristóbal Mejía and Hernando de Ecija to four - besides having to pay substantial fines. Their principal female follower, María González, received a hundred lashes and three years imprisonment.[15]

A question which still remains to be solved is the extent to which the conventicles of Extremadura were composed of *conversos*. Alonso de la Fuente insisted on their prominence, claiming that in Zafra, the centre of the movement, the *alumbrados* 'were *conversos* for the most part' and that 'of seventy priests sixty were Jews.'[16] In reality the proportion of New Christians would seem to have been far smaller. Of the nineteen *alumbrados* given penances at the *auto de fé* in Llerena in 1579 no more than five appear to have been of Jewish descent: Hernando Alvarez himself, three of his most active male followers, and one of his female devotees. A similar proportion emerged when the inquisitors extended their investigation to Andalusia and, in the city of Jaén, proceeded against a group of enthusiastic *beatas* and clerics whose errors corresponded to those of the *alumbrados* of Llerena.[17] The leader was the prior of the church of San Bartolomé, Gaspar Lucas, who was allegedly inspired by the great Flemish mystic Jan Ruusbroeck, a work by whom was found in his possession. He was seconded by a *beata*, María Romero, and was sentenced with his followers at an *auto de fé* held in Cordova in 1590. He himself was deprived of his sacerdotal functions, banished from the diocese of Jaén, and sentenced to ten years reclusion in a monastery, while nearly all his followers were flogged. Gaspar Lucas, alone of the eight culprits, is stated to have been of *converso* extraction.

Teresa of Avila

Alonso de la Fuente's pursuit of *alumbrado* groups in Extremadura and later in Andalusia became part of a campaign to discredit mysticism of any kind. One of the most illustrious victims was the greatest contemporary writer of mystical works, Teresa of Avila. The Carmelite reformer had had various dealings with the Holy Office in her lifetime. She had been denounced to the tribunal of Cordova in 1574. She was in Seville in 1575 and 1576 when the investigation into the *alumbrados* of Llerena was at its height.[18] Engaged in the foundation of a reformed Carmelite convent, she was denounced by a former novice for spreading a doctrine consisting of superstition and fraudulence and with a dangerous emphasis on mental prayer. Thereupon the local inquisitors asked the *Suprema* to allow them to examine the manuscript of her confessions which was in the hands of Fray Domingo Báñez in his Dominican convent in Valladolid. The *Suprema* refused and investigations were abandoned, even if suspicion remained attached to Teresa's foundation in Seville and the mystical enthusiasm fomented by her imitators. At the same time, moreover, Teresa herself was acquainted with the other reformers who had fallen foul of the Inquisition or who were about to be tried by it. Besides John of Avila, whom she greatly admired, she knew his disciples Bernardino de Carleval and Diego Pérez de Valdivia.[19]

The true campaign against Teresa, however, started two years after her death with the publication of her works in 1588. In 1589 and 1590 Alonso de la Fuente addressed a number of letters and reports to the Holy Office imploring the inquisitors to prohibit her writings.[20] She was, he assured the Inquisition, one of the *alumbrados*. The doubts about the source of her inspiration which induced her to compose her autobiography in 1562 were fully justified: it was the devil. All the saint's expressions of humility were given the darkest interpretation. Her incapacity to find a satisfactory confessor was taken as a sign of her deeply rooted disobedience to the Church. The early Massilians, Tauler, the Beghards, Luther and the *alumbrados*, said Fray Alonso, were her forefathers.[21]

The points which Fray Alonso found particularly dangerous were the general accessibility of Teresa's method of meditation, the emphasis on feeling, and the description of mystical union. When condemning the speed with which the saint claimed that mystical progress could be achieved, he quoted the *alumbrado* Juan García who maintained that his disciples could attain perfection within three days. He indicated the perils of the idea that anyone - the clergy, the religious, the married, the weak and the imperfect of any state or profession - could advance to perfection by following her method of prayer. The favours which God bestowed and which produced the trances and visions described by Teresa and experienced by her followers were rare in the extreme and might be accorded, he suggested, once in a thousand years. He was equally appalled by what Teresa described as the feeling of the presence of God in the soul (a concept which he associated with the *alumbrados*), and by her claim that God and heaven could be found within ourselves, words, he said, reminiscent of Tauler. Teresa's insistence on mental prayer led Fray Alonso to conclude that she rejected oral prayer out of hand. This was in keeping with what he detected as the idea, condemned in some of the leading medieval mystics, of an essential union with God, and with the complete passivity of the senses such a union entailed. That, he decided, was little more than Lutheranism disguised.[22]

Although Teresa's defenders prevailed over her detractors and her works were approved and published, Alonso de la Fuente found support among other Dominicans - Fray Juan de Orellana and Fray Juan de Lorenzana (who coupled Teresa with the contemporary Flemish mystic

Blosius).[23] But he also met with the agreement of certain secular theologians, such as the historian Francisco de Pisa. Even if Teresa's opponents did not always go as far as Fray Alonso in maintaining that her inspiration was diabolical, they were all preoccupied by the effects the spread of her writings could have on the laity and the growing number of *beatas*, particularly in Andalusia.

The Alumbrados of Seville

In the late sixteenth and early seventeenth century Andalusia had its share of fraudulent visionaries who could be accused of *alumbradismo*. There was also the more serious episode of the Congregación de la Granada in Seville, a pious association whose main doctrinal error seems to have been its insistence on secrecy and a sacred leadership transmitted from one 'heir of the Holy Ghost' to another.[24] Its gravity was largely due to the distinction of some of those involved - the Jesuit Rodrigo Alvarez, the sculptor Juan Martínez Montañés and others - but its investigation did not lead to discoveries quite as scandalous as those made about the last sizeable *alumbrado* movement, the '*alumbrados* of Seville' arrested between 1622 and 1628.[25]

Although they were detected up to fifty years later than the movements in Extremadura and the north of Andalusia investigated by Alonso de la Fuente, the *alumbrados* of Seville were regarded as part of the same phenomenon. The direct links with individuals arrested in Extremadura, however, were slight: one of the leaders of the Seville group, the *beata* Catalina de Jesús, had been a devotee of John of Avila's disciple Pedro de Hojeda, the rector of the university of Baeza who was tried in 1590. Yet the charges made against the *alumbrados* of Seville were almost identical with those against the '*alumbrados* of Llerena', and the edict issued against the former in 1623 was largely the same as that issued in 1574.[26]

The sudden activity of the inquisitors in Seville in the 1620s can be attributed to the efforts of Philip IV's powerful favourite, the Count Duke of Olivares, to reorganise the *Suprema* and to inspire that lethargic body with greater enthusiasm.[27] Manned by a more dynamic staff, the tribunal of Seville proceeded to the arrest in 1622 of the two leaders of the movement, against whom denunciations were accumulating: Catalina de Jesús[28] had already been tried in 1611 on account of her claims to divine favour, but had then got away with a warning and had retained her reputation for visions and miraculous gifts; the other, Juan de Villalpando, a former Carmelite acting as priest of the parish of San Isidoro, was a preacher of immense popularity.

The edict read in the churches in June 1623 elicited a number of denunciations unprecedented in the history of the tribunal. In assessing the teachings of the sect as they can be extracted from the brief accounts of some of the trials, the sentences, and the reports drawn up by a group of industrious Dominicans, a certain caution should, however, be exercised. Not only were the condemned propositions frequently the same as those in the edict of Llerena, but the Dominicans who composed the reports venerated the memory of Alonso de la Fuente and had been profoundly influenced by the accounts he had written fifty years earlier.[29] The similarities in the beliefs attributed to movements divided by a long period of time raise legitimate doubts about the accuracy of their description, but there is no other documentation by which to judge them.

Again the group is described as a sect in which the leaders demanded absolute obedience and absolved their followers of any duty towards their worldly or ecclesiastical superiors. Vocal prayer was derided and mental prayer commended; confessions were received within the sect but no orthodox penances imposed; communion was administered with frequency; the state of the *beata* was described as the most perfect while that of matrimony and religious ordination was scorned; the Inquisition was mocked pitilessly; worship of the saints and images was regarded as an impediment; the female members were required to wear humble clothes even if ascetic practices were discouraged; and the members were sure of their impeccability. Although Villalpando and some of his male colleagues seem to have kissed and caressed their female penitents, the *alumbrados* of Seville were less prone to debauchery than the *alumbrados* of Extremadura and avoided orgiastic excesses.[30]

The male participants were nearly all priests from Seville and the vicinity - Cristóbal Blasco, Juan Crisóstomo de Soria, Francisco de Villaescusa. Some, like Villalpando himself, had once been in religious orders, and others - the Augustinian Nicolás de Santamaría and the Mercedarian Diego de Montiel - still were. The sentences were markedly lighter than those pronounced in Llerena. At the *auto de fé* held at the end of February 1627 Catalina de Jesús, who had provided the inquisitors with a full confession shortly after her arrest, was sentenced to abjure *de levi* and to six years reclusion in a monastery. Juan de Villalpando had to retract all his heretical propositions at the same *auto de fé* and was further sentenced to four years confinement, a fine of 200 ducats and some spiritual penances. The sentences of their followers, some of whom were flogged or banished, were not much heavier. With the exception of a couple of accused of Muslim descent those involved are not stated to have been New Christians.[31]

One of the more interesting aspects of the Seville movement is the book which its members read with particular fervour: the recent edition, published in 1618, of the *Noche oscura* by John of the Cross. Just as Alonso de la Fuente had made use of the *alumbrados* of Extremadura to discredit Teresa of Avila and other mystics, so the Dominicans of Seville tried to discredit Teresa of Avila's companion, this other great Carmelite reformer.

The most ardent, Fray Domingo Farfán, claimed to have detected statements condemned in the edict of 1623 in John of the Cross's work. He referred to three propositions, all of which concern the state of quiet accompanying union with the Almighty. According to the first those praying in the presence of God should not even meditate on the passion of Christ or pause to think of His humanity. According to the second it was possible to attain such a state of perfection that grace annihilated all activity and the soul could neither recede nor advance. According to the third, if the Almighty ordered the soul of the perfect to be good it would become substantially virtuous and at that point would not have to work, love or do anything.[32]

Such was Fray Domingo's insistence on the dangers contained in John of the Cross's book that a copy of the *Noche oscura* was dispatched to Madrid in order to be examined. In Madrid it was submitted to the judgement of the Augustinian professor at the university of Salamanca, Basilio Ponce de León. The reply was a persuasive defence of its orthodoxy. Ponce de León pointed out that all works, beginning with the Scriptures, contained statements which, if taken out of context, could be interpreted heretically.[33] In a letter to the *Suprema* written in September 1625 the inquisitors of Seville themselves came to a similar conclusion. They emphasised the dangers of mystical works read without the necessary theological knowledge and without fulfilling the basic conditions stipulated by the writers.[34] Although John of the Cross, like Teresa, Osuna and other mystics before them, provided meticulous instructions for mystical progress and insisted on the high moral requirements attending it, the *alumbrados* of Seville had leapt to the last part of his work describing the all but total immobility of the senses, the state of union with God, and the ensuing feeling of divinity. They had overlooked the warnings which preceded it.

From Alumbrados to Quietists

The *alumbrados* of Seville are generally regarded as marking the end of the history of the movement. Certainly this was the last group to be known exclusively by that name, but it was not the last group of its kind and its condemnation was not the last occasion on which the term *alumbrado* was used.

Groups bearing some resemblance to the conventicles of Seville came to light throughout the seventeenth century. The best known were the nuns of the Benedictine convent of San Placido in Madrid who were denounced to the Inquisition in 1631.[35] But although their confessor, Francisco García Calderón, held ideas similar to those of Juan de Villalpando in Seville about the benefits of intimate contacts with his penitents, and although he was accused of being an *alumbrado*, the episode was ultimately diagnosed as a case of diabolical possession. A less known incident was investigated in Valencia in 1668.[36] The term *alumbrado* was not applied, even if the group of eight individuals who assembled round the twenty-five year-old Gertrudis Tosca had more affinities with the *alumbrados* of Llerena and Seville than the nuns of San Placido. Gertrudis Tosca was married. She laid high claims to sanctity, maintaining that she could read the mind of God, that only she knew whether the souls of the deceased went to heaven, and that she herself was another God on earth. Her followers, who abandoned themselves to the divine will, were convinced of her impeccability. Her male disciples included three priests who expressed their devotion by becoming her lovers. One of them, José Torres, to whom she would administer the eucharist, cherished the belief that whenever they performed the sexual act a soul would be released from purgatory. Determined to depopulate purgatory as best he could, he went as far as to copulate with her in the communion chapel of a local parish church.

The word *alumbrado*, at the same time, was used still more by writers on mysticism than by the Inquisition. It was taken to designate the type of heterodox piety which the practitioners of mysticism abhorred and it served to stress their own orthodoxy. When describing the final stage of union with God the orthodox mystics of the sixteenth century had resorted to the traditional divisions of the soul to allow some slight activity to one of its faculties. Francisco de Osuna argued for the activity of the intelligence,[37] Bernardino de Laredo for that of the loving will.[38] Teresa of Avila, too, admitted the continuous 'occupation' of the will, but not of the memory or the understanding.[39] The complete quiet of the senses, the passive surrender to God in which the *via unitiva* seemed to culminate, remained one of the greatest perils for writers on mysticism. For later authors an attack on the *alumbrados* was a convenient way of circumventing it.

In the last years of the sixteenth century the Carmelite Juan Aravalles was warning his readers of the dangers of the *alumbrados*.

The warning was repeated in the following century by the Jesuit Alonso Rodríguez, by the Minim Juan Bretón, and by the distinguished Mercedarian mystic Juan Falconi.[40] Most insistent of all was the Franciscan Félix Alamín, later in the seventeenth century. He amalgamated the *alumbrado* groups of Toledo and Llerena with the Protestants of Valladolid and Seville, and regarded them all as descendants of the 'heretics of Durango'.

> They started well and with a great desire for betterment; but they then chose as their means the kind of prayer of contemplation here described, appearing in the presence of God without images or matter or meditation, behaving passively, believing they were governed in everything by the Holy Spirit; and since this kind of prayer, in which the operations of the understanding and the will are suspended, is so dangerous, they were little by little deceived by the devil . . . and precipitated from one error to another.[41]

In the late seventeenth, and even in the early eighteenth, century other theologians, stimulated by the Quietist controversy, continued to look back on what was by then a well-established national heresy - the Discalced Trinitarian Rafaél de San Juan, the Carmelite Francisco de Santo Tomás, and, in 1712, the Franciscan Juan de Ascargota.[42]

Alumbradismo thus lingered on as an accusation. The term was still being used by the Inquisition in the eighteenth century for isolated cases of imposture. It was also employed in works on mysticism even when it was on the way to being replaced by the new heresy condemned at the end of the seventeenth century - Molinosism or Quietism. With this another term came into currency which could be applied to that combination of mystical exuberance and lasciviousness with which the *alumbrados* had been associated for almost two hundred years.

The man who gave his name to the movement, Miguel de Molinos,[43] was born close to Saragossa and had been educated by the Jesuits. In 1663 he settled in Rome, where he became a most popular confessor and spiritual adviser. He published his celebrated *Guía espiritual* in 1675, the year in which John of the Cross was beatified in the face of strong opposition. Mysticism had numerous enemies and Molinos's book was promptly attacked by both Dominicans and Jesuits. Nevertheless, for ten years it looked as though Molinos had triumphed. He was protected by the pope, Innocent XI, by Italian and Spanish princes of the Church, and by leading members of the Roman aristocracy. In the end, like Carranza, he fell victim to the political struggles at the Vatican. French hostility prevailed and in 1685 he was arrested. His doctrine was officially condemned in November 1687 and he was sentenced to an imprisonment which lasted until his death in 1696.

Some of the sixty-eight propositions in the bull condemning Molinos, *Caelestis Pastor*,[44] closely resembled propositions ascribed to the *alumbrados* of Toledo and repeated, in slightly different forms, in the edicts issued in 1574 and 1623. The propositions describe a similar desire to banish images from the mind engaged in prayer, a similar condemnation of activity as an obstacle to perfection, the same idea of abandonment to the divine will which precludes even the struggle against temptation. But did they really reflect the teaching of Molinos? The statements condemned were taken mainly from letters which have not survived. It is fruitless to search for traces of such ideas in the *Guía espiritual*, where Molinos displays the utmost caution in his description of the mystical way and stresses the rôle of the Church as an intermediary.

The first attacks drove Molinos to write his *Defensa de la contemplación*, which has remained in manuscript.[45] In order to justify his spirituality he too resorted to a lengthy attack on the *alumbrados*, false mystics whose doctrine should be compared to the true mysticism which he himself was teaching. The *alumbrados*, he wrote, had decided to live in idleness, rejecting any activity, be it praise of God or gratitude to God. They believed they had reached a state of such perfection that they were above the practice of virtues which were only the recourse of the imperfect soul. They refused even to resist temptation and thus showed that their 'entire object . . . was to procure the pleasure of the carnal and natural appetite'. How different from his own teaching!

> Theirs was idleness and repose of the flesh, impure and sensual,
> a quest for their own pleasure, for themselves, and in no way for
> God. But this other doctrine of the mystics and the saints is a
> spiritual quiet with which the soul waits on God, adoring Him,
> believing in Him and hoping in Him, the complete abandonment
> into His hands with loving and resigned devotion so that He may
> do with the soul what He likes and how He likes.[46]

The words of Molinos provide a suitable ending to a study of the *alumbrados*. They show how the heresy which had assumed different forms in the course of the sixteenth and seventeenth centuries continued to serve a purpose as a bugbear. Yet, as Quietism advanced and spread through the most exalted intellectual circles in Europe, the essentially Spanish heresy of the 'poor little women and the ignorant' gradually faded away.

Conclusion

How should the *alumbrados* be assessed? There has been a tendency in Spanish historiography, which can already be perceived in the sixteenth century, to look at the *alumbrados* with a certain sense of affection: they were indeed heretics, but they were Spanish heretics; their heterodoxy was the outcome of excessive zeal rather than of any deep hostility to Catholicism. The *alumbrados* of Toledo came close to Lutheranism, but they did not go as far as Lutheranism. Contemporaries and later theologians could thus point to them in order to show how lightly Spain had been let off and to express their gratitude to the Inquisition which had guarded the peninsula so effectively.

In judging the heresy we must make certain distinctions. We must distinguish between what the *alumbrados* of Toledo actually taught and how their teaching was presented by the inquisitors. At an early stage the movement was associated with manifestations of hysteria and of moral depravity which were altogether alien to the doctrine of Isabel de la Cruz, Alcaraz and María de Cazalla. We must then detach Isabel de la Cruz and her followers from the later groups of Extremadura and Andalusia, even if the presence of the disciples of John of Avila makes the distinction sometimes less obvious than it might at first seem.

There is no doubt of the evangelical aspirations of the first *alumbrados*, however formless and contradictory their doctrine may sometimes seem to have been. What they would have become had the Inquisition not intervened when it did, how far they would have dared to go in a society preponderantly hostile to them, are among the many questions thrown up by history which can only be answered with speculation. Elsewhere in Europe we see men and women, undaunted by a persecution far more ferocious, who persisted in their beliefs and finally succeeded in founding churches of their own. The most obvious examples are the Anabaptists and certain groups of Protestants. Would the first *alumbrados* ever have wished to go so far?

If we take the development of Juan de Valdés as an indication the answer would appear to be no. Valdés was always cautious in his attitude to the Catholic Church: he never broke with it and enjoyed his ecclesiastical benefices until his death. Such behaviour may have been the result of indifference. The senselessness he attributed to all ceremonies led him and his followers in Naples to practise a form of 'Nicodemism' or simulation, outwardly conforming but actually retaining their own evangelical beliefs. After his death, a few of Valdés's admirers did indeed leave the Church of Rome and go over to Protestantism, while others remained loyal to the papacy. Valdés's later works were published by Protestants north of the Alps, but were repeatedly condemned by the more orthodox members of the Reformed Churches.[1]

In Spain men with a similar background to the first *alumbrados* and who were directly or indirectly associated with the movement also adopted different positions. Their sentences to the stake suggest that Juan del Castillo, Juan López de Celain and perhaps Alonso Garzón had committed themselves to Protestantism to an unacceptable degree. The majority, however, remained attached to Roman Catholicism. Miguel de Eguía was thus buried in a Franciscan habit, while his brother, with Manuel de Miona and Miguel de Torres, joined the Jesuits. Indeed, the Society of Jesus, which managed to combine so many elements that had seemed to be in conflict with one another earlier on in the century, was an obvious haven for men once attracted by evangelism and who continued to believe in the reform of the Catholic Church.[2]

By 1600 the Jesuits were firmly established in Spain. Dominican hostility persisted, but Loyola's movement had won. It was, as it always had been, many-sided. There were cases of apocalypticism, of members of the Society who adopted the same Joachist ideas which had once been popular among the Franciscans and who were persuaded that the Jesuits were the men of providence prophesied by the Cistercian.[3] There were also cases of mystical extravagance, of raptures and trances. Yet what prevailed was a more sober spirituality. Loyola's *Ejercicios espirituales*, considerably emended since its presentation to the prayer groups in Alcalá, was read more widely than ever in the seventeenth century, but another highly popular work, first published in Seville in 1609, was Alonso Rodríguez's *Ejercicio de perfección y virtudes christianas*. Far longer than Loyola's book, Rodríguez's *Ejercicio*, reprinted over the years and circulated throughout the world, lays an emphasis on the asceticism which was to characterise Catholic orthodoxy rather than on mysticism.

With the other writers on mystical practices Rodríguez provided the standard aspersions of the *alumbrados*, condemning their passivity. We must, he said, cooperate with God at all times, even when practising a kind of mental prayer 'extraordinary and outstanding', '*extraordinaria y aventajada*', which could not be taught, which was rare and brief, which must not be aimed at but could only be received, and about which Rodríguez was wary in the extreme.[4]

The acclaim with which Rodríguez's book was greeted reflected the changes which had taken place in the Society after the death of its more mystical members, Antonio Cordeses and Baltasar Alvarez. By the early seventeenth century the Jesuits owed much of their influence both to their gifts as educators and to the confraternities, composed almost entirely of laymen, which they had managed to organise all over Europe.[5] Like the other sodalities which abounded in the sixteenth century and later, these too had their forerunners in the Middle Ages. But the Jesuit congregations combined devotional practices, including meditation, with an active participation in propagating the Catholic faith and the performance of works of charity, and can perhaps be regarded as the most successful descendants of the prayer groups which Loyola had assembled in Alcalá in the 1520s.

But prayer groups, as the history of the *alumbrados* shows, could also lead in different directions. The *alumbrado* conventicles in the south of Spain had been reading respectable devotional literature, including Loyola's *Ejercicios espirituales*. They had connections with men of unquestioned piety, Jesuits and disciples of John of Avila. Yet, convinced of their own incapacity to sin, they drew ever further away from the orthodox teaching of the Church, practised religious ceremonies and performed religious duties only among themselves, and at the same time indulged in various degrees of lasciviousness.

The *alumbrados* of Llerena and Seville could hardly have been further removed in beliefs and practices from the followers of Isabel de la Cruz. Ecstatic manifestations of mystical unity with the Almighty seem to have held a central place in the conventicles of Extremadura and Andalusia, while it was these very manifestations which the *alumbrados* of Toledo had repudiated. Their social situation was also different. The later *alumbrados* may occasionally have been able to beguile reputable members of the Church, but they were far from having the protection of the aristocracy and the support of the learned which characterised the *alumbrados* of Toledo.

The *alumbrados* of the late sixteenth and early seventeenth century are more reminiscent in their behaviour of eccentric religious movements elsewhere in Europe. In the north, in England, the Low Countries and Germany, certain sectarians, members of the Family of Love and of other groups descended from the Anabaptists, displayed the same belief in their own divinity in the 1560s and 1570s. Their members had read works of mysticism, especially the late medieval *Theologia Germanica* with its description of the 'godded' man. And however common the accusation of lechery, advanced indiscriminately by enemies of heterodoxy, it would certainly appear to have been justified where some of the Familists and their fellow sectarians were concerned.[6] The relative lack of official control in many parts of northern Europe meant that it was possible for sects to flourish in remote areas. Their members could intermarry or simply copulate; they could organise their own religious services and improvise their own form of priesthood, without too much danger of denunciation and prosecution.

The glimpses we are afforded of the *alumbrado* groups in Extremadura and Andalusia suggest that they had little future, even if they were part of a recurrent phenomenon. They were regarded as aberrations - examples of the misunderstanding to which the most orthodox devotional literature can lend itself. They played into the hands of the enemies of mysticism who used them, in more or less good faith, to discredit the teaching in all its forms.

The evangelism of the *alumbrados* of Toledo, on the other hand, was attended by a genuine desire to reform the Church which found its way into various channels, both orthodox and heterodox, and did have a future, although historians may disagree as to what it was.

Abbreviations

AHN = Archivo Histórico Nacional, Madrid
AHSJ = Archivum Historicum Societatis Jesu
ARG = Archiv für Reformationsgeschichte
ARSJ = Archivum Romanum Societatis Jesu
Bataillon, *Erasme* = Marcel Bataillon, *Erasme et l'Espagne*, ed. Daniel Devoto
& Charles Amiel, 3 vols., Geneva 1991, (reprint of 1937 edition with
corrections and supplements)
BAC = Biblioteca de Autores Cristianos
BHisp = Bulletin Hispanique
BHR = Bibliothèque d'Humanisme et Renaissance
BHS = Bulletin of Hispanic Studies
BRAH = Boletín de la Real Academia de Historia
CHE = Cuadernos de Historia de España
CTom = Ciencia Tomista
HeyJ = Heythrop Journal
HispR = Hispanic Review
HispSac = Hispania Sacra
Huerga, *Alumbrados*, = Alvaro Huerga, *Historia de los Alumbrados*, 4 vols.,
Madrid 1978-88
Márquez, *Alumbrados*, = Antonio Márquez, *Los alumbrados: orígenes y
filosofía (1525-1559)*, Madrid 1980²
MHSJ = Monumenta Historica Societatis Jesu
Proceso de Alcaraz = Proceso de Pedro Ruiz de Alcaraz, Archivo Histórico
Nacional (Madrid), Inquisición de Toledo, Leg. 106, no. 5
Proceso de Beteta = José Manuel Carrete Parrondo, *Movimiento alumbrado y
Renacimiento español: Proceso inquisitorial contra Luis de Beteta*, Madrid
1980
Proceso de Bivar = Alastair Hamilton, *El proceso de Rodrigo de Bivar (1539)*,
Madrid 1979
Proceso de María de Cazalla = Milagros Ortega Costa, *Proceso de la
Inquisición contra María de Cazalla*, Madrid 1978
Proceso de Ortiz = Proceso de Fray Francisco Ortiz, Universitäts-und
Landesbibliothek Sachsen-Anhalt in Halle (Saale), Yc.2⁰.20
RABM = Revista de Archivos, Bibliotecas y Museos
RET = Revista Española de Teología
RFE = Revista de Filología Española
Selke, *Ortiz* = Angela Selke de Sánchez, *El Santo Oficio de la Inquisición:
Proceso de Fr. Francisco Ortiz (1529-1532)*, Madrid 1968

Notes

Introduction. pp.1-5

1. A survey of the most important publications is provided by M. Andrés Martín, 'Alumbrados de Toledo de 1525 e Inquisición, procesos y procesados' in: *Historia de la Inquisición en España y América*, ed. J. Pérez Villanueva & B. Escandell Bonet, I, Madrid 1984, pp. 488-520. There is also a useful and broader survey by A. Gordon Kinder, *Spanish Protestants and Reformers in the Sixteenth Century: a bibliography*, London 1983. Dr Kinder is preparing a bibliography on the *alumbrados* of which he has kindly allowed me to see a typescript. The standard Spanish study on the *alumbrados* of Toledo is still Antonio Márquez, *Los alumbrados: orígenes y filosofía (1525-1559)*, Madrid 1980².

2. Extensive extracts - but only extracts - had been published earlier from the trial of Juan de Vergara (John E. Longhurst, 'Alumbrados, erasmistas y luteranos en el proceso de Juan de Vergara' in: *CHE*, 27, 1958, pp. 99-163; 28, 1958, pp. 102-65; 29-30, 1959, pp. 266-92; 31-2, 1960, pp. 322-56; 35-6, 1962, pp. 337-53; 37-8, 1963, pp. 356-71) and from the trial of Francisco Ortiz (Angela Selke de Sánchez, *El Santo Oficio de la Inquisición: Proceso de Fr. Francisco Ortiz (1529-1532)*, Madrid 1968). Since then the trials have been published in full of Rodrigo de Bivar (Alastair Hamilton, *El proceso de Rodrigo de Bivar (1539)*, Madrid 1979), Luis de Beteta (José Manuel Carrete Parrondo, *Movimiento alumbrado y Renacimiento español: Proceso inquisitorial contra Luis de Beteta*, Madrid 1980), and María de Cazalla (Milagros Ortega Costa, *Proceso de la Inquisición contra María de Cazalla*, Madrid 1978). This last trial, edited with exemplary precision, is a particularly important contribution to the history of the *alumbrados*.

3. Alvaro Huerga, *Historia de los Alumbrados*, 4 vols., Madrid 1978-88. Vols. I, II and IV contain numerous documents concerning Extremadura and Andalusia. Vol III is on the New World.

Chapter I. Reform and Enthusiasm. pp.7-23

1. Cf. A. Domínguez Ortiz, *Los Judeoconversos en España y América*, Madrid 1971, pp. 18-19. For a recent study of the Inquisition *see* Henry Kamen, *Inquisition and Society in Spain*, London 1985.

2. *Luzero de la vida cristiana*, Sevilla 1528, fo. 2r.

3. *Retablo de la vida de Christo*, Alcalá 1577, fo. 5r.

4. Cf. Luis Fernández de Retana, *Cisneros y su siglo*, 2 vols, Madrid 1929-30. For the climate Cisneros created see Bataillon, *Erasme*, I, pp. 1-75; II, pp. 25-45.

5. *Opus epistolarum*, Paris 1670, p. 61.

6. Cf. José García Oro, O.F.M., *Cisneros y la Reforma del Clero español en tiempo de los Reyes Católicos*, Madrid 1971.

7. Cf. M. Andrés Martín, *Los Recogidos: Nueva visión de la mística española (1500-1700.)*, Madrid 1976, pp. 29-47.

8 García de Cisneros, *Obras completas*, 2 vols, Montserrat 1965, II, p. 454.

9 Cf. M. Andrés, *Los Recogidos*, pp. 64-70.

10 *Tratado llamado Via Espiritus*, Salamanca 1541, fo. 2v.

11 Francisco de Osuna, *Tercer abecedario espiritual*, ed. M. Andrés Martín, (*BAC* 333) Madrid 1972, pp. 436-43. On Osuna see Fidèle de Ros, O.F.M., *Un maître de sainte Thérèse: le Père François d'Osuna*, Paris 1936.

12 *Tercer abesedario*, pp. 403, 597.

13. Ibid., pp. 123, 270, 281, 376, 391.

14. Ibid., pp. 210, 221, 223, 225.

15. *Arte para servir a Dios* in: *Místicos Franciscanos Españoles*, I, (*BAC* 38) Madrid 1948, p. 182. Cf. p. 104.

16. *Subida del Monte Sión* in: *Místicos Franciscanos Españoles*, II, (*BAC* 44) Madrid 1948, p. 350.

17. Bataillon, *Erasme*, I, p. 183. The full text of the *Tractatus de vita spirituali* is in *Biografía y escritos de San Vicente Ferrer*, (*BAC* 153) Madrid 1956, pp. 476-541.

18. On *beatas* see William A. Christian, Jr., *Local Religion in Sixteenth-Century Spain*, Princeton 1981, pp. 16-17; id., *Apparitions in Late Medieval and Renaissance Spain*, Princeton 1989², pp.185-7. The episode of the *beata* of Piedrahita is reconstructed in Vicente Beltrán de Heredia, O.P., *Historia de la reforma de la Provincia España (1450-1550)*, Roma 1939, pp. 78-142. Cf. also José Manuel Blecua's introduction to María de Santo Domingo, *Libro de oración*, Madrid 1948, a facsimile edition of the *beata's* devotional work.

19. Cf. Marjorie Reeves, *The Influence of Prophecy in the Later Middle Ages: A Study in Joachism*, Oxford 1969, pp. 72, 146, 175-241.

20. See José María Pou y Martí, O.F.M., *Visionarios, beguinos y fraticelos catalanes (siglos XIII-XV)*, Vich 1930.

21. Cf. J.H. Hillgarth, *Ramon Lull and Lullism in Fourteenth-Century France*, Oxford 1971, pp. 283-8; Joan Fuster, *Rebeldes y heterodoxos*, Barcelona 1972, pp. 26-31; For a survey of the tradition of prophecy in fifteenth-century Spain see Américo Castro, *Aspectos del vivir hispánico*, Madrid 1970, pp. 13-45.

22. Bataillon, *Erasme*, I, pp. 65-75.

23. Cf. Ottavia Niccoli, *Prophecy and People in Renaissance Italy*, Princeton 1990.

24. *Proceso de Beteta*, p. 70.

25. Proceso de Ortiz, fos. 239r.-240v.

26. See below p. 58.

27. Cf. Alister McGrath, *The Intellectual Origins of the European Reformation*, Oxford 1987, pp. 12-28.

28. Proceso de Alcaraz, fo. 367v. Carlos Gilly, 'Juan de Valdés: Uebersetzer und Bearbeiter von Luthers Schriften in seinem *Diálogo de Doctrina*' in: *ARG*, 74, 1983, pp. 257-305, esp. pp. 296-7, argues, on grounds which I cannot accept, that the *alumbrados* only started preaching in 1519.

29. Proceso de Alcaraz, fo. 367v.

30. Proceso de Petronila de Lucena, A.H.N., Inquisición de Toledo, Leg. 111, no. 14, fo. 2r. The statement was made by Diego Hernández, see below p. 83.

31. The words of Hernando Pecha, excerpts from whose *Historia de las vidas de los excelentisimos señores duques del Infantado y sus progenitores*, written in the second half of the sixteenth century, are quoted in the standard history of the Mendoza family, Francisco Layna Serrano, *Historia de Guadalajara y sus Mendozas en los siglos xv y xvi*, 3 vols, Madrid 1942-3, III, p. 38. Cf. also Helen Nader, *The Mendoza Family in the Spanish Renaissance, 1350-1550*, New Brunswick, 1979.

32. On Villena see Alonso López de Haro, *Nobiliario genealógico de los Reyes y Titulos de España*, 2 vols, Madrid 1622, II, pp. 287-8; Francisco Fernández de Béthencourt, *Historia genealógica y heráldica de la Monarquía Española*, 10 vols, Madrid 1897-

1922, II, pp. 195-219.

33. See below pp. 53-5.

34. For biographical and genealogical details see A. López de Haro, *Nobiliario*, I, p. 339. On Don Fadrique's military career *see* Prudencio de Sandoval, *Historia de la vida y hechos del emperador Carlos V*, Pamplona 1634, I, pp. 362-541.

35. *Proceso de Beteta*, p. 158.

Chapter II. The Piety of the *Alumbrados* of Toledo. pp. 25-42

1. On Isabel de la Cruz see John E. Longhurst, 'La beata Isabel de la Cruz ante la Inquisición 1524-1529', *CHE*, 25-6, 1957, pp. 279-303. The summary of her trial and those of Alcaraz and Gaspar de Bedoya is published in Márquez, *Alumbrados*, pp. 243-93. We are reminded by Milagros Ortega (*Proceso de María de Cazalla*, p. 24) that there were two women called Isabel de la Cruz who appear in the *alumbrado* trials, and the distinction between them is not always clear.

2. Brief excerpts from Alcaraz's trial were published by M. Serrano y Sanz, 'Pedro Ruiz de Alcaraz, iluminado alcarreño del siglo XVI', *RABM*, 8, 1903, pp. 1-16, 126-39, but the trial itself has remained unpublished. For Alcaraz's genealogy *see* Proceso de Alcaraz, fos. 3r.-4r. AHN, Inquisición, Libro 245, fo. 16v. shows that Alcaraz owned a house and a vineyard in Guadalajara.

3. Proceso de Alcaraz, fo. 188r.

4. A cook and a maidservant would earn about 1,632 maravedís a year in this period and a labourer about 35 a day. Cf. Earl J. Hamilton, *American Treasure and the Price Revolution in Spain, 1501-1650*, Cambridge (Mass.) 1934, p. 395.

5. Proceso de Alcaraz, fos. 67v., 280v.

6. Ibid., fos. 205r., 233v. For the indentification of certain works see Michel Ange Sarraute, O.F.M., 'La vie franciscaine en Espagne entre les deux couronnements de Charles Quint ou le Premier Commissaire Général des provinces franciscaines des Indes Occidentales', *RABM*, 29, 1913, p. 182.

7. *Proceso de María de Cazalla*, pp. 569-70.

8. The effects of incarceration are discussed in J.-P. Dedieu, *L'administration de la foi: L'Inquisition de Tolède XVIe-XVIIIe siècle*, Madrid 1989, pp. 80-94.

9. *Proceso de María de Cazalla*, pp. 101-2.

10. A version of the edict was published by Vicente Beltrán de Heredia, O.P., 'El edicto contra los alumbrados del reino de Toledo' in: *RET*, 10, 1950, pp. 105-30. An improved version is contained in Márquez, *Alumbrados*, pp. 229-38.

11. *Proceso de María de Cazalla*, pp. 99-101; *Proceso de Bivar*, pp. 25-7.

12. For a discussion of the term *see* Márquez, *Alumbrados*, pp. 70-6.

13. For the authors of the various propositions *see* Milagros Ortega Costa, 'Las proposiciones del edicto de los alumbrados. Autores y calificadores' in: *Cuadernos de Investigación Histórica*, 1, 1977, pp. 23-36.

14. Proceso de Alcaraz, fo. 367v.

15. Selke, *Ortiz*, p. 232.

16. Ibid., pp. 246-9.

17. Proceso de Alcaraz, fo. 93v.

18. Selke, *Ortiz*, p. 236.

19. Proceso de Alcaraz, fos. 57v., 77r.

20. Proceso de Alcaraz, fo. 93v.

21. 'Que estando en el dexamiento no avían de obrar porque no pusiessen obstáculo a lo que Dios quisiesse obrar y que se desocupassen de todas las cosas criadas e que aun pensar en la humanidad de Christo estorvaba el dexamiento en Dios; e que desechassen todos los pensamientos que se les ofreciessen aunque fuessen buenos, porque a sólo

Dios debían buscar; e que era mérito el trabaxo que en desechar los tales pensamientos se tenía; y que estando en aquella quietud por no distraerse tenía por tentación acordarse de Dios.' (Márquez, *Alumbrados*, p. 232).

22. Selke, *Ortiz*, p. 175.

23. Ibid., p. 237; Longhurst, 'Proceso de Vergara', *CHE*, 27, 1958, p. 144.

24. Proceso de Alcaraz, fo. 39r.

25. *Proceso de María de Cazalla*, p. 116. For Ecija see below, pp. 59-60.

26. Proceso de Alcaraz, fo. 359r.

27. For Alcaraz's quotations of Hugh of Balma *see* Proceso de Alcaraz, fos. 166r., 189r., 196v., 200v., 203r. On Alcaraz as a mystic *see* Márquez, *Alumbrados*, pp. 119-35, 199, 213.

28. Proceso de Alcaraz, fos. 32r., 172r., 355r.

29. Ibid., fos. 115v., 117v., 385r.

30. *Proceso de Beteta*, pp. 66-7.

31. Proceso de Alcaraz, fos. 32v.-35r.; 163r.-167v., 172r., 178r., 179r., 185r., 291r. On Alcaraz and the *Imitation of Christ* cf. Alastair Hamilton, 'A recent study in Spanish Mysticism', *HeyJ*, 18, 1977, pp. 191-9, esp. pp. 196-7.

32. *Tercer abecedario*, pp. 380, 384.

33. *Proceso de María de Cazalla*, pp. 99, 110, 119, 223.

34. Proceso de Alcaraz, fos. 7r., 56r.-58r. Attention is rightly drawn to Alcaraz's use of the Johannine Epistles by José C. Nieto, *Juan de Valdés and the Origins of the Spanish and Italian Reformation*, Genève 1970, pp. 63-97.

35. Proceso de Alcaraz, fos. 5r., 19r.-20v., 415v.

36. Ibid., fos. 3r.-6v., 112r.

37. Cf. Angela Selke de Sánchez (=Angela Sánchez Barbudo), *Algunos aspectos de la vida religiosa en la España del siglo XVI: los Alumbrados de Toledo*, unpublished PhD thesis, University of Wisconsin, 1953, p. 92.

38. Proceso de Alcaraz, fo. 4v.

39. Ibid., fos. 14r.-15v.

40. Ibid., fos. 431r.-433v.

41. Ibid., fos. 388r.-390v.

42. *Tratado llamado Excelencias de la fe . . .*, Burgos 1537, sig. Llr.-v.

43. Fermín Caballero, *Conquenses ilustres II. Vida del Illmo. Melchor Cano*, Madrid 1871, p. 541.

44. Proceso de Alcaraz, fos. 114r.-v.

45. Ibid., fos. 60v., 102r.-103v.

46. Ibid., fo. 22v.

47. Ibid., fos. 7r., 56r.-58r.

48. *Proceso de María de Cazalla*, pp. 109, 125, 390, 399-400.

49. For a discussion of the term see Eva-Maria Jung, 'On the nature of Evangelism in sixteenth-century Italy' in: *Journal of the History of Ideas*, 14, 1953, pp. 511-27.

50. This important discovery was made by Carlos Gilly, 'Juan de Valdés, pp. 273-80. See below p. 80.

51. Cf. J.C. Nieto, *Juan de Valdés*.

52. *Diálogo de Doctrina Christiana y el Salterio*, ed. Domingo Ricart, México 1964, p. 48.

53. Ibid., p. 113.

54. Ibid., p. 76.

55. Cf. Massimo Firpo, *Tra alumbrados e "spirituali": Studi su Juan de Valdés e il valdesianesimo nella crisi religiosa del '500 italiano*, Firenze 1990, pp. 43-84.

56. Cf. the comments on 'inchoate evangelical movements' in northern Europe in Alastair Duke, *Reformation and Revolt in the Low Countries*, London 1990, pp. 1-28.

Chapter III. Tradition and Discussion. pp. 43-50

1. 'Que tenía sospecha que tenían el amor de Dios en ellos por el mismo Dios e que hazían
   burla de quien andaba por méritos o dezía por más merescer hago esto o lo otro
   teniendo ellos por cierto que quien estubiera en lo que ellos estaban hubiera todo
   mérito, e diziendo una persona que abía más mersecimientos en unas personas que en
   otras, dixo, O, quién no oyesse este más o menos' (Prop. 34) According to the
   qualification: 'dezir que alguno puede venir a tan gran perfección que no pueda más
   merescer es proposición condenada por la yglesia contra los vegardos.' The other
   proposition, no. 43, is 'Diziendo cierta persona que su intención era servir a Dios e
   hazer penitencia e guardar sus mandamientos, dizo que no estaba en aquello la summa
   perfección'. The qualification runs: 'Esta proposición es herrónea y herética, condenada
   en otro tiempo contra los vegardos'. (Márquez, *Alumbrados*, pp. 236-7). For the text
   of the bull *Ad nostrum* see H. Denzinger & A. Schönmetzer S.J., *Enchiridion
   Symbolorum*, Freiburg-Roma 1967[34], p. 282.
2. Proceso de Alcaraz, fos. 376r.-377r.
3. Cf. Robert E. Lerner, *The Heresy of the Free Spirit in the Later Middle Ages*, Berkeley
   1972, for a revision of the accepted view of the Beghards. *See also* Herbert Grundmann,
   Religiöse Bewegungen im Mittelalter, repr. Hildesheim 1961.
4. J.M. Pou y Martí, *Visionarios*, pp. 34-110; Eugenio Asensio, 'El erasmismo y las
   corrientes espirituales afines' in: *RFE*, 36, 1952, pp. 31-99, esp. pp. 75-6. See also
   Marcelino Menéndez Pelayo, *Historia de los Heterodoxos Españoles*, 2 vols, (*BAC*
   150-1), Madrid 1965-7, I, pp. 516-25.
5. Livarius Oliger, O.F.M., *De secta spiritus libertati in Umbria saec. XIV: Disquisitio et
   documenta*, Roma 1943.
6. *Proceso de Bivar*, pp. 30-1.
7. For accounts of his career, beliefs and statements see Juan de M. Carrianzo, 'Precursores
   españoles de la Reforma: los herejes de Durango (1442-1445)' in: *Actas y Memorias
   de la Sociedad Española de Antropología, Etnografía y Prehistoria*, 4, 1925, pp. 35-
   69; and above all Dario Cabanelas, O.F.M., 'Un Franciscano heterodoxo en la
   Granada Nasrí: Fray Alfonso de Mella' in: *Al-Andalus*, 15, 1950, pp. 233-50.
8. Cf. Friederich Stegmüller, 'Pedro de Osma. Ein Beitrag zur spanischen Universitäts-,
   Konzils- und Ketzergeschichte' in: *Römische Quartalschrift für christliche
   Altertumskunde und für Kirchengeschichte*, 43, 1935, pp. 205-66.
9. *Proceso de Bivar*, pp. 24, 27, 59-60, 69-70.
10. The whole matter is discussed in a note by John E. Longhurst, 'Proceso de Vergara',
    CHE, 27, 1958, p. 161.
11. For suggestions of his implication *see* Márquez, *Alumbrados*, p. 62 and Milagros
    Ortega Costa, s.v. Cazalla in: *Diccionario de Historia Eclesiastica de España*, Madrid
    1972, p. 394, who provides biographical details.
12. Cf. Bataillon, *Erasme*, I, pp. 69-75; II, pp. 44-5.
13. Proceso de Alcaraz, fos. 42v., 49v., 209v.-211v., 236r., 428v.
14. Cf. ibid., fos. 188v., 282v.; Selke, *Ortiz*, pp. 244-5; Longhurst, 'Proceso de Vergara',
    CHE, 27, 1958, p. 138; Bataillon, *Erasme*, I, pp. 200-1, 228-9.
15. Cf. E. Asensio, 'El erasmismo', p. 77, who gives as a source the Master of Sentences.
    Peter Lombard, however, was a far more distant source for the *alumbrados* than Juan
    de Cazalla.
16. The text, together with its influence on the *alumbrados*, is studied by I.S. Révah, *Une
    source de la spiritualité péninsulaire au XVIème siècle: la 'Théologie Naturelle' de
    Raymond Sebond*, Lisboa 1953. Cf. also the introduction to Juan de Cazalla, *Lumbre
    del alma*, ed. J. Martínez Bujanda, Madrid 1974, pp. 11-44.
17. *Lumbre del alma*, pp. 121-4.

18. Cf. Roger Boase, *The Troubadour Revival. A Study of Social Change and Traditionalism in Late Medieval Spain*, London 1978.

19. Cf. Charles F. Fraker, Jr., 'The "Dejados" and the *Cancionero de Baena*' in *HispR*, 33, 1965, pp. 97-117.

20. *Cancionero de Juan Alfonso de Baena*, ed. José María Azaceta, 3 vols, Madrid 1966, II, pp. 519-20, 523, 528, 552-3; III, pp. 1018-22, 1060. Cf. also Charles F. Fraker, Jr., 'The theme of predestination in the *Cancionero de Baena*' in: *BHS*, 51, pp. 228-43.

21. Cf. Francisco Márquez Villanueva, *Investigaciones sobre Juan Alvarez Gato*, Madrid 1960.

22. Juan Alvarez Gato, *Obras completas*, ed. J.A. Rodríguez, Madrid 1928, pp. 175, 181-3, 207-10.

23. *Cancionero de diversas obras de nuevo trobadas*, Sevilla 1537, fos. 17v., 75v. On Montesino see Marcel Bataillon, 'Chanson pieuse et poésie de dévotion. Fr. Ambrosio Montesino' in: *BHisp*, 27, 1925, pp. 228-38.

24. Cf. Michèle Gendreau-Massaloux, 'Des *Quinquagenas* aux *Quatrocientas Respuestas*, Fray Luis de Escobar Témoin du XVIe siècle espagnol' in: *Les cultures ibériques en devenir. Essais publiés en hommage à la mémoire de Marcel Bataillon (1895-1977)*, Paris 1979, pp. 171-80.

25. *Quinquagenas*, Valladolid 1526, fos. 71r.-v.

26. Ibid., fos. 35r.-49v.

27. Proceso de Alcaraz, fo. 69v.

28. The inquisitors seem to have been reluctant to approach the higher nobility in this period. When María de Cazalla gave the name of the Duchess of Infantado as a witness in her defence the inquisitors crossed it out (*Proceso de María de Cazalla*, p. 273). Nevertheless, in 1538 the fourth Duke's eldest son, the Count of Saldaña, was fined for blasphemy after appearing spontaneously before the inquisitor Vaguer (J.-P. Dedieu, *L'Administration de la foi*, p. 267).

Chapter IV. The First Arrests. pp. 50-63

1. Proceso de Alcaraz, fos. 41r.-42r.

2. *Records of the Trials of the Spanish Inquisition in Ciudad Real*, ed. Haim Beinart, 4 vols, Jerusalem 1974-85, II, pp. 240-319.

3. Proceso de Alcaraz, fos. 266v., 367v.

4. *Proceso de María de Cazalla*, pp. 63-5, 356-7.

5. Proceso de Alcaraz, fos. 48v., 49r., 187r., 226r., 227r.-v., 264r.-265r.

6. The first major study on Francisca Hernández was Edward Boehmer, *Francisca Hernández und Frai Francisco Ortiz. Anfänge reformatorischer Bewegungen in Spanien unter Kaiser Karl V*, Leipzig 1865, now superseded by Selke, *Ortiz*.

7. Proceso de Ortiz, fos. 228v., 243r., 245r.-246v.

8. See Angela Selke de Sánchez, 'El caso del Bachiller Antonio de Medrano, iluminado epicúreo del siglo XVI' in: *BHisp*, 58, 1956, pp. 393-420.

9. Proceso de Alcaraz, fos. 42r.-43v., 53r.-55v., 60r.

10. By Márquez, *Alumbrados*, pp. 64, 170.

11. Cf. J.H. Elliott, *Imperial Spain 1469-1716*, Harmondsworth 1990[3], pp. 135-59.

12. Layna Serrano, *Historia de Guadalajara*, III, pp. 71-5.

13. The following trials were in progress: AHN, Inquisición de Toledo, Leg. 137, no. 13; Leg. 150, no. 12; Leg. 156, no. 2; Leg. 157, no. 4; Leg. 158, no. 9; Leg. 159, no. 15; Leg. 165, no. 7; Leg. 173, no. 1; Leg. 203, no. 1. Cf. Inquisición, Libro 572, fos. 331r.-49v.

14. The interrogation by Mendoza is mentioned in Proceso de Alcaraz, fos. 22r., 22v., 23v., 98r., 187r., 213r., 357r. According to one witness (fo. 98r.) Mendoza told Alcaraz that if he wanted to be devout he should take a crucifix to his room and be devout there and nowhere else.

15. Proceso de Alcaraz, fo. 51r.

16. Ibid., fo. 187r.

17. Ibid., fo. 359r.

18. Ibid., fos. 278v., 280v,; Selke, *Ortiz*, p. 194; Longhurst, 'Proceso de Vergara', *CHE*, 27, 1958, p. 143.

19. *Proceso de María de Cazalla*, pp. 87-8, 100.

20. Proceso de Alcaraz, fos. 68r.-69v.

21. Ibid., fos. 63r., 68v.

22. Ibid., fos. 9v.-10r., 279r., 281r.

23. Ibid., fo. 1r.

24. The Franciscans seem to have been 'subjected absolutely to the inquisitor-general' by a brief of 16 June 1525. H.C. Lea, *A History of the Inquisition of Spain*, 4 vols, New York 1906-7, II, p. 32.

25. Proceso de Alcaraz, fo. 279r.

26. Lucas Wadding, *Annales Minorum ab origines Ordinis ad annum 1540*, 25 vols, Roma 1731-1886, XVI, pp. 237-8.

27. Proceso de Alcaraz, fo. 10r.

28. L. Wadding, *Annales*, XVI, p. 217. Cf. Selke, *Ortiz*, p. 230.

29. The arrest of Alcaraz took place in the convent of Santa Clara in Toledo. Cf. *Proceso de Beteta*, p. 129, and the first unnumbered folio of Alcaraz's own trial.

30. Proceso de Alcaraz, fo. 259r. This was not the first time that Don Diego interceded on behalf of a victim of the Inquisition. In 1517 he appears to have tried to secure the release of the *converso* surgeon Maestro Juan Serrano sentenced to perpetual reclusion as a Judaizer. The marquess also interceded on behalf of Rodrigo Alvarez who was absolved of his penances at the marquess's request on 28 August 1529 (AHN, Inquisición, Libro 573, fo. 114v.).

31. Proceso de Alcaraz, fo. 262r.

32. Proceso de Alcaraz, fos. 366r.-368v.; *Proceso de María de Cazalla*, pp. 469-72, 454-6. On the reluctance with which the Inquisition resorted to torture see Bartolomé Bennassar, 'L'Inquisition ou la pédagogie de la peur' in: *L'Inquisition espagnole XVe-XIXe siècle*, ed. Bartolomé Bennassar, Paris 1979, pp. 104-12.

33. Proceso de Alcaraz, fo. 7r.

34. *Proceso de María de Cazalla*, pp. 542-61.

35. Proceso de Alcaraz, fos. 445r.-451r.

36. Ibid., fos. 458r.v., 460r.-v.

37. AHN, Inquisición, Libro 573, fo. 168r.

38. *Proceso de María de Cazalla*, p. 254.

39. Ibid., pp. 497-504.

40. *Proceso de Beteta*, pp. 177-8.

41. *Proceso de Bivar*, pp. 107-17.

42. Proceso de Alcaraz, fo. 341r.

43. E.g. the trial of Juan Serrano (see above n. 30), which lasted from 1515 to 1520 and in which both Cardinal Cisneros and Adrian of Utrecht intervened in order to obtain Serrano's release.

44. Proceso de Alcaraz, fos. 376r.-377r., 380r.-382r.

45. Ibid., fos. 374v.-375r., 378r.-379v.

46. *Tratado llamado Excelencias de la Fe*, sig. D1r.

Chapter V. The *Alumbrados* between Two Heresies. pp. 65-75

1. Cf. Jean-Pierre Dedieu, 'Les quatre temps de l'Inquisition' in: *L'Inquisition espagnole XVe-XIXe siècle*, pp. 13-39; id., 'The archives of the Holy Office of Toledo as a source

for historical anthropology' in: *The Inquisition in Early Modern Europe. Studies on Sources and Methods*, ed. Gustav Henningsen & John Tedeschi, Dekalb (Ill.) 1986, pp. 158-89.

2. *Records of ... Ciudad Real*, I, p. xix.

3. This idea prompted Hernando de Talavera to write his *Católica impugnación* in 1478. See the introduction to Fray Hernando de Talavera, O.S.H., *Católica impugnación*, ed. Francisco Martín Hernández, Barcelona 1961.

4. H.C. Lea, *A History of the Inquisition of Spain*, I, p. 125.

5. *Records of ... Ciudad Real*, IV, p. 41 *passim*.

6. Ibid., III, pp. 1-302.

7. For a brief survey see Antonio Domínguez Ortiz, *Los Judeoconversos*.

8. Albert A. Sicroff, *Les Controverses des estatuts de 'pureté de sang' en Espagne du XVe au XVIIe siècle*, Paris 1960, pp. 79-87, 90, 96-139.

9. *Proceso de María de Cazalla*, p. 101; *Proceso de Alcaraz*, fos. 3r.-4r. *Proceso de Beteta*, pp. 110-12; *Proceso de Bivar*, pp. 37, 57, 93.

10. Marcel Bataillon, 'Les nouveaux-chrétiens de Ségovie en 1510', *BHisp*, 58, 1956, pp. 207-31.

11. AHN, Inquisición de Toledo, Leg. 156, no. 2.

12. AHN, Inquisición de Toledo, Leg. 165, no. 7.

13. AHN, Inquisición de Toledo, Leg. 165, no. 5. To these we can add Leg. 144, no. 5, the trial of Elvira de Ayala, whose husband worked for the Duke of Infantado and who was arrested in error in 1516 and Leg. 173, no. 13, the trial of Luis Alvarez's son-in-law Juan de Pastrana.

14. Proceso de Ortiz, fo. 232v.

15. For examples of such prophecies see Fritz Baer, *Die Juden im christlichen Spanien*, 2 vols, Berlin 1929-36, II, pp. 513-5, 528-42.

16. For *conversos* charged with blasphemy rather than Judaizing by the tribunal of Toledo between 1510 and 1530 see AHN, Inquisición de Toledo, Leg. 43, no. 26; Leg. 44, no. 10 and Leg. 47, no. 51; for *conversos* tried for uttering 'scandalous words' see Leg 199, no. 25 and Leg. 205, no. 40; and for defending 'heretical propositions' see Leg. 222, no. 6.

17. All these propositions occur in the following trials judged by the Tribunal of Toledo between 1510 and 1540 and conducted by the same inquisitors who conducted the *alumbrado* trials: AHN, Inquisición de Toledo, Leg. 131, no. 14; Leg. 132, no. 2; Leg. 133, no. 19; Leg. 137, nos 13, 20; Leg. 138, no. 1; Leg. 143, no. 19; Leg. 147, no. 12; Leg. 150, no. 9; Leg. 155, no. 3; Leg. 160, no. 9; Leg. 162, no. 5; Leg. 165, no. 13; Leg. 167, nos 6-8; Leg. 171, no. 2; Leg. 172, no. 5; Leg. 175, nos 2-6; Leg. 178, no. 10; Leg. 179, no. 1; Leg. 181, no. 13; Leg. 183, no. 9; Leg. 184, no. 4; Leg. 185, nos 1, 18.

18. AHN, Inquisición de Toledo, Leg. 203, no. 9.

19. Giornata terza, novella decima: 'Alibech divien romita, a cui Rustico monaco insegna rimettere il diavolo in inferno ... '

20. Proceso de Ortiz, fo. 203v.

21. Proceso de Alcaraz, fos. 14r.-15v.

22. Ibid., fos. 18r., 23v.

23. Ibid., fo. 164v.

24. Ibid., fo. 332r.

25. Ibid., fo. 91v.

26. Selke, *Ortiz*, pp. 36, 64-6.

27. The best study of Luther's early influence in Spain, on which the following reconstruction is based, remains A. Redondo, 'Luther et l'Espagne de 1520 à 1536', *Mélanges de la Casa de Velazquez*, 1, 1965, pp. 109-65. See also John E. Longhurst, *Luther's Ghost in Spain (1517-1546)*, Lawrence (Kansas) 1969. Referring to the years

before 1520 the humanist Juan de Vergara later said: 'no abia ni podia aber en España
notiçia particular de las opiniones de Lutero: ni libro de sus errores: porque a la sazon
començava la secta en Alemaña e solamente en España se sonava una fama general
de un hereje que en Alemaña se levantava'. (Longhurst, 'Proceso de Vergara', (*CHE*,
31-2, 1960, pp. 327, 339).

28. Longhurst, 'Proceso de Vergara', *CHE*, 28, 1958, p. 158; 31-32, 1960, p. 355.
29. *Proceso de Beteta*, p. 70.
30. Proceso de Alcaraz, fos. 14r.-15v. On the *alumbrados* and Lutheranism see
Angela Selke de Sánchez, 'Algunos datos nuevos sobre los primeros alumbrados:
El edicto de 1525 y su relación con el proceso de Alcaraz' in: *BHisp*, 54, 1952, pp.
125-52; José C. Nieto, *Juan de Valdés*, pp. 63-97.
31. Proceso de Alcaraz, fos. 36v.-39r.
32. Ibid., fos. 399r.-v.
33. Cf. José Luis G. Novalín, *El Inquisidor General Fernando de Valdés (1483-1568)*,
2 vols, Oviedo 1968-71, I, p. 40; Milagros Ortega Costa, 'San Ignacio de Loyola
en el *Libro de los alumbrados*; nuevos dates sobre su primer proceso, in: *Arbor*, 107,
1980, pp. 23-4, esp. pp. 25-6.
34. Cf. Alastair Hamilton, 'An episode in Castilian Illuminism: The case of Martín
Cota' in: *HeyJ*, 17, 1976, pp. 413-27.
35. Proceso de Alcaraz, fos. 400r.-402r.
36. J.L.G. Novalín, *El Inquisidor General Fernando de Valdés*, II, pp. 215-21. See
below p. 106.

Chapter VI. Humanism Attacked. pp. 77-89

1. *A Dialogue between Reginald Pole and Thomas Lupset*, ed. K.M. Burton, London
1948, pp. 128-9.
2. On Erasmus's relations with Spain in this period see Bataillon, *Erasme*, I, pp. 77-109;
II, pp. 47-54.
3. Quoted in ibid., I, p. 134. On Zúñiga and Erasmus see the introduction to Erasmus,
Apologia respondens ad ea quae I.L. Stunica taxaverat (= *Opera omnia Des. Erasmi
Roterodami* IX-2), ed. H.J. de Jonge, Amsterdam 1983, pp. 3-49. Cf. also Erika
Rummel, *Erasmus and his Catholic Critics 1515-1536*, 2 vols, Nieuwkoop 1989, I,
pp. 145-77.
4. Erasmus, *Opus Epistolarum*, ed. P.S. Allen, 11 vols, Oxford 1906-58, VII, pp. 244-5
(Ep. 1904).
5. Cf. Miguel Avilés, *Erasmo y la Inquisición (El libelo de Valladolid y la Apología de
Erasmo contra los frailes españoles)*, Madrid 1980.
6. Proceso de Alcaraz, fos. 338r.-v.
7. Cf. C. Gilly, 'Juan de Valdés', pp. 273-80.
8. Cf. Angela Selke de Sánchez, 'Vida y muerte de Juan López de Celain' in: *BHisp*, 62,
1960, pp. 136-62.
9. Cf. Alastair Hamilton, 'A Flemish "Erasmian" in the Spain of Charles V: the case of
Ana del Valle' in: *BHR*, 41, 1979, pp. 567-73.
10. *Proceso de Beteta*, pp. 93-4. According to Mari Ramírez, Francisca Hernández's
maid, 'el señor almirante los tenia alli pensando que eran muy buenas personas e que
despues que vido que era cosa del diablo los echó de alli.'
11. Cf. R. Emmet McLaughlin, *Caspar Schwenckfeld, Reluctant Radical: His Life to
1540*, New Haven-London 1986, pp. 23-4.
12. *Proceso de Bivar*, pp. 35-6, 51-2.
13. Cf. AHN, Inquisición de Granada, Leg. 2604, caja 1.
14. See John E. Longhurst, 'The Alumbrados of Toledo: Juan del Castillo and the

Lucenas' in: *ARG.*, 45, 1954, pp. 233-53.

15. Cf. A. Redondo, 'Luther et l'Espagne', p. 153.

16. Selke, *Ortiz*, p. 33.

17. Longhurst, 'Proceso de Vergara', *CHE*, 27, 1958, pp. 127-30.

18. *See* A. Selke de Sánchez, 'El caso del Bachiller Antonio de Medrano' for a reconstruction of his life and trials.

19. Proceso de Medrano, fo. 11v.

20. Selke, *Ortiz*, pp. 207-8.

21. Proceso de Medrano, fos. 200r.-203v.; 205r.

22. Ibid., fos. 262r.-272v.

23. Longhurst, 'Proceso de Vergara', *CHE*, 27, 1958, pp. 127-39.

24. For the Vergara family see *Contemporaries of Erasmus. A Biographical register of the Renaissance and Reformation*, ed. Peter G. Bietenholz & Thomas B. Deutscher, 3 vols, Toronto 1985-7, III, pp. 338-9, 383-7.

25. Longhurst, 'Proceso de Vergara', *CHE*, 28, 1958, pp. 154, 161; 31-2, 1960, pp. 335, 342; 35-6, 1962, p. 356. Cf. Bataillon, *Erasme*, I, pp. 473-508; II, pp. 144-50.

26. Bataillon, *Erasme*, I, pp. 514-22; II, pp. 151-3.

27. Henry De Vocht, *Monumenta Humanistica Lovaniensia*, 2 vols, Louvain-London 1934, II, p. 435. Cf. Bataillon, *Erasme*, I, p. 529; II, p. 156.

28. Bataillon, *Erasme*, I, p. 541; II, p. 166.

29. *Proceso de María de Cazalla*, pp. 127-30.

30. Ibid., pp. 80, 88, 118.

31. Ibid., pp. 105-20.

32. Proceso de Medrano, fos. 276v., 280r., 293r., 300r., 304r., 305r.

33. Selke, *Ortiz*, pp. 363-82.

34. Cf. J. Goñi Gaztambide, 'El impresor Miguel de Eguía procesado por la Inquisición (c. 1495-1546)', in: *HispSac*, 1, 1948, pp. 35-88.

35. *Las causas y raçones de la contradiçion del estatuto de Toledo* (University of Salamanca, Ms. 455, fos. 70-87) is discussed in A.A. Sicroff, *Les Controverses*, p. 118. The *Tratado de las ocho questiones del templo, propuestos por el Illustrissimo señor Duque del Infantadgo, y responsidas por el doctor Vergara, Canonigo de Toledo* was published in Toledo in 1552. For Vergara's sentence *see* Longhurst, 'Proceso de Vergara', *CHE*, 37-8, 1963, pp. 356-71.

36. Longhurst, 'Proceso de Vergara', *CHE*, 28, 1958, pp. 117-18.

37. Cf. Vicente Beltrán de Heredia, O.P., 'Documentos inéditos acerca del proceso del erasmista Alonso de Virués' in: *Boletín de la Biblioteca Menéndez y Pelayo*, 17, 1935, pp. 242-57.

Chapter VII. The Fear of Novelty. pp. 91-114

1. Proceso de Alcaraz, fos. 400r.-402v.

2. Extracts from the censor's report are reproduced in Alfonso de Valdés, *Diálogo de Mercurio y Carón*, ed. José F. Montesinos, Madrid 1954, pp. 241-6.

3. Cf. Luis Fernández, 'Iñigo Loyola y los alumbrados' in: *HispSac*, 35, 1983, pp. 585-680, esp. pp. 617-23.

4. Cf. John E. Longhurst, 'Saint Ignatius at Alcalá 1526-1527' in: *AHSJ*, 26, 1957, pp. 252-6.

5. Milagros Ortega Costa, 'San Ignacio de Loyola', pp. 32-3.

6. Cf. the editor's account in San Ignacio de Loyola, *Obras completas*, ed. I. Iparraguirre (BAC 86), Madrid 1963, pp. 179-85.

7. Cf. the comments of E. Allison Peers, *Studies of the Spanish Mystics*, 3 vols, London 1926-60, I, pp. 11-12; III, pp. 175-7.

8. For the trials at Alcalá see *MHSJ, Monumenta Ignatiana, Series Quarta, Scripta de Sancto Ignatio de Loyola*, I, Madrid 1904, pp. 598-623; cf. M. Ortega Costa, 'San Ignacio Loyola', pp. 23-31.

9. On this charge see Ricardo García Villoslada, S.J., *Loyola y Erasmo, dos almas, dos epocas*, Madrid 1965, p. 114.

10. The event is recounted in Loyola's 'autobiography', *MHSJ, vol. 66, Monumenta Ignatiana, Series Quarta, Scripta de Sancto Ignatio*, I, Roma 1943, pp. 452-60. Cf. Vicente Beltrán de Heredia, O.P., 'Estancia de San Ignacio de Loyola en San Esteban de Salamanca' in: *CTom*, 83, 1956, pp. 507-28.

11. Victoriano Larrañaga, S.J., 'La revisión total de los Ejercicios por San Ignacio ¿en París, o en Roma?' in: *AHSJ*, 25, 1956, pp. 396-415.

12. Marcello Del Piazzo & C. de Dalmases, S.J., 'Il processo sull'ortodossia di S. Ignazio e dei suoi compagni svoltosi a Roma nel 1538' in: *AHSJ*, 38, 1969, pp. 431-53.

13. On Miguel (or Cristóbal) de Torres *see* C. Gilly, *Juan de Valdés*, pp. 290-5. On Manuel de Miona and hostility towards the Jesuits *see* Marcel Bataillon, 'D'Erasme à la Compagnie de Jésus' in: Bataillon, *Erasme*, III, pp. 279-304.

14. A.A. Sicroff, *les Controverses*, pp. 270-90.

15. ARSJ, Persecutiones Fratrum 1576-1608, fos. 3v., 6v. Cano also referred to Loyola's arrest and flight to Rome in a letter dated 28 March 1556 (F. Caballero, *Vida*, p. 500). For Cano's persecution of the Society of Jesus in Spain *see* Antonio Astrain, S.J., *Historia de la Compañía de Jesús en la Asistencia de España*, 7 vols, Madrid 1902-25, III, pp. 54-65; M. Andrés, *Los recogidos*, pp. 450-5.

16. J.A. de Polanco, *MHSJ, Vita Ignatii Loiolae et rerum Societatis Jesu Historia*, Madrid 1895, pp. 503-24.

17. ARSJ, Persecutiones Fratrum 1567-1608, fo. 59r.

18. John of Avila's life is recounted by Luis Sala Balust in the introduction to San Juan de Avila, *Obras completas, I, Biografía. Audi, filia 1556 y 1574*, ed. Luis Sala Balust & Francisco Martín Hernández, (*BAC* 302), Madrid 1970. On John of Avila as a mystic *see* M. Andrés, *Los recogidos*, pp. 668-88.

19. The surviving documents concerning the trial are published in C.M. Abad, S.J., 'El proceso de la Inquisición contra el Beato Juan de Avila' in *Miscelanea Comillas*, 6, 1946, pp. 97-167. Cf. also Marcel Bataillon, 'Jean d'Avila retrouvé' in: *BHisp*, 57, 1955, pp. 5-44.

20. Juan de Avila, *Obras completas, V, Epistolario*, ed. Luis Sala Balust & Francisco Martín Hernández, (*BAC* 313), Madrid 1970, p. 26.

21. Ibid., pp. 24, 38, 777-90.

22. Ibid., pp. 573-6.

23. Ibid., p. 260.

24. Ibid., p. 52.

25. Ibid., p. 750.

26. *Audi, filia* in *Obras completas*, I, p. 496. Cf. p. 682.

27. *Obras completas*, V, p. 636.

28. *Obras completas*, I, pp. 108-94.

29. V. Beltrán de Heredia, O.P., 'Los alumbrados de la diócesis de Jaén. Un capitulo inédito de la historia de nuestra espiritualidad' in: *RET*, 9, 1949, pp. 161-222, 445-88, esp. pp. 181-3.

30. Juan de Avila, *Obras completas*, I, pp. 144, 343-56.

31. Cf. Ugo Rozzo & Silvana Seidel Menchi, 'Livre et Réforme en Italie' in: *La Réforme et le livre: L'Europe de l'imprimé (1517-v.1570)*, ed. Jean-François Gilmont, Paris 1990, pp. 327-74.

32. For a survey of this situation *see* Dermot Fenlon, *Heresy and Obedience in Tridentine Italy: Cardinal Pole and the Counter Reformation*, Cambridge 1972.

33. Cf. M. Firpo, *Tra alumbrados e "spirituali"*, pp. 127-53.

34. Cf. William Monter, *Frontiers of Heresy: The Spanish Inquisition from the Basque Lands to Sicily*, Cambridge 1990, pp. 231-52.

35. The standard study on the subject is still Ernst Schäfer, *Beiträge zur Geschichte des spanischen Protestantismus und der Inquisition im sechzehnten Jahrhundert*, 3 vols, Gütersloh 1902. For Valladolid see I, pp. 233-344, and Seville, I, pp. 345-400. Cf. also Bataillon, *Erasme*, I, pp. 560-87, II, pp. 175-88. For further literature *see* A. Gordon Kinder, *Spanish Protestants and Reformers*.

36. On Pedro de Cazalla's relationship with María see *Proceso de María de Cazalla*, p. 92. As the editor points out, Pedro is sometimes referred to as María's brother, but she does not mention him in her genealogy.

37. Cf. A. Gordon Kinder, 'Le livre et les idées réformées en Espagne' in: *La Réforme et le livre*, pp. 301-26, esp. pp. 314-22.

38. This is stressed by J. Ignacio Tellechea Idígoras, 'El protestantismo castellano (1558-1559): Un *topos* (M. Bataillon) convertido en tópico historiográfico' in: *El Erasmismo en España*, ed. M. Revuelta Sañudo & C. Morón Arroyo, Santander 1986, pp. 305-21.

39. A point clearly made by A. Gordon Kinder, *Casiodoro de Reina, Spanish Reformer of the Sixteenth Century*, London 1975.

40. J.L.G. Novalín, *El Inquisidor General Fernando de Valdés*, II, pp. 215-21.

41. Cf. E. Schäfer, *Beiträge*, I, p. 291; III, pp. 730-7.

42. Huerga, *Alumbrados*, II, pp. 122-3.

43. For Carranza's life *see* J. Ignacio Tellechea Idígoras, *El arzobispo Carranza y su tiempo*, 2 vols, Madrid 1968. Carranza's trial is published in *Fray Bartolomé Carranza, Documentos históricos*, ed. J. Ignacio Tellechea Idígoras, Madrid 1962 ff.

44. J. Ignacio Tellechea Idígoras, 'Textos inéditos sobre el fenómeno de los alumbrados' in: *Ephemerides Carmeliticae*, 13, 1962, pp. 768-74.

45. Cf. Anthony Grafton, 'Inventions of Traditions and Traditions of Invention in Renaissance Europe: The Strange Case of Annius of Viterbo' in: *The Transmission of Culture in Early Modern Europe*, ed. Anthony Grafton & Ann Blair, Philadelphia 1990, pp. 8-38, esp. p. 27.

46. *Fray Bartolomé Carranza, Documentos hisóricos*, 2-I, pp. 264-6.

47. Cano's criticisms are published in F. Caballero, *Vida*, pp. 536-615. Cf. J. Ignacio Tellechea Idígoras, 'Melchor Cano y Bartolomé Carranza, dos Dominicos frente a frente' in: *HispSac*, 15, 1962, pp. 5-89; Antonio Márquez, 'Origen y caracterización del iluminismo (según un parecer de Melchor Cano)' in: *Revista de Occidente*, 21, 1968, pp. 320-33.

48. *Comentarios sobre el Catechismo christiano*, ed. José Ignacio Tellechea Idígoras, 2 vols, *(BAC Maior 1-2)*, Madrid 1972, I, pp. 131-2.

49. F. Caballero, *Vida*, pp. 536-7, 544-54.

50. Ibid., pp. 572-8.

51. Ibid., pp. 582-9, 592-9.

52. Alvaro Huerga, *Fray Luis de Granada: Una vida al servicio de la Iglesia*, *(BAC 496)*, Madrid 1988, pp. 146-52.

53. F. Caballero, *Vida*, pp. 593, 597-8.

54. *Index de l'Inquisition Espagnole 1551, 1554, 1559* (= *Index des Livres Interdits*, V), ed. J.M. de Bujanda, Genève 1984, pp. 303-592, 625-86.

55. *Libro de la vida* in: Santa Teresa de Jesús, *Obras completas*, ed. Efrén de la Madre de Dios, O.C.D. & Otger Steggink, O. Carm., *(BAC 212)*, Madrid 1967, p. 117.

56. Cf. Bataillon, *Erasme*, pp. 759-67; II, pp. 290-301.

57. Cf. A.A. Sicroff, *Controverses*, pp. 145-8.

58. W.A. Christian, *Local Religion*, pp. 170-1; Huerga, *Alumbrados*, II, pp. 307-36.

59. *Aviso de gente recogida*, ed. Alvaro Huerga, Madrid 1977, pp. 312-35, 716-22.

60. Ibid., pp. 101, 810-19.
61. Huerga, *Alumbrados*, II, pp. 175-201.

Chapter VIII. The *Alumbrados* of Llerena and Seville. pp. 115-129

1. *See* Alvaro Huerga's introduction to Fray Luis de Granada, O.P., *Historia de Sor María de la Visitación y Sermón de las caídas públicas*, ed. B. Velado Graña, Barcelona 1962, pp. 3-112. On the changing attitude to visions, which were first investigated by the Inquisition at about the time of the first *alumbrado* trials see W.A. Chrstian, *Apparitions in Late Medieval and Renaissance Spain*, pp. 150-87.
2. Cf. H.C. Lea, *History of the Inquisition of Spain*, IV, pp. 81-94; V. Beltrán de Heredia, O.P., 'Un grupo de visionarios y pseudo-profetas que actúa durante los últimos años de Felipe II y repercusión de ello sobre la memoria de Santa Teresa' in: *RET*, 7, 1947, pp. 373-97, 483-534; Richard L. Kagan, *Lucrecia's Dreams: Politics and Prophecy in Sixteenth-Century Spain*, Berkeley (Cal.) 1990. The situation in the New World is examined in Huerga, *Alumbrados*, III.
3. *Diez lamentaciones del miserable estado de los ateistas de nuestros tiempos*, ed. Otger Steggink, O. Carm., Madrid 1959, pp. 174-5.
4. Huerga, *Alumbrados*, I, pp. 49-97.
5. Ibid., pp. 394-6, 417, 430.
6. Ibid., p. 349.
7. Ibid., p. 119.
8. Ibid., pp. 257-71, 515-39.
9. Ibid., pp. 174, 405.
10. Ibid., pp. 571-2. Cf. Beltrán de Heredia, 'Los alumbrados de la diócesis de Jaén', pp. 169-70.
11. *Vita della Beata Caterina Adorni da Genova*, Firenze 1589, pp. 11, 15, 17, 34, 61, 64-5, 102, 145, 149, 185.
12. Huerga, *Alumbrados*, I, pp. 373-7.
13. Ibid., pp. 114, 340.
14. Beltrán de Heredia, 'Los alumbrados de la diócesis de Jaén', pp. 164-5; Huerga, *Alumbrados*, I, pp. 148-9.
15. Ibid., pp. 272-8.
16. Ibid., p. 363.
17. Huerga, *Alumbrados*, II, pp. 215-58, 540-614; Beltrán de Heredia, 'Los alumbrados de la diócesis de Jaén', pp. 445-88.
18. Huerga, *Alumbrados*, IV, pp. 112-36; Enrique Llamas Martínez O.C.D., *Santa Teresa de Jesús y la Inquisición Española*, Madrid 1972, pp. 29-38, 53-219.
19. Ibid., pp. 29-32.
20. Published in ibid., pp. 395-433.
21. Ibid., pp. 396-7, 403-4, 409-10.
22. Ibid., pp. 401-3, 405, 407, 409, 416.
23. Ibid., pp. 434-5, 444-85.
24. Cf. Antonio Domínguez Ortiz, 'La Congregación de la Granada y la Inquisición de Sevilla (un episodio de la lucha contra los alumbrados)' in: *La Inquisición española: Nueva visión, nuevos horizontes*, ed. Joaquín Pérez Villanueva, Madrid 1980, pp. 637-46; Huerga, *Alumbrados*, IV, pp. 217-37.
25. Ibid., pp. 176-216.
26. The edict is published in Joseph de Guibert, S.J., *Documenta Ecclesiastica Christianae Perfectionis Studium Spectantia*, Roma 1931, pp. 229-40.
27. Huerga, *Alumbrados*, IV, p. 177.

28. Cf. Mary Elizabeth Perry, 'Beatas and the Inquisition in Early Modern Seville' in: *Inquisition and Society in Early Modern Europe*, ed. Stephen Haliczer, London 1987, pp. 147-68.

29. Huerga, *Alumbrados*, IV, p. 404.

30. Ibid., pp. 455-75.

31. Ibid., pp. 509-20.

32. Ibid., pp. 495-8.

33. Ibid., pp. 247-50.

34. Ibid., pp. 446-50.

35. Cf. José Deleito y Piñuela, *La vida religiosa española bajo el cuarto Felipe: santos y pecadores*, Madrid 1963, pp. 301-9.

36. Cf. Stephen Haliczer, *Inquisition and Society in the Kingdom of Valencia 1478-1834*, Berkeley (Cal.) 1990, pp. 277-9.

37. *Tercer abecedario*, pp. 594-5.

38. *Subída del Monte Sión*, pp. 321, 429.

39. *Obras completas*, p. 85.

40. Cf. E. Allison Peers, *Studies of the Spanish Mystics*, II, pp. 352-5, 380; III, pp. 12, 117, 208.

41. Quoted in M. Andrés, *Los recogidos*, p. 351.

42. E. Allison Peers, *Studies of the Spanish Mystics*, III, pp. 78, 144, 244.

43. Cf. Leszek Kolakowski, *Chrétiens sans Eglise. La conscience religieuse et le lien confessionel au XVIIe siècle*, Paris 1969, pp. 492-566; the introduction to Miguel de Molinos, *Guía espiritual*, ed. J. Ignacio Tellechea Idígoras, Madrid 1973, pp. 15-53.

44. Denzinger-Schönmetzer, *Enchiridion*, pp. 470-7.

45. Extracts are included in Miguel de Molinos, *Guía espiritual seguida de la Defensa de la Contemplación*, ed. José Angel Valente, Barcelona 1974, pp. 257-324.

46. Biblioteca Apostolica Vaticana, Ms. Vat. Lat. 8604, fo. 59r.

Conclusion. pp. 129-132

1. On the reception of Juan de Valdés cf. Domingo Ricart, *Juan de Valdés y el pensamiento religioso europeo en los siglos XVI y XVII*, México 1958, pp. 50-132; M. Firpo, *Tra alumbrados e "spirituali"*, pp. 84-103.

2. Cf. M. Bataillon, 'D'Erasme à la Compagnie de Jésus' in: Bataillon, *Erasme*, III, pp. 279-304.

3. Cf. M. Reeves, *The Influence of Prophecy in the Later Middle Ages*, pp. 274-90.

4. *Ejercicio de perfección y virtudes cristianas*, 3 vols, Barcelona 1889, I, pp. 220-3.

5. Cf. Louis Châtellier, *The Europe of the Devout: The Catholic Reformation and the Formation of a New Society*, Cambridge-Paris 1989; Christopher F. Black, *Italian Confraternities in the Sixteenth Century*, Cambridge 1989; Maureen Flynn, *Sacred Charity: Confraternities and Social Welfare in Spain, 1400-1700*, London 1989.

6. Cf. Alastair Hamilton, *The Family of Love*, Cambridge 1981, pp. 48-9, 117-19; Jean Dietz Moss, *"Godded with God": Hendrik Niclaes and His Family of Love*, Philadelphia 1981, pp. 23-6, 70-4. For a general survey of these and similar groups *see* George H. Williams, *The Radical Reformation*, London 1962.

Index

Acquaviva, Claudio, 97
Acuña, Juan de, Count of
  Buendía, 54
Admiral of Castile, *see*
  Enríquez, Fadrique
Ad nostrum (bull), 43
Adrian VI, Pope, *see*
  Adrian of Utrecht
Adrian of Utrecht, Cardinal
  (later Pope Adrian VI),
  53, 54-5, 71-2, 140
Alamín, Fray Félix, 127
Alba, Duke of, *see* Alvarez
  de Toledo, Fadrique
Albadán, Pedro de, 56
Alcalá de Henares, 10, 16,
  46, 52, 57, 93-5, 130-1
Alcalá de Henares,
  university of
  (Complutensian
  university), 2, 46, 47,
  102; founded, 11;
  alumbrado influence at,
  27, 53, 60; humanists
  suspected of Lutheran-
  ism and *alumbradismo*
  at, 40, 77, 78-9, 81-2,
  84-7, 91, 105, 106;
  Loyola and, 93-5; John
  of Avila at, 97
Alcaraz, *see* Ruiz de
  Alcaraz
Aldeanueva, 17
Aleander, Jerome, 72
Almendralejo, 118
Almorox, 50
alumbrado, passim., term
  defined, 1, 28; different
  meanings of, 2-3, 77, 83-
  4, 91-2, 113, 115-16,
  131-2; used by orthodox
  mystics as a bugbear,
  126-8
alumbrados of Baeza, 3,
  113

alumbrados of Jaén, 121
alumbrados of Llerena, 2-3,
  4-5, 97, 117-21, 123-4,
  126, 127, 131
alumbrados of Seville, 2-3,
  4-5, 123-6, 131
alumbrados of Toledo,
  passim., doctrine of, 1-2,
  27-42; careers and trials
  of, 25-7, 51-75, 87-9;
  compared with
  alumbrados of Llerena
  and Seville, 2-3, 116-17,
  120, 127, 131
Alvarez, Baltasar, 133
Alvarez, Hernando, 118-21
Alvarez, Luis, 68, 141
Alvarez, Rodrigo (Jesuit),
  123
Alvarez, Rodrigo
  (Judaizer), 140
Alvarez de Toledo,
  Fadrique, Duke of Alba,
  17
Alvarez Gato, Juan, 49
Amalric of Bena, 63
Anabaptists and
  Anabaptism, 29, 116,
  129, 131-2
Andalusia (*see also*
  alumbrados of Baeza,
  Jaén and Seville), 8, 26;
  alumbrados in, 2, 5, 113-
  14, 118, 121, 129, 131-2;
  John of Avila in, 97-8,
  102
Angela of Foligno, St, 13,
  26
Anghiera, Pietro Martire d',
  10
Annius of Viterbo, 108
Anselm, St, 29
antinomianism, 35-6, 45,
  83-4, 112, 114, 119-20,
  126, 131

Antwerp, 108
Arabs, 7
Aragon, 7, 8, 17, 44, 83
Aragón, Isabel de, 4th
  Duchess of Infantado
  (formerly Countess of
  Saldaña), 27, 47, 139
Aravalles, Fray Juan, 126
Arcos, Duke of, *see* Ponce
  de León, Luis Cristóbal
Arenas, Luisa, 93
Arias, Fray García, 100,
  107
Arnaldo de Vilanova, 18
Ascargota, Fray Juan de,
  127
Augustine, St, 29, 98
Avendaño, Fray Alonso de,
  97
Avila, John of, *see* John of
  Avila, St
Avila, Teresa of, *see* Teresa
  of Avila, St
Ayala, Elvira de, 141

Badajoz, 117-8
Baena, Cancionero de, 48-9
Baeza, (*see also*
  alumbrados of),
  university of, 102, 112-
  13, 123
Baeza, Antonio de, 26, 33,
  60, 80-1
Bailén, Count of, *see* Ponce
  de León, Rodrigo
Báñez, Fray Domingo, 121
Barbarossa (Kheireddin),
  71
Barcelona, 14, 92, 93, 95,
  113
Barco de Avila, 17
Barreda, Fray Diego de, 30-
  1, 38, 44, 56, 60-1
Barrios, Pedro de, 60
Basel, 41, 96

Basque lands, 8, 44, 73
beatas, 16-7, 98, 102, 113-14, 116, 118-19, 121, 123-4
Bedoya, Gaspar de, 28, 36, 56, 60, 62-3
Beghards and Beguines, 43-4, 45, 63, 109, 116, 120, 122, 138
Benedict, St, 26
Benedictines, 12-13
Benet, Fray Cipriano, 73
Bernard, St, 26
Beteta, Luis de, 62, 67-8, 81, 86
Bible, read and quoted by *alumbrados* of Toledo, 2, 34, 37-9, 47; translations of, in the vernacular, 9, 105; Complutensian polyglot edition of, 11, 45, 78, 85; Juan de Valdés's treatment of, 41-2; Erasmus's studies on, 78, 82, 100; John of Avila and, 97-8, 100, 102; on 1559 Index, 111
Biel, Gabriel, 11, 47
Bilbao, 44
Bivar, Rodrigo de, 28, 40, 46, 56, 62, 67, 82
Bivero, Beatriz de, 105
Bivero, Costanza de, 105
Bivero, Francisco de, 105
Bivero, Juan de, 105
Bivero, Leonor de, 105
Blasco, Cristóbal, 124
blasphemy, cases of, 65, 69
Blosius, Ludovicus, 123
Boccaccio, Giovanni, *Decameron*, 70
Bologna, 80
Bonaventure, St, 13
Borja, Francisco de *see* Francis Borgia, St
Bovelles, Charles de, 19, 29, 47
Brethren of the Common Life, 12
Bretón, Fray Juan, 127
Brevissimo atajo e arte de amar a Dios, *Hun*, 14
Bridget of Sweden, St, 33
Brussels, 77

Bucer, Martin, 106
Buendía, Count of, *see* Acuña, Juan de
Bullinger, Heinrich, 106
Burgos, 60, 63
Burgundy, 54
Buytrago, García de, 56

Caelestis Pastor (bull), 128
Calvin, Jean, 106, 109
Campo, Pedro del, 58-9
Campuzano *el mozo*, 56
Cano, Fray Melchor, 37, 97, 108-10, 117, 144
Carafa, Cardinal Gian Pietro (later Pope Paul IV), 103-4, 106, 110-12
Carleval, Bernardino de, 102, 112, 122
Carmelites, 23, 116, 121-2, 125
Carnesecchi, Pietro, 40
Carranza, Fray Bartolomé, archbishop of Toledo, 2, 104, 107-10, 120, 127; *Comentarios sobre el catechismo christiano*, 108-10
Carrillo, Alfonso, arch-bishop of Toledo, 46
Carrillo, de Mendoza, Diego, 3rd Count of Priego, 26, 51-2
Carrillo, de Mendoza, Luis, 4th Count of Priego, 26, 57
Carvajal, Fray Luis, de, *Apologia monasticae religionis*, 79
Castile, (*see also alumbrados* of Toledo), 7, 8, 18, 44, 53, 54, 83, 118
Castillo, Alonso del, 80
Castillo, Diego del, 86
Castillo, Juan del, 81-3, 86, 87, 89, 93, 130
Catalina de Jesús, 123-4
Catalonia, 7, 12, 17, 44, 104
Catherine of Genoa, St (Caterina Adorno), 119-20
Catherine of Siena, St, 13, 26
Cazalla family, 27, 105-6

Cazalla, Agustín de, 105, 107
Cazalla, Juan de, career of, 27, 46-7; and *alumbrados* of Toledo, 28, 29, 46-8, 73, 84; *Lumbre del alma*, 48, 111, 138; trial of, 86
Cazalla, María de, 46, 82, 84, 105, 129, 145; character and life, 25, 27, 87; and Mendoza family, 27, 139; trial and sentence, 28, 61-2, 87-8; and *recogimiento*, 31; and sin, 34; and Erasmus, 34, 87; and Bible, 37; and works, 39; denounced, 51-3; proselytises, 55-7; *converso* descent of, 67-8
Cazalla, Pedro de, 53, 105, 145
Cazorla, 26
Cerda, Alonso de la, 27
Cerda, Juan de la, Duke of Medinaceli, 27
Chamizo, Cristóbal, 119, 120
Charles V, Holy Roman Emperor, King of Spain as Charles I (formerly Charles of Ghent), 18, 20, 22, 40, 54, 58, 71-3, 77-8, 83, 84, 86, 89
Charles VIII, King of France, 12
Chaves, Sor Francisca de, 105
Cifuentes, 30, 56, 59, 60
Ciruelo, Pedro de, 94
Cisneros, *see also* Jiménez de Cisneros
Cisneros, Benito, 26, 57
Ciudad Real, 8, 65, 66
Ciudad Real, Fray Antonio de, 14
Clare, St, 26
Colonna, Vittoria, Marchioness of Pescara, 40
commandments of the Church, 29, 47, 79, 118-19

communion, sacrament of, 84, 93, 99, 111, 114, 119, 124, 126
comuneros, revolt of the, 22, 53-5, 63, 72
confession, status of, 45-6
Constable of Castile, *see* Fernández de Velasco, Iñigo
Constance, Council of, 33
Contarini, Cardinal Gasparo, 95, 103
conventicles (*see also* prayer meetings), 91-2, 98, 101, 105, 112-13, 131
conversos passim., and *alumbrados* of Toledo, 2, 26-8, 53, 63; and Spanish Inquisition, 7-8, 67-71, 144; situation of, 49, 65, 91; and Lutheranism, 72, 103; humanists and courtiers, 91; and Jesuits, 96-7; and John of Avila, 97, 101-2, 112; and *alumbrados* of Llerena and Jaén, 121; and *alumbrados* of Seville, 125
Cordeses, Antonio, 133
Cordova, 66, 99, 115, 121
Corro, Antonio del, 106
Coruña, Count of, *see* Suárez de Figueroa y Mendoza, Bernardino
Coruña, Countess of, *see* Manrique de Sotomayor, María
Cota, Martín, 74
Croy, Guillaume de, archbishop of Toledo, 85
Cruz, Fray Antonio de la, 63
Cruz, Isabel de la, 27, 80, 84, 115, 129, 136; proselytises, 1-2, 55-7; and Admiral of Castile, 23; early life of, 25; heretical utterances of, 28, 31; and Franciscans, 29, 60; scepticism of, 32; and antinomianism, 34, 35; and Bible, 37-8, 91; and mysticism, 39, 42;

denounced, 51-3; investigated, tried and sentenced, 59-63; *converso* descent of, 68, 71; and Luther, 73; and María de Cazalla, 88; and *alumbrados* of Llerena, 131
Cruz, Isabel de la (*beata* often confused with her namesake), 136
Cuenca, 40
Cyprian, St, 29

Dávalos, Gaspar, 60
dejamiento and *dejados* (*see also alumbrados* of Toledo), 28, 63; term defined, 1-2; contrasted with *recogimiento*, 29-32; and temptation, 34-6; and reading of Bible, 38-9; practitioners of, 56; associated with Judaism, 70-1; and Lutheranism, 73, 83, 106; described by Jeronimo Gracián, 116
Denis the Carthusian, *De Quatuor Novissimis*, 26
Devotio Moderna, 12, 93
Deza, Fray Diego de, 66
Díaz, Hernando, 51-2, 56, 57, 80
Dominicans (Order of Preachers) and *alumbrados* of Llerena, 5, 107-8; and Inquisition, 8; reformed, 11; and prophecy, 16-19; and *estatutos de limpieza*, 67; and Erasmus, 79; and Jesuits, 95-7, 130; and John of Avila, 102, 112; and Carranza, 107-10; and Teresa of Avila, 122-3; and *alumbrados* of Seville, 124-5; and Molinos, 127
Dorland, Pierre, *Viola animae*, 48
Dueñas, 54
Durango, heretics of, 18, 44-5, 63, 127

Ecija, 98, 100
Ecija, Fray Andrés de, 32, 59-60
Ecija, Hernando de, 120
edicts of faith; 1525 edict against *alumbrados* of Toledo, 2, 27-9, 43, 46, 47, 74, 128; 1574 edict against *alumbrados* of Llerena, 3, 120, 123, 124, 128; 1623 edict against *alumbrados* of Seville, 3, 123-4, 128
Eguía, Diego de, 93, 96, 130
Eguía, Miguel de, 40, 79-82, 86, 88, 93, 96, 130
Eiximenis, Francesc, 13
Enbid, Nicholás de, 30-1
Encina, Juan del, 111
England, 107-8, 131
Enríquez family, 66
Enríquez, Fadrique, Admiral of Castile, 22-3, 49-50, 54, 72, 80-1, 88, 142
Enríquez, Juana, Marchioness of Villena, 22, 50, 57, 60, 71
Erasmus, Desiderius, Spanish readers of, attacked, 2, 4, 82-7, 103, 104; admired in Spain, 22, 47, 59, 77-80, 82-7; *Enchridion militis christiani*, 34, 78, 79-80, 87, 110; and Valdés brothers, 40, 41, 92; *Adagia*, 77; *Moriae encomium*, 78, 110; *Institutio principis christiani*, 78; *Novum Testamentum*, 78; attacked in Spain, 78-80, 94; New Testament paraphrases, 82, 100; *Colloquia*, 86-7, 110; and Loyola, 93, 96; and John of Avila, 98, 100; condemned in Spain, 110-11
Erigena, John Scotus, 44
Escalona, 22, 26, 40, 48, 50, 57-60, 61

Escobar, Fray Luis de, *Quinquagenes* and *Quatrocientas Respuestas*, 49-50
Espina, Fray Alonso de, 8
Espinosa, Diego de, 56
Esquina, Fray Reginaldo de, 32, 80
estatutos de limpieza, 67, 89, 96-7, 112
Estella, 88
evangelism, 77, 89, 91; and *alumbrados* of Toledo, 2, 23, 130, 132; in northern Europe, 29; and Juan de Valdés, 39-42; in Italy, 95, 103; and John of Avila, 100; and Protestantism, 106; and Carranza, 109; and Jesuits, 130
Exsurge Domine (bull), 71
Extremadura (*see also alumbrados* of Llerena), 2-3, 5, 102, 113-14, 117-21, 123, 125, 129, 131-2

Falconi, Fray Juan, 127
Family of Love, 132
Farfán, Fray Domingo, 125
Ferdinand, King of Aragon, 1, 7, 8, 9, 10, 17, 18, 22, 54, 66
Fernández, Guiomar, 68
Fernández Pacheco, Juan, 1st Marquess of Villena, 22
Fernández de Portocarrero, Luis, Count of Palma, 27, 99
Fernández de Velasco, Iñigo, Constable of Castile, 54, 72
Ferrer, Vincent, *see* Vincent Ferrer, St
Figueroa, Fray Alonso de, 50, 57
Flaminio, Marcantonio, 40
Flanders, *see* Netherlands
Flor, María de la, 95
Flos sanctorum, 26, 111
Fonseca, Alonso de, archbishop of Toledo, 78, 85-6, 95

France, 18
Franche-Comté, 54
Francis, St, 12, 20, 44, 55, 59
Francis I, King of France, 21, 58
Francis Borgia, St, 111
Franciscans (Order of Friars Minor) and mysticism, 2, 12-16, 99, 113, 127; and Inquisition, 8, 140; and Cardinal Jiménez de Cisneros, 10, 11-12; and prophecy, 17-20, 58, 130; and *alumbrados* of Toledo, 21, 25, 46, 55-6; and nobility, 22; and *dejamiento*, 30-1; and medieval heresy, 44-5, 48-50; and Francisca Hernández, 52; and Alcarez, 57-60, 69; and *estatutos de limpieza*, 67; Luther read by, 73; and Erasmus, 79; and Francisco Ortiz, 84
Francisco de Santo Tomás, Fray, 127
Fraticelli, 44
Free Spirit, movement of the, 43
freedom of the will, 35, 44, 48, 49, 50, 63, 79
Frías, Martín, 95
Fuente, Fray Alonso de la, 97, 110, 112, 124, 125; and *alumbrados* of Llerena, 117-18, 120-1; and Teresa of Avila, 121-3
Fuente de Cantos, 118
Fuente del Maestre, 118

Gansfort, Wessel, 12
García, Juan, 119, 120, 122
García Calderón, Francisco, 126
García de Santa María, Gonzalo, 9-10
Garzón, Alonso, 89, 93, 132
Gastón, Juan, 70
Gattinara, Mercurino, 78, 83
Gelassenheit, 43

Germany, 20, 73, 83, 103, 104, 105, 132
Gerson, Jean Charlier de, 13, 33; *Mystica theologia*, 13; *De probatione spirituum*, 33
Gil, Juan (Dr Egidio), 105
Gonzaga, Giulia, 40
González, Elvira, 56
González, María (*alumbrada*), 120
González, María (Judaizer), 51
González de Mendoza, Cardinal Pedro, archbishop of Toledo, 9, 10
González Francés, Anton, 62-3
Gracián de la Madre de Dios, Fray Jerónimo, *Diez lamentaciones*, 116
Granada, 22, 45, 81-2, 99
Granada, Congregación de la, 123
Granada, Fray Luis de, 2, 99, 107, 110, 115, 117-18; *Libro de la oración*, 110, 117, 119; *Guía de pecadores*, 110, 119; *Manual de diversas oraciones*, 110
Gregory, St, 29
Gregory XIII, Pope, 108
Guadalajara, 10, 49; *alumbrados* of Toledo in, 1, 21-2, 25-7, 31, 47, 52, 55-6, 58-62, 73, 80, 82, 116; *comunero* revolt in, 55; Judaism in, 68
Guas, Enrique, 21
Guas, Juan, 21
Gutiérrez, Sebastián, 60
Guzmán, Diego de, 107
Guzmán, Gaspar de, Count Duke of Olivares, 123
Guzmán, Fray Tomás de, 81

hell, denial of, 44, 46, 53, 69-70
Henry IV, King of Castile, 22
Hernández, Diego, 80, 83, 87, 93, 137

Hernández, Francisca, 19-
20, 31, 34, 47; first
investigated by the
Inquisition, 52-3; and
Alcaraz, 56-7, 58, 60, 71;
denounces others, 61,
80-4, 87, 105, 142
Hernández, Pedro, 81
Herp, Henricus, *Theologia
mystica*, 111
Herrera, Hernando de, 112
Hieronymites, 48, 67, 100,
106
Hojeda, Pedro de, 112, 123
Horche, 52
Hurtado de Mendoza,
Diego, 1st Duke of
Infantado, 26
Hurtado de Mendoza,
Diego, 3rd Duke of
Infantado, 80;
alumbrados of Toledo
connected with household
of, 21, 22, 27, 28, 49, 50,
55, 56; and *comunero*
revolt, 54; Judaizers in
household of, 68, 141
Hurtado de Mendoza,
Diego, Count of Saldaña
(son of 4th Duke of
Infantado), 139
Hurtado de Mendoza,
Pedro, *adelantado* of
Cazorla, 26, 51
Hus, Jan, 63

Ignatius Loyola, St, 99,
113; suspected of
alumbradismo, 2, 92-7,
98, 130-1, 144;
Ejercicios espirituales,
93-7, 119, 130-1; *Diario
espiritual*, 94
*Imitation of Christ
(Contemptus mundi)*, 13,
26, 32-3
imposture, cases of, 3, 113,
115-16, 120, 126, 127
Index of prohibited books
(1559), 110-12
Inestrosa, Leonor de, 100
Infantado, 3rd Duchess of,
see Pimentel, Mariá

Infantado, 4th Duchess of,
see Aragón, Isabel de
Infantado, 1st Duke of, *see*
Hurtado de Mendoza,
Diego
Infantado, 2nd Duke of, *see*
López de Mendoza,
Iñigo
Infantado, 3rd Duke of, *see*
Hurtado de Mendoza,
Diego
Infantado, 4th Duke of, *see*
López de Mendoza,
Iñigo
Innocent XI, Pope, 127
Inquisition, Holy Office of
the, in Rome, 103
Inquisition, Holy Office of
the, in Spain, *passim.*,
foundation of, 3, 7-8;
medieval Inquisition in
Aragon, 8, 46; and
alumbrados of Toledo,
51-75, 87-9; and
Judaizers, 65-71; and
Lutherans, 71-5, 81-3,
87-9, 104-7; and
humanists, 83-7; and
conventicles, 91-2; and
Loyola, 94-7; and John
of Avila and his disciples,
98-9, 101-2, 112-14; and
Carranza, 107-10; and
alumbrados of Llerena,
117-21; and Teresa of
Avila, 121-2; and
alumbrados of Seville,
123-5
Isabella, Queen of Castile,
1, 7, 8, 9, 10, 22, 66
Italy, 79, 83, 103-4, 116

Jaén (*see also alumbrados*
of), 26, 113
Jerome, St, 11, 78
Jerusalem, 1, 10, 19, 58, 93
Jesuits (Society of Jesus),
23, 91, 103; foundation
of, 92, 95-7; joined by
men implicated in
alumbrado trials, 96,
130; and John of Avila
and his disciples, 101,

102-3; and Molinos, 127;
future of, 130-1
Jews (*see also conversos*;
Judaizers and Judaism),
1, 7-8, 9, 19, 96
Jiménez, Agueda, 56
Jiménez, Francisco, 30-1, 56
Jiménez, Mencía, 56
Jiménez de Cisneros,
Cardinal Fray Francisco,
archbishop of Toledo,
22, 25, 27, 45, 85, 111,
140; as an ecclesiastical
and cultural reformer, 3,
10-12; encourages
devotional literature in
the vernacular, 13-14,
26, 29; and prophecy and
visionaries, 16-20, 33,
113, 115; Juan de
Cazalla and, 46-8;
Judaizers in household
of, 66; and Erasmus, 78
Jiménez de Cisneros, Fray
García, 12-13;
*Ejercitatorio de la vida
espiritual*, 12-13, 26
Jiménez de Préjano, Pedro,
*Luzero de la vida
christiana*, 9, 110-11
Joachim of Fiore and
Joachism, 17-18, 44, 45,
48, 130
John of Avila, St, 23;
suspected by the
Inquisition, 2, 98-9, 112;
disciples of, 3, 112-14,
123, 129, 131; and
Jesuits, 96, 101; life of,
97-102; *Audi, filia*, 99-
101, 107, 110, 117, 119
John of St Victor, 29
John of the Cross, St, 33,
127; *Noche oscura*, 125
John Chrysostom, St, 100
John Climacus, St, *Spiritual
Ladder*, 13, 26
Judaizers and Judaism (*see
also conversos*), 4, 7-8, 36,
51, 53, 65-71, 104, 143
justification by faith, 2, 20-
1, 41-2, 43, 72-3, 103-4,
108-9

Laínez, Diego, 96
Laredo, Fray Bernardino
  de, 111, 126; *Subida del
  Monte Sión*, 16
Lea, H.C., 66
lechery, cases of, 83-4, 119,
  124, 132
Lefèvre d'Etaples, Jacques,
  47
Lerma, Pedro de, 46, 86
Le Sauvage, Jean, 78
Lisbon, 110, 115, 119
Llerena, *see alumbrados* of
Loarte, Gaspar, 102
López, Juan, 56
López de Ayala, Pero, 48
López de Celain, Juan, 80-
  2, 86, 87, 89, 130
López de Husillos, Diego,
  47, 81, 86
López de la Palomera,
  Alonso, 28, 32, 60-1, 73
López de Mendoza, Iñigo,
  2nd Duke of Infantado,
  49
López de Mendoza, Iñigo,
  4th Duke of Infantado
  (formerly Count of
  Saldaña), 32, 51, 55, 56,
  68, 89, 142
López de Mendoza, Iñigo,
  Marquess of Santillana, 26
López de Zúñiga, Diego, 75
López Pacheco, Diego, 2nd
  Marquess of Villena, 48,
  66; career of, 21-2; and
  Alcaraz, 26, 50, 57-60;
  and Juan de Valdés, 40,
  41; intercedes for
  prisoners of the
  Inquisition, 140
López Sebastián, Alonso, 56
Lorenzana, Fray Juan de,
  122-3
Louvain, 72, 82
Loyola, Ignatius, *see*
  Ignatius Loyola, St
Lucas, Gaspar, 121
Lucena, Gaspar de, 86, 93
Lucena, Petronila de, 82,
  86, 93
Ludolph of Saxony, *Vita
  Christi*, 10, 26

Lull, Ramon, 18, 19
Luna, Alvaro de, 22, 48
Lupset, Thomas, 77
Luther, Martin (Lutheran-
  ism and Lutherans), 11,
  22, 50, 92, 113, 122;
  Spanish readers of
  Luther accused of being
  alumbrados, 2, 83, 85-7;
  alumbrados of Toledo
  suspected of Lutheran-
  ism, 3, 34, 36, 62, 74-5,
  81-5, 129; Spanish fear
  of Lutheranism, 4, 20,
  37, 55, 65, 74-5;
  knowledge of Luther
  among the *alumbrados*
  of Toledo, 19, 73, 41,
  87; Duke of Infantado
  rumoured to admire
  Luther, 21; Lutherans of
  Valladolid and Seville,
  23, 101, 104-7, 110;
  Lutheranism and
  evangelism, 40, 77, 89,
  103-4; Luther read by
  Juan de Valdés, 41, 80;
  influence and transmis-
  sion of Lutheran ideas in
  Spain, 43, 47, 71-3, 85,
  104, 106, 142; admira-
  tion for Luther in Spain,
  61, 71-3, 82-3; Erasmus
  and Luther, 78-80;
  Decem Praecepta, 80;
  *Explanatio dominicae
  orationis*, 80; John of
  Avila and Lutheranism,
  100-1; Luther's
  opposition to compro-
  mise with Catholicism,
  103; Carranza and
  Lutheranism, 108-9

Madrid, 57, 58, 59, 120,
  125
Madrid, Fray Alonso de,
  14, 25, 111; *Arte para
  servir a Dios*, 16, 39
Magdalena de la Cruz, Sor,
  115
Majorca, 17, 44, 83
Maluenda, Fray Luis de,

37, 111; *Excelencias de
  la fe*, 63
Manresa, 92-3
Manrique, Alonso,
  archbishop of Seville, 81,
  82, 86; orders investiga-
  tion into *alumbrados* of
  Toledo as inquisitor
  general, 27, 62, 74; and
  Erasmus, 79; disgraced,
  83; and Virués, 89; and
  John of Avila, 97
Manrique, Rodrigo, 86-7
Manrique de Lara family, 83
Manrique de Lara, Antonio,
  Duke of Nájera, 88, 92
Manrique de Lara,
  Francisco, 92
Manrique de Sotomayor,
  María, Countess of
  Coruña, 49
María de la Visitación, Sor,
  115
María de Santo Domingo,
  Sor (*beata* of Piedrahita),
  17-19
Mariana, Alonso de, 62-3, 70
Marquina, Pedro de, 36-7,
  41, 60
Marta, Madre, 17, 19, 47
Martínez Montañés, Juan,
  123
Martínez Silíceo, Juan,
  archbishop of Toledo, 67
Mary I, Queen of England,
  107
Massilians, 122
Maximilian I, Holy Roman
  Emperor, 54
Medina de Ríoseco, 22, 49,
  80-2, 84, 86, 88
Medinaceli, Duke of, *see*
  Cerda, Juan de la
Medrano, Antonio de, 52-3,
  61, 83-4, 88, 92
Mejía, Alonso, 58-9, 63, 94
Mejía, Cristóbal, 120
Melanchthon, Philip, 41,
  103, 106; *Enchiridion
  elementorum puerilium*,
  80
Melchor, Fray, 19, 29, 47
Meléndez, Antonio, 68

Meléndez, Mayor, 68
Mella, Fray Alfonso de, 44-5, 63
Mendoza family (see also Carrillo de Mendoza; Hurtado de Mendoza; López de Mendoza; Suárez de Figueroa y Mendoza), 21, 27, 49, 51, 54, 66, 68, 81
Mendoza, Brianda de (daughter of 3rd Duke of Infantado), 27
Mendoza, Brianda de (sister of 3rd Duke of Infantado), 68
Mendoza, Juan de, 53, 55, 139
Mendoza, Marina de, 49
Mendoza, Mencía de, 38
Mennonites, 29
Mesa, Francisco de, 119, 120
Mexía, see Mejía
Milan, 111
Miona, Manuel de, 86, 93, 96, 130
Molinos, Miguel de, 3, 127-8; Guía de pecadores, 127-8; Defensa de la contemplación, 128
Molinosism, 3, 127-8
Mombaer, Jan, Rosetum exercitiorum spiritualium, 12
Monte, Fray Lope del, 49
Montemayor, Jorge de, 111
Montesino, Fray Ambrosio, 47; Epístolas y evangelios, 10
Montiel, Fray Diego de, 124
Montilla, 100
Montserrat, 12, 92
Morone, Cardinal Giovanni, 40, 103-4
Muslims, 7, 9, 10, 19, 47, 60, 68, 124
Mysticism, passim., see also alumbrados; dejamiento; Franciscans; Osuna, Francisco de; recogimiento

Nájera, Duke of, see Manrique de Lara, Antonio
Naples, 8, 40, 42, 54
Navarre, 8, 83, 88
Navarrete, 88
Nebrija, Antonio de, 45
Netherlands, 12, 54, 71-2, 73, 82, 85, 105, 108, 116, 131
New Christians, see conversos
New World, 115
Nicholas of Cusa, 47
Nicholas of Lyra, 100
Nicodemism, 130
Noguerol, 60
Nominalism, 11
North Africa, 1, 46
Núñez, Mari, 47, 51-3, 55-7, 61, 80

Ocaña, Fray Francisco de, 20, 58-60
Ochino, Bernardino, 103, 111
Ochoa, Fray Juan de, 120
Oecolampadius, Johannes, 41, 106; In Iesaiam, 80
Olesa, Jaime, 73
Olivares, Count Duke of, see Guzmán, Gaspar de
Olivares, Jerónimo, 30-1
Olmillos, Fray Juan de, 57-9, 71
Oran, 46
Orellana, Fray Juan de, 122
Origen, 44
Ortiz, Fray Francisco, 70, 81, 96; and Francisca Hernández, 20, 84; and Admiral of Castile, 23, 88; and recogimiento, 30-1; and Alcaraz, 56-7, 58; arrest and trial of, 61, 84, 88; converso descent of, 69, 71
Ortiz, Pedro, 96
Ortiz de Angulo, Diego, 58, 62, 71
Osma, Pedro de, 45-6, 70; De confessione, 45

Osuna, Fray Francisco de, 25, 39; and recogimiento, 14-16, 30, 38, 125, 126; Tercer abecedario, 14, 22, 33-4, 99, 111-12; Gracioso convite, 22, 111; and nobility, 23; on scepticism, 58; admired by John of Avila, 99; and 1559 Index, 112

Pacheco family, 66
Padilla, Juan de, Retablo de la vida de Christo, 9, 26
Palencia, 81, 104
Palma, Count of, see Fernández de Portocarrero, Luis
Palma, Bernabé de, 14, 99, 111
Palma del Río, 27
Pamplona, 92
Paris, 93, 95, 96
Pascual, Mateo, 86
Pastrana, 28, 30-1, 47, 56, 58, 59, 61, 116
Pastrana, Fray Antonio de, 30, 56
Pastrana, Juan de, 141
Paul III, Pope, 95-6, 103
Paul IV, Pope, see Carafa, Gian Pietro
Pavia, Battle of, 21
Pedroche, Fray Tomás de, 97
Pedrosa, 105
Pelagians, 109
Peña, Fray Juan de la, 108
Pérez de Pineda, Juan, 111
Pérez de Valdivia, Diego, 107, 112-14, 122; Aviso de gente recogida, 113-14
Peter Lombard, 138
Philip II, King of Spain, 107
Philip IV, King of Spain, 123
Philip, Duke of Burgundy, 10
Piedrahita, beata of, see María de Santo Domingo
Pimentel, María, 3rd Duchess of Infantado, 56

Pisa, Francisco de, 123
Pius IV, Pope, 104
Pius V, Pope, 108
Pizarro, Fray Domingo, 43,
    44, 62-3
Pole, Cardinal Reginald, 40,
    77, 95, 103-4, 107
Ponce de la Fuente,
    Constantino, 105, 107,
    111
Ponce de León, Fray
    Basilio, 125
Ponce de León, Juan, 105,
    107
Ponce de León, Luis
    Cristóbal, Duke of
    Arcos, 105
Ponce de León, Rodrigo,
    Count of Bailén, 105
Portugal, 47, 116, 117, 118
Poza, Marquess of, see
    Rojas, Juan de
prayer, discussions of
    superiority of mental to
    vocal, 29, 85, 92, 93-4,
    109-10, 113, 119, 122
prayer meetings (see also
    conventicles), 91-2, 93-
    5, 98-9, 105, 112-13,
    118-19, 131
predestination, 48-9
Priego, Counts of, see
    Carrillo de Mendoza
Priego, Marquess of, see
    Suárez de Figueroa,
    Lorenzo
prophecy and prophets, 3,
    17-20, 46-7, 58-9, 69,
    114, 115
Protestantism (see also
    Luther, Martin), 65, 69,
    73-4, 81, 91, 103-7, 111,
    112, 117, 127, 129, 130
Provence, 44
Pseudo-Augustine,
    Meditaciones, Soliloquio
    y Manual, 26, 29
Pseudo-Bonaventure,
    Estimulo de amor, 26
Pseudo-Dionysius, 12;
    Mystical Theology, 13, 14
Puerto de Santa María, 56

Quietism, 3, 127-8
Quiñones, Fray Francisco
    de, 60

Rafael de San Juan, Fray,
    127
Ramírez, Beatriz, 93
Ramírez, Diego, 66
Ramírez, Juan, 66
Ramírez, Mari, 142
Raymond of Sebonde,
    Liber creaturarum sive
    Theologia naturalis, 48
recogimiento, 38; defined,
    12, 14-15, 21; contrasted
    with dejamiento, 30-2
Regensburg, Conference of,
    103-4
Reina, Casiodoro de, 106
Rhineland, 44
Ribera, Juan de, 117-18, 119
Richard of St Victor, 12
Rodríguez, Alonso, 127;
    Ejercicio de perfección,
    130-1
Rodríguez Lucero, Diego,
    66
Rojas, Cristóbal de, 118
Rojas, Fray Domingo de,
    104, 107
Rojas, Juan de, Marquess of
    Poza, 104
Rome, 40, 58, 86, 93, 95,
    96, 97, 108, 112, 120,
    127-8
Romero, María, 121
Rueda, Lope de, 27, 34
Rueda, Pedro de, 38
Ruiz de Alcaraz, Hernando,
    56
Ruiz de Alcaraz, Pedro, 1,
    20, 106, 116, 129, 136,
    139; character and
    career, 25-7; author of
    condemned propositions,
    28; and dejamiento , 31;
    and spiritual consola-
    tions, 32-4, 113; views
    on salvation and love of
    God, 34-6, 44, 109; and
    ceremonies and
    commandments of the

Church, 36-7; and Bible,
    37-9; and Juan de
    Valdés, 40-1; and Juan
    de Cazalla, 47; and
    Johannine Epistles, 49;
    and Marquess of Villena,
    50; denounced, 51-3,
    142; proselytises, 55-60;
    arrest and sentence of,
    60-3, 143; suspected of
    Judaism, 67-71;
    suspected of Lutheran-
    ism, 73-5; and Erasmus,
    79-80
Ruusbroeck, Jan, 121

Saa, Calixto de, 95
Sahagún, Fray Antonio de,
    52
Salamanca, 52-3, 95;
    university of, 45, 95, 96,
    97, 125
Salceda, convent of La, 10,
    14, 19
Saldaña, Counts of, see
    Hurtado de Mendoza;
    López de Mendoza
Saldaña, Countess of, see
    Aragón, Isabel de
San Isidro del Campo
    (Seville), convent of,
    100, 105-6, 107
San Juan de los Reyes
    (Toledo), convent of, 10,
    14, 58-9, 60, 84
San Plácido (Madrid), nuns
    of, 126
Sánchez, Gaspar, 118
Sánchez, Graviel, 30, 56
Sánchez Calavera, Ferrán,
    48-9
Santa Cruz, Diego de, 118
Santamaría, Fray Nicolás
    de, 124
Santillana, Marquess of, see
    López de Mendoza, Iñigo
Saragossa, 45, 127
Sardinia, 8, 54
Savonarola, Girolamo, 17,
    110
scandalous words, utterance
    of, 65, 69-70

Schwenckfeld, Caspar, 81
Scotism, 11
Segovia, 68
Seneca, 49
Serrano, Juan, 140
Seso, Carlos de, 104-5, 107
Seville (see also alumbrados of), 55, 61, 82, 97, 100, 117, 120, 121-2, 130; Protestants of, 105-7, 111, 112, 127
Sicily, 54
Soria, Juan Crisóstomo de, 124
Spirit of Freedom, sect of the, 44
Starkey, Thomas, Dialogue between Reginald Pole and Thomas Lupset, 77
Suárez de Figueroa, Lorenzo, Marquess of Priego, 100
Suárez de Figueroa y Mendoza, Bernardino, Count of Coruña, 52, 55, 68

Talavera, Fray Hernando de, archbishop of Granada, 9; Católica impugnación, 111, 144
Tauler, Johannes, 122
Tejeda, María de, 34, 57
Tendilla, Fray Cristóbal de, 30, 32, 47
Teresa of Avila, St (Teresa de Jesús), 33, 111, 116, 126-7; accused of alumbradismo, 2, 121-3; and John of Avila, 99; Libro de su vida, 111, 115, 121-2; attacked by Alonso de la Fuente, 117, 121-3, 125
Theologia Germanica, 132
Thomas Aquinas, St, 38
Thomas of Villanova, St, 107
Thomism, 11, 94
Toledo (see also alumbrados of), 22, 51-2, 54-61, 67, 68, 81, 82, 86, 88, 97, 108
Toledo, María de, 16

Toro, 104
Torrelaguna, 23, 88
Torres, José, 126
Torres, Miguel de, 86, 96, 132
Tosca, Gertrudis, 126
Tovar, Bernardino de, 81, 82, 89, 93; and Francisca Hernández, 52-3, 61; trial of, 84-6; and María de Cazalla, 87, 88
Trent, Council of, 4, 20, 103-4, 107
troubadours, 48-50
Turks, 69, 71

Ubeda, 112
Umbria, 44
Usagre, 118

Vado, María del, 93-5
Vaguer, Dr, 83, 139
Valdés, Alfonso de, 40, 72-3, 78, 86, 111; Diálogo de Mercurio y Carón, 92
Valdés, Fernando de, 74-5, 77, 106-7, 110-12
Valdés, Juan de, 4, 92, 103; Diálogo de doctrina christiana, 22, 40-1, 80, 87-8; at Escalona, 37, 40, 60; life of, 40-2; reads Luther, 41, 73; Cento e dieci divine considerazioni, 41; trial prepared against, 86; read by Spanish Protestants, 106; and Carranza, 107; on 1559 Index, 111, cautious attitude to Catholic Church, 129-30
Valencia, 8, 17, 44, 60, 73, 126
Valencia, Fray Diego de, 48
Valencia, Juana de, 51-2
Valera, Cipriano de, 106
Valla, Lorenzo, 15
Valladolid, 22, 48, 52-3, 81, 82, 84, 108, 110, 121; conference on Erasmus at, 79, 83; Protestants of, 104-7, 111, 113, 127

Valle, Ana del, 81, 86
Valtanás, Fray Domingo de, 112
Vega, Gabriel de, 56-7
Velázquez, Luisa, 93-5
Vélez, Dr, 92
Vélez, Sancho, 51, 70
Venegas, Alejo, 81
Venice, 95, 96, 111
Vergara, Fray Alonso de, 112
Vergara, Francisco de, 84
Vergara, Juan de, 81, 84, 143; and institution of confession, 46; on Luther, 72, 142; and Erasmus, 78; trial of, 85-6, 120; sentence of, 88-9
Vermigli, Pietro Martire, 103
Villacreces, Fray Pedro de, 12
Villaescusa, Francisco de, 124
Villafaña, Gaspar de, 81, 86
Villalpando, Juan de, 123-4, 126
Villareal, Diego de, 52-3
Villena, 1st Marquess of, see Fernández Pacheco, Juan
Villena, 2nd Marquess of, see López Pacheco, Diego
Villena, Marchioness of, see Enríquez, Juana
Vincent Ferrer, St, 7, 9, 17, 113; Tractatus de vita spirituali, 16, 26, 33, 113
Virués, Fray Alfonso de, 86, 89
Vives, Juan Luis, 86

William of Paris, 9
Worms, Diet of, 72-3, 85

Yáñez, Juan, 84

Zafra, 118-19, 121
Zamora, 44
Zamora, Francisco, 118
Zerbolt, Gerard, Tractatus de spiritualibus ascensionibus, 12

DATE DUE

			Printed in USA